What the Negro
Can Do About Crime

WHAT THE NEGRO CAN DO ABOUT CRIME

**J. A. Parker and
Allan C. Brownfeld**

ARLINGTON HOUSE·PUBLISHERS

NEW ROCHELLE, N. Y.

Manufactured in the United States of America

Library of Congress Cataloging in Publication Data

Parker, J   A   1936-
    What the Negro can do about crime.

    1. Crime and criminals--United States. 2. Victims of crime--United States. 3. Negroes. 4. Crime prevention--United States. I. Brownfeld, Allan C., 1939-   joint author. II. Title.
HV6791.P37   364   74-6195
ISBN 0-87000-231-7

To the black man in blue
and those of all races
who work for
a decent, free and safe society

Contents

Tables

Chapter 1

Crime: The Problem

Both the United States and the remainder of the world face an unprecedented crisis of crime and violence. Men and women feel afraid to leave their homes. Newspapers no longer feature murders, rapes, and other such crimes as headline news, for we are becoming increasingly accustomed to such events. They have, unfortunately, become part of our way of life.

There is no doubt that government has failed in its primary domestic task, that of preserving order and providing an atmosphere within which honest citizens may go about the business of living. There is also little doubt that the sense of community we once knew has vanished, and that citizens do not provide one another with assistance at critical moments. More and more, we find ourselves isolated and alone in the midst of massive urban areas. More and more, we are victimized by crime and do not know what to do about it. Men run for public office promising that if they are elected strong measures will be taken to stem the rising tide of crime. We elect them—and see crime increase even more. Something is wrong, and we do not know quite what it is.

One of the nation's leading psychiatrists, Dr. Bruno Bettelheim of the University of Chicago, described the "violence syndrome." He said, "There's a lawlessness at large. Up to World War II, what was glorified was the respectable, hard-working citizen. Now there is the attitude that 'Everybody owes me a living—I have to get what I want right now, or I'll burn the house down, and if I have no roof, then the Government has to give me another roof.' Today violence is being glorified, and respectable behavior is never shown. All the students who riot are on the screen; the students who stay at their studies are not. A few draft-card burners are written up, but not the 50,000 boys who lost their lives in Vietnam—nobody glorifies them."

Dr. Frederic Wertham, noted psychiatrist and author of numerous books and articles dealing with violence, noted that "younger and younger people are committing more and more crimes of greater and greater violence. Children of 12 and 13 are killing now. This was not so 15 years ago. We seem to be running a sort of 'head start' program for violence, with all the emphasis we give it in films, on television, and in those awful comic books."

In the ten years from 1960 to 1970, crime almost tripled, rising 176 percent, according to FBI reports published in 1970. On a nationwide average, each American has one chance in 36 of becoming a victim of some kind of serious crime—murder, rape, robbery, aggravated assault, burglary, larceny or car theft. For those living in big cities, the odds are even closer—one chance in 19 of being victimized.

For the criminal, chances of being caught are only one in five. Police solved about 20 percent of all crimes in 1970. A decade earlier, in 1960, they solved approximately 31 percent. Factors in the decline of solutions, the FBI said, "include court decisions which have resulted in restrictions on police investigative and enforcement practices and increases of police workloads in criminal and noncriminal matters—riots, disturbances, marches, etc."

The police record is best on "crimes against the person." Police cleared 86 percent of all murder cases in 1970, 65 percent of aggravated assaults and 56 percent of rapes. On the other hand, only 29 percent of robberies, 19 percent of burglaries and 17 percent of auto thefts were cleared.

In the period from 1960 to 1970 murders were up 76 percent; forcible rapes were up 121 percent, robberies were up 224 percent, aggravated assaults were up 117 percent, burglaries were up 142 percent, larcenies were up 245 percent and auto thefts were up 183 percent.

Violent crime in the nation's suburbs is increasing nearly twice as fast as in the large cities. While this is true, suburban crime rates, on a per capita basis, are still so low that even at the present rate of increase there is no chance that suburbanites will soon be in as much danger of violence as city residents.

According to FBI uniform crime reports for 1971, crimes of violence in the 57 cities with more than a quarter of a million people rose by

7.5 percent over 1970, while in the suburbs the increase was 13.4 percent. What the numbers really mean is that for every 100,000 persons in the suburbs, 206 were victims of violent crimes while in the large cities the number was 1,048.

In the residential suburbs in the New York metropolitan area, violence is so relatively rare that local police spend only a small amount of their time on those crimes compared to crimes against property. "Violence? Gosh, it's so rare here it's like asking me how many rabies cases we've had in the last 20 years," said Chief Stephan Barran of the Greenwich, Connecticut, police. "More and more people are out walking at night, for their health."

Discussing his 14 years as a member of the police force in Yorktown, New York, in Westchester County, Lieutenant George Calcagnini declared, "I can't recall an act of violence associated with a burglary." Most acts of violence in Yorktown, he said, "occurred between people who were already acquainted."

The fact that the suburban crime rate is far below that for large cities does not mean that suburbanites are not vitally concerned. In fact, it seems that fear of crime is growing in the suburbs even faster than the crime rate itself. In 1969, a study comparing suburban and inner city areas of Baltimore found that the suburban residents were five times more likely to be afraid of crime—although actually five times less likely to become victims of crimes—than the inner city residents.

Marvin Wolfgang, one of the nation's leading criminologists, says there are three reasons why the fear of crime in the suburbs outstrips the reality. First, he says, the rate of crime increase actually has been greater in the suburbs. Although the numbers are still modest, rising crime is a reality. The second reason is the increase in drug-related offenses, which are particularly frightening to suburban parents. Third, he says, the knowledge that crimes such as burglary are often committed by people from outside the community creates the special fear of falling victim to "invaders from the outside," a fear of random attacks.

Writing in the *New York Times* of May 20, 1968, David Burnham pointed out that "predatory, often senselessly savage, the mugger looms as the most menacing figure in the public concern over crime."

A mugging is a type of robbery that involves a physical attack. It is a crime that is reported to the police in Manhattan more than 16,000 times each year. Mr. Burnham states, "Although muggings represent only a fraction of all serious crimes reported to the police, the mugger exacts a high toll in terms of physical and mental anguish and personal property loss, and he diminishes the quality of life in a fearful city."

A recently revitalized element of street crime in the nation's large cities is that of the marauding teenage gang—of the kind romanticized in the musical "West Side Story." These gangs seemed to fall out of fashion in the late 1950s due to a number of factors, including the breakup of gang neighborhoods by urban renewal, the attraction of hard drugs which turned warriors into apathetic addicts, and the fact that anti-poverty programs sought to buy off gang leaders.

Today, at New York's newest high school in the Bronx, half of the lavatories are kept locked so security guards can better cope with the rash of assaults and robberies aimed largely at white students by black and Puerto Rican gangs. A nationwide check of 12 cities indicated that the violence is concentrated in the nation's four largest urban areas— New York, Philadelphia, Chicago and Los Angeles. During the four years from 1968 to 1972, Philadelphia had 160 killings attributed to street gangs. *Newsweek* magazine reports that "the zip guns, car-radio antennas and switchblades that served as weapons in the 1950s have been replaced by pistols, carbines, sawed-off shotguns and sub-machine guns. And the violence has mounted along with the technology."

Edward Muir of the United Federation of Teachers of New York declared that "the tragic element that distinguishes this from earlier gang activity is the proliferation of handguns among teenagers. The 'Saturday night special' has hit the high schools."

In Los Angeles, members of a black gang specialize in mass muggings. About 20 of them stomped to death a 15-year-old highschool football star outside the Hollywood Palladium when the boy refused to hand over his prized black leather jacket. In New York City, gang violence has reached unprecedented heights. The New York gangs are blamed for 15 killings in the first three months of 1972.

In New York, 15 members of two Puerto Rican street gangs called the Savage Nomads and the Seven Immortals invaded a party in the Bronx to redress an alleged wrong done to one gang member. They proceeded to shoot and stab two men, then raped a girl three times before killing her with a shotgun blast in the chest. "I don't really think they make any connection between shooting and death," says John Nolan, a special assistant to the commissioner of New York's Youth Services Agency. "A 15-year-old came to me recently to talk about a killing, and he said, 'Yeah, Joey did a Roy Rogers on him.' Now to that kid, killing was something you only see in the movies."

While some city gangs are white, the majority are black or Puerto Rican. *Newsweek* notes that "While the gangs' style of dress and their swagger is reminiscent of the old Hell's Angels of California, their rhetoric is politically conscious, more in the manner of the Black Panthers and Young Lords. Their rules on drugs are notably strict. Most gang members have no aversion to dropping acid or blowing grass, but sticking a needle in their arms is seldom tolerated. In the Javelins, for instance, the penalty for messing with heroin is 20 lashes if you're a girl and a thrashing if you're a boy."

14

Much violence is being directed by gang members against schools and teachers. In New York's Taft High School, the teachers have become so terrified that they have taken to locking their classroom doors once the students are all inside. When one teacher forgot to lock up, her room was invaded by half a dozen members of a neighborhood gang. While the students cowered in the back of the room, the gang members threatened to rape the teacher. In the confusion, one pupil managed to escape and raced up and down the hall trying to find help. The other teachers, however, were afraid to open their locked doors. Only when the boys in the class resisted the invasion did the gang members leave. "It's much worse than in the blackboard jungle days," says Mario Raimo, the Bronx representative of the United Federation of Teachers. "Then you really had only the vocational-type schools with gang problems. Now they're everywhere."

In Los Angeles a confederation of black gangs known as the Crips has arisen. Numbering between 200 and 1,000, they are spread through the city in small groups. The gang members identify themselves by wearing black leather jackets and a wide-brimmed hat known in Los Angeles as a "liquor store hat," because it can be purchased where liquor is sold. Unlike Eastern gangs who fight among themselves, the Crips consider the ordinary citizen their primary target. They specialize in mugging, street-corner extortion and "car clouting," which means stealing everything from a car that they can carry away.

The terror caused by the Crips has instilled widespread fear. William F., a typical retired pensioner, will not leave his apartment after dusk. The mother of a 15-year-old girl who was raped by gang members decided that her daughter would not press charges after two weeks of late-night phone calls threatening fire-bombing and window smashing if she did.

In mid-February, 1972, the day after the son of the late actor Ed Begley was beaten, stomped and stabbed by a gang of 25 black youths in Los Angeles in the third such incident of the afternoon, the Los Angeles City Council ordered a police crackdown. Billy G. Miles, council president pro tem, said that the increase in murders and assaults had imposed a "crisis of intimidation and fear" on parts of Los Angeles "by roving groups of young people ranging in age from 10 to 30."

Americans increasingly live in fear. A Crime Commission survey found that one-third of a representative sample of all Americans say that it is unsafe to walk alone at night in their neighborhoods. Slightly more than one-third say they keep firearms in the house for protection against criminals and 28 percent say they keep watchdogs for the same reason. In addition, 43 percent of those responding say that they stay off the streets at night because of their fear of crime and 35 percent say that they do not speak to strangers because of their fear of crime.

An analysis in the *National Observer* states: "One current estimate has it that 50 percent of the population of the nation's larger cities are afraid to walk the streets at night."

At a time when crime is mounting, law enforcement seems less and less effective in dealing with it. A study of serious crimes in New York has found that only 5.89 percent of the robberies, 1.35 percent of the burglaries and 2.2 percent of the grand larcenies assigned to detectives result in arrests by them.

This study, conducted for the police department by New York's Rand Institute, analyzed the serious crimes reported to the police during the first six months of 1967. It concluded that detectives wasted a great deal of time investigating cases that could not be solved and that different methods of following up crimes could be more productive.

The Rand Institute study, conducted by Dr. Peter W. Greenwood, raised questions about how policemen are assigned to apprehend criminals, both in New York and elsewhere. The study said that more than half of the arrests for crimes of profit—burglary, robbery and grand larceny—were made at the scene of the crime and that only an "extremely small" fraction of such crimes were solved by investigating detectives.

"This state of affairs suggests that a great deal of detective manpower that is possibly wasted investigating unsolvable cases might be saved or made more productive by improving the procedures for selecting cases to be investigated and those to be closed without detective follow-up," Dr. Greenwood said.

Street patrol, which has been de-emphasized for economic reasons in many police departments, has been shown to be the most effective means of capturing criminals. Dr. Greenwood compared different methods of apprehending criminals for major crimes. A detective on street patrol, he found, averaged 2.15 such arrests each month. A detective on regular investigative duty averaged 0.86 arrests and uniformed patrolmen 0.22 arrests for serious crimes each month. "The implications of this analysis," Dr. Greenwood said, "are that shifting men from either uniform patrol or case investigation to detective patrol will enhance the number of primary arrests made by the department."

Of increasing concern to city dwellers is the fact that even though a criminal has been apprehended by the police, he still remains a danger to the community. In Washington, D.C., more than 1,400 persons charged with crimes and freed by local courts, either while awaiting trial or following conviction for an offense, were rearrested and charged with new crimes during an eight-month period in 1971, according to a District police study.

During July, August and September alone, 92 persons released on personal recognizance by the US District and Superior Courts were rearrested while awaiting trial and charged with robberies or attempted robberies in the city. And during a four-month period ending August 16, 1971, eight District men released prior to trial—in four instances while facing felony charges—were charged with murder while they were free.

In one of the homicide cases, the 25-year-old suspect had been released on personal recognizance—his promise to appear for trial—in January 1971, while awaiting trial for armed robbery and again the following month after being arrested on a second armed robbery charge. He is accused, according to the police study, of first-degree murder in the shooting death of a 68-year-old man during an attempted robbery at the victim's apartment.

The report was prepared by the Metropolitan Police Major Violators Bureau, a unit formed to assemble rearrest data on known criminal offenders in the city. A total of 955 persons were rearrested while released on personal recognizance by the courts between February 1 and September 30. During approximately the same period, 388 persons placed on probation by the District Superior Court were arrested and charged with new crimes.

In one case, a 19-year-old man was charged with burglary and released on personal recognizance by a judge of the Superior Court. He was convicted subsequently, the report said, and placed on probation. Twenty days after his conviction he was arrested again—on another burglary charge—and released once again on his own recognizance. At the time of the police study, the man was free in the community.

Washington, D.C., is also notoriously lenient in its treatment of rapists. According to the *New York Post,* "By conservative estimate, a man committing rape in Washington has a 90 percent chance of escaping arrest or identification." On a national basis, according to the FBI, 62 percent of the crimes of forcible rape are cleared by arrests. In Washington, it seems that about 10 percent of the rape cases are cleared up.

Despite the fact that congressmen, senators, presidents and judges of both parties continue to declare that the fight against crime is our single most important domestic priority, the nation's Capitol, which is effectively under their control, is a laboratory not of how best to fight crime, but of how to combat it least effectively.

The now defunct *Washington Daily News* had the following headline in its paper of November 4, 1971: "MURDER PACE HERE EPIDEMIC. 7 IN 10 D.C. SLAY SUSPECTS GO FREE." Reporter Patrick Collins wrote, "The homicide rate in the District is more than twice that of New York City and the man who kills here has a seven out of ten chance of getting away with a murder. Although the District homicide squad boasts of the fact that it solves 90 percent of its cases, only half of the suspects captured get indicted and only a third of the suspects indicted get convicted." In addition, only 15 percent of those arrested for carrying a gun on a Washington street serve time in jail. Forty-five percent of the cases never reach a judge, and of those that do come before the court, 79 percent result in convictions, but two thirds of those convicted never spend a single day in jail.

The District of Columbia Health Department, which charts the mortality rate, says that District residents between the ages of 14 and 44 have a better chance of being murdered than of being killed by a heroin overdose, automobile accident or any natural cause. The city medical examiner has called the homicide rate "epidemic" and the U.S. Attorney calls it "alarming."

Some of the findings of a study of District homicides conducted by the *News* include the following:

• In an eight-year period 1,361 homicides were reported and police say they solved 1,230 of them by arrests. But of the 1,230 homicide suspects arrested, 534 were never indicted by a grand jury and another 115 were released after the indictment when the U.S. Attorney decided the case was not strong enough to take to court.

• The U.S. Attorney's office has obtained convictions of only 444 of the 1,230 homicide suspects.

• The District of Columbia averages 37 homicides per 100,000 people while New York reports 17 homicides per 100,000.

• In the eight years from 1963 to 1970 the number of murders has increased 250 percent while the number of convictions has climbed 95 percent.

Describing the number of Washington homicides as "astronomical" and the rate of murders as "epidemic," District Medical Examiner James Luke says the right people don't care about the homicide problem.

"Homicide is still a ghetto problem," Dr. Luke said, "like the drug problem was years ago. There have been very few homicides of whites here and until the homicides affect the people of influence—the people who make decisions—nothing will be done. Homicide is a problem that has not been dealt with at all."

Dr. Luke declared, "Our job is to have a dialogue with the dead, and many people would expect us to be hardened to it. But these are real people who are brought in here. We see their faces. We see their families and we see a potentially productive life wiped out each day. It's not a game. The more we see, the more we become sensitized to the problem."

Each day the financial toll of crime in America rises. The crime burden has now reached more than $51 billion a year, equal to more than 5 percent of the gross national product.

In 1967, a study on the economic impact of crime was made by a presidential crime commission. Its estimate then was $21 billion. More recently, improved methods of tracking down crime costs show that the estimate was far too conservative. In addition, crime rates themselves have risen spectacularly. Crime in the 1960s increased 11 times as fast as the population. Serious crimes, which include murder, rape, robbery, aggravated assault, burglary, larceny of $50 and over and auto theft, were up 148 percent.

The cost of crimes against the person—murder, assaults and rapes— is estimated to have totaled $2 billion in a typical year. Bigger than this are two other forms of crime. Organized crime, which makes business enterprises out of such activities as narcotics peddling, illegal gambling, hijacking and "loan sharking," is costing the nation $19.7 billion a year. Business and property crimes, ranging from embezzlement to shoplifting and vandalism, are draining off another $13 billion from the nation's economy. Together, these two types of crime account for more than three of every five dollars of the annual crime bill.

Shoplifting is one crime which is by no means confined to the inner city, but has moved to the nation's most fashionable suburbs. A group of affluent high-school students in Connecticut's Fairfield County, for example, were taking part in an encounter session, and when the subject got around to shoplifting they had no trouble comparing experiences and recounting exploits.

As reported in the *New York Times* of October 17, 1972, one girl was asked, "What have you stolen?" Laughing, she struggled to recall the harvest of several years: "Shirts, eyeliner, eyeshadow, nail polish, cartons of cigarettes, earrings, bracelets, rings, candy, wallets, belts, underwear, purses, tapes (about $200 worth), combs, necklaces, scarves . . . ."

According to the Retail Merchants Association, shoplifting cost more than $3.5 billion in 1971. Security experts estimate that more than 50 percent of shoplifters are juveniles, with women in their thirties and forties providing another substantial group. Mrs. Joy Walker, a Fairfield County teacher who conducts communications workshops and human relations classes with her high-school students, sees shoplifting as a rite of passage, a way that teen-agers test themselves and prove their resourcefulness and courage.

"They find shoplifting daring in the same way that diving off a high rock ledge into a river is daring," she said. "Though they place honesty high on their list of values, they see no connection between shoplifting and dishonesty."

Judge Margaret Driscoll of the Juvenile Court of Fairfield County said that parents' reactions vary when their children are caught shoplifting. "Some parents think it's much ado about nothing and some parents are shocked. They can't imagine their child doing it."

In many instances, the use of crime statistics tends to make us think of various criminal acts as being impersonal. As a result, we tend to fail in our appreciation of the very great shock which acts of violence have produced in our large cities, and the atmosphere of fear which seems, more and more, to pervade our urban areas.

Consider some of the individual criminal cases which took place in 1972. These were not different in nature from crimes which occurred in previous years, or which will occur in the future. Nevertheless, the picture they paint is far more revealing than a discussion limited to the recitation of facts and figures.

In October, eight members of a group called "De Mau Mau" gang, made up of dishonorably discharged Vietnam veterans, were charged in a series of nine murders, including the mass killings of two families, which terrorized the Chicago area for more than five months. Police said that the slayings appear to have been racially motivated and the victims picked at random by members of the gang, former students at Malcolm X University, a black city university on Chicago's West Side. Dr. Charles Hurst, president of Malcolm X University, said that members of the gang were expelled from the school in the spring after they had beaten up students and intimidated teachers.

Hurst said that the Mau Mau were formed in Vietnam and that the men got together when they returned with dishonorable discharges to the United States. The men were accused of the murder of nine whites, including four people in the home of a retired insurance executive, Paul M. Corbett, in well-to-do Harrington Hills. The other victims were three members of a farm family slain near Monee, Illinois, a serviceman shot as he napped in a pickup truck on the Edens Expressway and a Southern Illinois student whose body was discovered near a downstate highway.

Also in October, in New York, a Brooklyn schoolteacher, leading a class of fifth graders on a field trip in Prospect Park, was beaten and robbed as 10 children and a woman aide watched helplessly. The assailant hit the 58-year-old teacher, Mrs. Ruth Greer, three times on the head with a small log as she bent over, talking about a piece of worm-eaten bark a girl had found.

Bleeding profusely from gashes behind her right and left ears, Mrs. Greer struggled to regain her feet as the man fled with her pocketbook, which contained $13 and five credit cards. She was taken to Methodist Hospital by a motorist who had been flagged down, and later was transferred to Caledonian Hospital, where 16 stitches were taken to close the head cuts. "I'm glad he didn't beat me to death," Mrs. Greer said. "If I had been flat on the ground, he might have. I'm really sorry for the children. They're impressionable and this experience will stay with them. With me, it will mellow."

In March, District Attorney Burton D. Roberts of the Bronx announced the conviction of a rape suspect who had been arrested one year after his crimes because of a police sketch a detective always carried with him. Convicted of rape, sodomy, burglary and other crimes against two women graduate students at Fordham University was Peter Lotz, 29 years old. "Lotz had two prior arrests for rape dismissed because of an inability to corroborate each and every elaborate detail of his crimes," Mr. Roberts said, adding: "This points up the need to change the archaic rape law which exists."

New Yorkers were shocked when, on September 20, Dr. Wolfgang G. Friedmann, professor of International Law and Director of International Legal Research at Columbia University, was robbed and stabbed to death three blocks from the campus. The police, responding to an anonymous call, found the body of the 65-year-old scholar and refugee from Nazi Germany in front of Public School 36 on Amsterdam Avenue between 122nd and 123rd streets. Witnesses told detectives that they had seen three youths between 15 and 17 years old wrest a wallet from Dr. Friedmann's pocket. They said that his assailants had tried to seize his wrist watch and that the professor had resisted. A struggle ensued in which he was stabbed near the heart and then the youths fled.

Dr. Friedmann had been attacked once before, but he had been successful in fighting off his assailants. In 1956, he was walking through Riverside Park on his way home from classes when two youths attacked him. One punched him in the eye, but the Professor fought back, punching and wrestling with the two youths and throwing one to the ground. Then his attackers fled.

Dr. Friedmann, who was born in Berlin on January 25, 1906, fled Germany after the Nazis came to power. During World War II he served with the political intelligence department of the British Foreign Office and with the Allied Military Government from 1944 to 1947. He was the author of numerous works on international law, legal aspects of foreign investment, world politics, social change and finance. Michael I. Sovern, dean of the Columbia Law School, said, "I grieve for him, for us, and for a world that violently carries off its men of peace."

On September 23, only two days after Dr. Friedmann's tragic death, a 60-year-old psychiatrist on his way home to White Plains was assaulted, robbed and stabbed near an East 125th Street bar that had been raided the previous summer as a suspected hangout of drug sellers and users.

The psychiatrist, Selwyn Brody, said that he was "happy to be alive." His accustomed route home from his office at 2 East 86th Street—up the Lexington Avenue subway to 125th Street and, on foot, over to the Penn Central Railroad stop at Park Avenue—was a perilous one, taking him down a block on one of the city's more violent, drug-ridden streets. Dr. Friedmann had been headed toward the same Penn Central stop when he was murdered.

Writing in the *New York Times* of September 24, 1972, Frank A. Prial noted that "the Penn Central station at 125th Street and Park Avenue, all dark wood and massive stone, looks like a fortress. 'And that,' said a railroad policeman who works there, 'is exactly what it is. People know that if they can make it here, they're safe.' "

"There is one mugging a night in the block—that we hear of," said Penn Central Patrolman John Faison, "and we're only supposed to deal with railroad property." Patrolman Faison was one of the two Penn Central policemen who went to Dr. Brody's assistance. "Two men ran in here and told us a man was lying in the doorway of the Carousel Bar," the patrolman said. "They said he looked like he'd been mugged."

The Penn Central police are often called upon to assist victims of muggers in the neighborhood. "The city police used to have foot patrolmen around all the time," said Patrolman Donald Santanastasio. "They say they just don't have the manpower any more."

Representative Mario Biaggi of the Bronx asserted that Dr. Friedmann's murder and the attack upon Dr. Brody could have been prevented if there had been a foot patrolman on the designated post near the scene of the crime.

Representative Biaggi, once a patrolman himself, declared that sources within the precinct had told him that only six of the precinct's 48 foot-patrol posts were covered on the afternoon of Dr. Friedmann's stabbing. He said that a patrolman on a scooter was no substitute for a foot patrolman, and blamed what he called Police Commissioner Patrick V. Murphy's "exotic programs and specialization of police" for the lack of foot patrolmen that he said might have deterred the crime. He also noted that many of the Commissioner's programs were a "suicidal course" for the department and were taking policemen further and further away from the community.

Also in September 1972, in daylight, with scores of people looking on, a prominent lawyer and civic worker was mugged and robbed in Manhattan, on 109th Street between Fifth Avenue and Madison Avenue. The victim, Herman B. Glaser, the 56-year-old director of the New York Academy of Trial Lawyers, said that he thought that about 100 people were watching while three youths beat and robbed him. They tore the watch off his arm and a pocket off his pants to get at his wallet.

"It was like a jungle, but I guess that's New York City," he said later in an emergency room at Lenox Hill Hospital. "I can't understand the apathy of all the people on that street." The police, who arrived three minutes after the assailants fled into Central Park, said about 60 people were on the street when they arrived on the scene.

Exactly one week before, when Dr. Friedmann was murdered, the street was also crowded with passers-by, the police said, but apparently no one went to Professor Friedmann's aid.

In Westport, Connecticut, in November 1972, a psychiatrist died of the effects of a mugging during a visit to a low-income housing project in Bridgeport, whose residents he had befriended. His family said that he and his wife, both civil rights activists, had gone there to deliver bail money and that the doctor had been attacked when he went outside to get some tobacco from his car. His death, following a hatchet murder of a University of Bridgeport professor, brought the number of murders in Bridgeport to 15 for the year.

In another instance in which people observed a violent murder and did nothing to assist the victim, a young black boy was beaten to death in New York's South Village on October 30, 1972. At that time, a gang of white teenagers armed with bats and clubs beat two black youths into unconsciousness. Derrick Samuel Johnson, a 15-year-old Harlem youth, never regained consciousness and died at St. Vincent's Hospital.

According to *New York Post* reporter John Mullane, "No one who witnessed the attack . . . has come forward . . . to speak to detectives who are investigating the case. Police fear that they may never be able to make an arrest because witnesses are reluctant to speak out against any of the youngsters in the tightly knit neighborhood."

A middle-aged woman who saw a portion of the attack from her apartment window agreed to talk with a reporter about what she saw after a guarantee of anonymity.

"I heard this shouting and screaming, so I ran down to the window. Down in the street there were about 20 or 30 kids chasing a black boy up Thompson Street. He was about four lengths ahead of them and it looked like he'd get away when one of the kids threw a baseball bat at him. It caught him in the legs and he fell to the sidewalk. The kids— they were only about 15 or 16 years old—were on top of him in an instant, and they just began beating him over the head with their bats." She estimated that some 30 or 40 blows were struck before the group dispersed, leaving the black youth lying in a pool of blood.

"There were lots of people in the street when the attack took place," explained the woman. "It was just before 9 o'clock when the morning papers came up." She added, "There was also the usual group standing in front of the Italian social club." She noted that the bystanders "were encouraging the kids to attack. They were shouting 'get the nigger' and 'kill the bastard.' "

Also in New York, an 86-year-old man, sleeping with his clothes and shoes on because he did not have the strength to undress himself,

23

was bound and suffocated by thieves in September 1972, in the rectory of a church on West 40th Street. The man had been given sanctuary there because he did not have a place to live.

In November 1972, the Right Rev. Paul Moore, Jr., Episcopal Bishop of New York, was robbed at knife-point in Central Park. The bishop, a much decorated marine veteran of World War II and former suffragan bishop of Washington, D.C., said that the stickup took place on the park's main road. He said that he would "still walk in Central Park, but I might be more careful."

It is possible to spend the entire text of a lengthy volume simply reporting acts of violence and terror which have occurred in the nation's urban areas. Most of the cases reported thus far have occurred in New York City in the period of several weeks. Police reports in Chicago, Los Angeles, Houston, Philadelphia, Detroit, and other large cities tell very much the same story.

What has occurred in our large cities as a result of the wave of violent crimes we have endured in recent years is an almost total change in the atmosphere of such areas, and a real decline in the quality of life. Former Chicago Police official O. W. Wilson describes a residential development, surrounded by a high masonry wall and protected by armed guards, as a "sort of penitentiary in reverse—the good people on the inside and the bad people outside." Our condition is perilous, Wilson says, when our society reaches the point where "it is necessary for the good people to bar themselves behind locked doors to protect themselves against murderers."

Fear is prevalent in most urban areas. The number of people who express fear of walking alone in their own neighborhood at night has risen sharply, particularly in smaller cities, over the last four years, according to an April 1972 Gallup poll.

Nearly six out of every ten women interviewed—58 percent—said that they were afraid to go out alone at night, an increase of 14 percent over the results of a similar question asked in 1968. Those interviewed who live in cities with a population from 2,500 to 50,000 showed the greatest percentage increase of those experiencing fear, up 19 percent from 1968, as compared with increases of 11 percent for cities which had a population of 50,000 to 500,000 and a rise of 9 percent in cities with a population over 500,000.

Discussing why he had left New York City to live in Santa Fe, New Mexico, journalist Robert Mayer said, "We left, quite frankly, out of fear. Fear of physical harm, and fear of what New York was doing to our psyches. Many of our friends were talking of leaving the city, but felt encumbered by their children, or by jobs they did not want to give up. We resisted the impulse to flee as long as we could. And then we fled."

Enumerating the reasons for leaving, Mr. Mayer declared:

We left because a fellow I know was knifed in the belly as he walked through Times Square, minding his own business . . . . We left because a woman I know was raped on the rooftop of her apartment building, and was lucky to escape with her life. We left because my car was stolen and wrecked. We left because a woman in my office was spat upon by a truck driver when she ignored his obscene remarks. We left because a panhandler grabbed my camera as I walked on Washington Square Park, and threatened to smash it unless I gave him money. We left because for the last two years my wife could not go out alone after dark without shaking. We left because one day, as I opened the elevator door in our building, a woman inside shrank back in terror, her face white, her eyes wide with fear. She was our next-door neighbor, but for a split second she had not recognized me, and thought I meant her harm. In that brief instant, I had become the villain. I had victimized her.

Comparing the atmosphere of fear which lurks in New York and other urban areas today with the tranquillity of a past which is not very long ago, Robert Mayer recalls his own youth and makes this troubling analogy: "When I was a kid growing up in the Bronx, there was an old crone dressed all in black who used to prowl the neighborhood, scrounging in garbage cans. 'The garbage lady,' we called her. She was the neighborhood bogey man. Whenever we would see the garbage lady coming, we would dash inside our houses and hide behind our beds. Our parents sometimes found her rather a convenience. If ever we did anything bad, they would warn, the garbage lady would come around and get us.

"Now," he points out, "30 years later, the garbage lady stalks throughout the city, a hag with needle scars on her arms and a knife in her pocket. And we don't know what it was that we did bad. Will someone please let us know when she goes away? We would like to come home."

One crime that has increased notably in our large cities is that of forcible rape. Nationwide, 1971 witnessed a seven percent increase in reported rapes. In 1971, 39,878 rapes were reported, compared to 37,270 in 1970. Criminologists widely believe that actual completed rapes are four times or more higher than the reported figures indicate.

The majority of accused rapists are never convicted, according to the FBI uniform crime report. A bureau spokesman declares that "27.7 percent of the accused in forcible rape cases are found guilty; 15.6 percent are found guilty of a lesser offense; 35 percent are acquitted. And 22 percent are referred to juvenile court."

In response to the appalling rape statistics and the general rise in violence, the National Organization of Women (NOW) has a list of demands to law enforcement officers and municipal officials in several cities calling for increased police protection. A group of women in Miami, Florida, marched to City Hall to demonstrate their outrage over the increased sexual attacks. In New York City, radical feminists have sponsored several "speak-outs" on rape and discussed forming rape vigilantes.

In Washington, D.C., diplomats have been victimized in a number of crimes, and mounting fear exists within that city's international community. Odetta Sara, a 29-year-old Jordanian who works as a secretary for the public information section of the Saudi Arabian embassy, was interviewed by the *Washington Post*. She declared that one thing she doesn't like about the United States is crime: "It is shameful for a man to attack or rape a woman. A Jordanian would be put in prison forever if he did that, without anybody trying to find out why he did it."

When Finnish Ambassador Leo Tuominen's residence was burglarized, he remarked: "I have been in the diplomatic service 38 years and have never been robbed. I have served in all the countries in Europe and South America . . . and after only two months in Washington I am robbed. All that I had of value was taken. It wasn't a very nice way to receive a diplomat in this country."

Crime also worries Aree Nalampang and her husband Anrangsee, staff members in the student department of the Royal Thai Embassy, who live in Silver Spring, Maryland. "When I first came here, I was not afraid of things or people. Now I am afraid to go places at night," said the 36-year-old mother of two teenage daughters. "We have robbery in Thailand, but not killing people and burning their houses," added her 34-year-old husband.

The shock that foreign visitors and diplomats express over crime in the United States should not be understood to mean that crime does not exist in other parts of the world, or that it is not mounting. It is.

Speaking in November 1972, Secretary General Kurt Waldheim of the United Nations called for UN action to cope with a world "crime crisis of growing proportions." In a report to the General Assembly, he suggested that it might wish to make a commitment to crime prevention, review trends in world crime and ask him for such reports in future years.

Disputing the theory that crime and poverty go hand in hand, Waldheim noted that "despite material progress, human life has never had a greater sense of insecurity than it is experiencing today." He spoke of "the ever-increasing tide of known homicides, robberies, burglaries and sex offenses which plague so many areas of the world," citing figures from Canada, Poland, Uganda and Japan among others.

"Some of the most affluent countries are most sorely afflicted," he said, because crime is not "always or necessarily retreating before

the quite considerable extensions of health, education, housing and other social improvement programs."

New and special problems exist, he declared, in youths who go over from social protest to real crime; narcotics addicts who "turn to aggressive personal criminality" to support their habits; organized crime "applying modern systems and managerial patterns to the accumulation of capital by unlawful means; bribery and corruption, and related white-collar business crimes against tax collectors, workers and consumers."

Great Britain has expressed mounting concern over its increasing crime. In 1968 and again in 1969 the crime rate rose by approximately 7 percent a year. The increase in crimes of violence in London in 1969 was 23 percent. In 1968, the total strength of the police actually fell, and in 1969 it rose only marginally. In 1970, the police were 16,000 men short of their authorized establishment. The London *Economist* notes that "morale is low because of the abolition of the death penalty, to which the three most recent killings of policemen have contributed." That was in 1970. Since then crime has increased steadily.

In November 1972, three late teenage men sat uneasily awaiting sentencing in an Old Bailey courtroom in London and were told by Judge Gerald Hines that the charge on which they had been found guilty "is so serious that the courts are taking the view that the overwhelming need is to put a stop to it." The judge added, "I am sorry to say that although the course I feel bound to take may not be the best for you young men individually, it is one I feel driven to take in the public interest."

Judge Hines then sentenced the trio to three years in jail for mugging a 48-year-old clerk and robbing him of seven pounds (about $17.50). It was one of the stiffest sentences ever handed out in England on that charge.

Mugging is becoming an increasingly difficult problem in London, a city which always had its footpads, but whose streets, subway stations and byways generally have been regarded as safe for any pedestrian or traveler. But the number of muggings in London is not excessive when compared with American cities. Unofficial estimates of the number reported for the first ten months of 1972 are approximately 600. In combination with the numbers of other crimes in London, however, muggings seem to be increasing.

They increasingly are marked by violence, and more and more involve young girls as muggers and the appearance of more young mugging gangs. In the fall of 1972, three teenagers assaulted a 68-year-old man near the Waterloo subway station in a mugging attack. He died from injuries sustained in the assault. At about the same time, three teenage girls were sent to a juvenile center for attacking a young lady schoolteacher at a bus stop, knocking her down, kicking her, stealing her watch and trying to tear her rings from her fingers. In sending them to a detention center, the judge said, "If you had been men there would have been prison sentences."

Reflecting Britain's anxiety about rising crime and violence, Home Secretary Robert Carr told a meeting of British magistrates that "offenses of this kind are in a special way offenses against society, and public opinion will rightly not be content unless you, acting on behalf of the community, deal with them firmly. I think it is right that some treatment is severe. We should not be ashamed of using the word 'punishment' when referring to the treatment given to serious offenders, particularly those who commit violent crimes."

Discussing recent crime figures in England, Professor Howard Jones, head of the Department of Sociology at the University of Keele, points out that "personal violence forms more than twice as large a proportion of the total number of offences known to the police as it did during the period 1935-39. Malicious injury to property increased even more strikingly to more than three times its prewar proportion. Robbery is also over three times as important in our total crime picture as it was . . . . There has been an increase in personal violence and the destruction of property."

Crime and delinquency in England, as in the United States, has seen its most dramatic growth among the very young. Professor Jones notes that "if we consider those found guilty of indictable offences among boys and girls between the ages of 14 and 21 on a basis of number of offenders per 100,000 in the age group, this amounted to 2,090 in 1938. However, by 1960, this figure had increased to 5,136. In the last few years the rate has further increased to 6,529 in 1965."

Similar conclusions were reached by F. H. McClintock's study of crimes of violence showing that the proportion of youths aged 14 to 17 committing these offenses increased by 216 percent, and of those aged 17 to 21 by 153 percent between 1950 and 1960.

Sweden provides another case in point concerning the rapid rise in crime. Slums do not exist in Sweden and despite the fact that Swedes enjoy the highest standard of living in Europe, its juvenile delinquency rate is also the highest. Between 1950 and 1966 the number of crimes reported to the police rose from 161,778 to 410,904, an increase of over 250 percent. The figures correspond to 23 and 52.6 per 1,000 inhabitants. In the same period crimes of violence rose from 12,665 to 26,862, or 1.8 to 3.4 per 1,000 inhabitants. Bank robberies, which in 1950 were virtually unknown, have become common. In Stockholm, a city of about 800,000, they take place at the rate of one per week. In 1970, more than 500,000 crimes were recorded.

Seventy-five percent of all crimes in Sweden are committed by children and youth between the ages of ten and 25. Despite "sexual liberation" and "enlightenment," rape increased by 65.2 percent between 1963 and 1967. In addition, Sweden is one of the nations with the fastest rising rate of narcotic users among its young people. Its suicide rate is one of the highest in the world.

Even in the Communist world, where statistics are not easily available and where crime has long been considered a part of the capitalist system and something that would cease under socialism, it seems that crime is mounting. In October 1971, for example, the Soviet Union's national police chief went on television to talk about law and order. Speaking in a Soviet version of "Meet the Press," the police chief, Nikolai A. Shchelokov, sought to assure the populace that his forces were doing their best to curb crime but evidently still had a long way to go.

Mr. Shchelokov, who is a longtime personal associate of Leonid I. Brezhnev, the party leader, stated that crime rates in the country were declining. Yet his television appearance on Saturday, a non-working day with a large viewing audience, as well as his comments, suggested, in the words of *New York Times* Moscow correspondent Theodore Shabad, "lively concern over the crime situation."

Reading from notes in response to questions submitted by five Soviet reporters, Mr. Shchelokov stated that although crime is viewed in the Soviet Union as a "survival of the past," it will take time and an "unrelenting struggle" to eradicate it. He declared that police and other law enforcement agencies will be more effective in their fight on crime if they enlist public support and work closely with local communities.

The police chief called for an increased effort to reduce youth crime—not, he contended, because it was on the rise, but "out of concern for the well-being of the next generation." He cited no national statistics, which are secret, but a report on juvenile crime in one Soviet Republic (Estonia) noted a relative increase in offenses by older children, aged 16 and 17, who tended to be involved in assault and robbery, sex crimes and the petty violations of public order that are categorized in the Soviet Union as "hooliganism."

Mr. Shchelokov conceded, "We are not yet able to control crime everywhere and complaints about lack of police action are being received." He described hooliganism as particularly common in some places and when asked what the police intended to do during the five-year plan of 1971-75, he said that not only daytime but night patrols would be expanded and educational requirements for policemen would be raised.

Times correspondent Shabad pointed out that "in the absence of national crime statistics, the recent Estonian report, though limited to a relatively small part of this vast nation, helped to illuminate an aspect of life that has long been regarded as highly sensitive by the Soviet authorities."

The report, published in the October 1971 issue of the monthly *Sovetskoye Gosudarstvo i Pravo,* or *Soviet State and Law,* was written by H. A. Randalu, a jurist associated with the Institute of Economics of the Estonian Academy of Sciences in Tallinn, the Estonian capital. Limiting his computer analysis of trial and police records to the preceding several years, he found that petty theft, usually committed by youngsters 14 and 15 years old, had declined from 1965 to 1970 while more serious crimes against persons and against public order, associated with 16- and 17-year-olds, had increased.

The total number of young offenders, Mr. Randalu said, had remained virtually unchanged during the study period except for slight year-to-year fluctuations. But, he added, beneath that stabilization the trend has been toward more serious crimes among older teenagers.

Correlating types of crime with the backgrounds of the offenders, he found that hooliganism, or petty violations of public order, was particularly common among working teenagers, who accounted for 55 percent of these offenses.

The finding was further supported by the fact that the rate of hooliganism was highest in the textile mill town of Narva, where the rate of teenage employment is also the highest in Estonia.

Assault and robbery, sex crimes and other serious offenses against persons were found to be most common among teenagers who were neither in school nor employed. Although this category accounted for only 16 percent of all offenses in the 14 to 17 age group, it was responsible for 19.4 percent of the youths' sex crimes, 21.5 percent of crimes against persons and one-third of all assaults with intent to rob.

Intoxication, which was found to have increased steadily during the 1965 to 1970 period, was found to be a factor in 44 percent of crimes against persons, 56 percent of assaults and robbery, 61 percent of rapes and 76 percent of hooliganism.

Communist China has also proved an exception to the Communist theory that crime is a result of the social distress caused by capitalist exploitation, and that with the elimination of capitalism, crime would disappear.

Writing in the *Washington Star* from Hong Kong, Henry S. Bradsher observed that "the main problem is with youths who were removed from school during the Cultural Revolution and sent to farms. Some have returned illegally to cities and supported themselves by crime."

Mr. Bradsher notes that around Peking, the farmers keep watchdogs, and in Shanghai bicycles, which are the private transportation of the slightly prosperous, are locked up when parked. In Canton, pickpocket operations, theft and robbery have been reported. When a Shanghai guide was asked about the locked bicycles he replied that, "The old remnants of social problems from before liberation are still there, but they are decreasing."

The young people who refuse to feed pigs or hoe crops are unable to obtain jobs in the tightly controlled urban labor market. In order to subsist in the cities, they turn to crime. Since statistics are not available, their numbers are difficult to estimate. The problem has, however, become serious enough to be discussed by the Chinese provincial press and radio.

Kunming Radio reported a directive of the Yunnan provincial committee of the Communist Party which held up store clerk Yen Chia-pin as a heroic example. A "class enemy" tried to rob the cooperative store and Yen sought to "protect state property." Stabbed three times, Yen managed to wound his attacker before dying.

Other reports tell of special squads in Canton to round up youths who were sent to farms but came back. A search in one month turned up 20 of them. Young pickpockets who are caught get one side of their heads shaved clean before being sent back to the farm. For more serious crimes there is "labor reform" or imprisonment.

In Japan, in 1972, a terrorist group known as Rengo Sekigun, the United Red Army, tortured and killed 14 of its members, using ice-picks and swords. In West Germany, despite increased security measures, more than 320 bank robberies were committed in 1971, often with hostages involved, prompting newspaper outcries that the country was becoming an "oversized Chicago." Nigeria's military government is putting armed robbers to death before the firing squad, sometimes in groups of a dozen or more. In Israel, an increase in bank robberies is blamed by police on an influx of guns since the Six Day War of 1967, and submachine guns, one official said, are "the cheapest and most obtainable weapon."

Despite the rise in crime throughout the world, the fact remains that the United States continues to lead almost all other nations in violent crime—armed robberies, assaults, rape and murder. From 1966 through 1971, such crimes rose by 90 percent. The number of policemen killed has risen from 57 in 1969 to 100 in 1970 to 125 in 1971. One law enforcement official declared, "We're back to medieval times when peasants worked their fields by day and returned at night to the castle for safety against marauding bands—only now it's the apartment house that is locked up and placed under guard."

Herman Kahn, the director of the Hudson Institute, told an interviewer for the *Intellectual Digest* that "since World War II, all developed countries have had a sharp increase in safety on the streets. The only developed country in the world where it is unsafe to walk the streets at night is the United States of America. I really mean that. Nobody would be surprised at a young girl walking around Paris at three in the morning. The most obvious characteristic of cities around the world is that they are safe day and night. Except here."

To those who have charged that calls for "law and order" were veiled appeals to racism, Kahn declared: "Crime in the streets is crime in the streets. Americans want that stopped. They want to be like the rest of the world. Law and order was never a code word for anti-Negro. It is only in the imagination of academics and reporters and editors for literate newspapers that law and order means racism .... It is correct that most of the crimes Americans were objecting to were committed by Negroes, but people would have been just as mad if the crimes were committed by whites."

Whether crime and violence in America will continue at their rapidly rising pace or will decrease is a question about which close observers express radically different opinions. Consider the views of Professor Martin E. Wolfgang, a criminologist at the University of Pennsylvania and president of the American Academy of Political and Social Sciences, and of Sir Leon Radzinowicz, director of Cambridge University's Center for Studies in Criminology and Criminal Law.

"If our American friends were less optimistic about being able to reduce crime," said Radzinowicz, "they would do more about having a decent system of criminal justice instead of waiting for the miracle that has not happened and will never happen. There has been a deterioration of law and order in the last 15 or 20 years—an increase in crime of at least 6 percent and sometimes 10 percent per year in the largest countries."

One characteristic of the current crime wave which was commented upon by both men was that of the increasing prevalence of women criminals. "It's probably too early to speculate that women's liberation is a major explanation," Professor Wolfgang said. "A lot of it is late adolescent and early female crime, and much of that is an increase in drug use." Sir Leon noted, "We witness a more intensive participation of women today in economic life. They become more vulnerable to pressures, and more tempted."

Sir Leon told the story of his arrival in a newly independent developing country at the very moment when a bank was being held up. When he saw the Minister of Justice he said, "Excellency, it is a little embarrassing that the arrival of a criminologist has been synchronized with an attack on one of your leading banks." "Not at all," the Minister replied. "We are very delighted. It means that we are becoming civilized."

The fact is that crime in the United States is at an all-time high and is mounting rapidly. Few Americans who fear to leave their homes at night, who hesitate to conduct their lives along familiar and traditional patterns because of such fear, would agree that crime and violence is, in some way, an index of "civilization." They feel, instead, that it marks a reversion to barbarism, and they wonder where it will end, as courts and the legal system continue to appear more sympathetic to the perpetrators than to the victims of crime.

They know that something is wrong, but often are unable to explain just what it is. Many find the easy answer—that Negroes commit most crimes of violence and that the crime problem is, therefore, essentially a racial problem, an explanation which, in some way, deals with reality.

Unfortunately, this explanation, while true on one level, introduces far more questions than it answers.

Chapter 2

Crime In The Black Inner City

When Americans reflect upon the rising crime and violence in their cities they have more and more come to the conclusion that in many respects the crime problem is a Negro problem.

Professor Marvin Wolfgang points out that "it is the black crime rate that most people are concerned about; it is the black crime rate that is high."

The figures released in 1971 by the Federal Bureau of Investigation make it clear that this concern is by no means based upon racial prejudice. Although the black population is 12 percent of the nation, blacks accounted for 66 percent of the reported arrests for robbery, 62 percent for murder, 50 percent for rape and 47 percent for assault. Clearly, blacks are the largest single group in the crime rate.

The black inner city of almost every major metropolitan area is a center of crime. Discussing the inner city of Washington, D.C., Paul W. Valentine noted that "the economy of Washington's ghetto, like most others in the country, is supported in part by a vital sprawling sub-economy called crime. Pimps, hustlers, fences, dope dealers, boosters and an assortment of other criminals pump millions of dollars into and out of the ghetto every day. At any given moment there are probably a minimum of 2,500 to 3,000 ghetto residents who are employed full-time in illegal livelihoods . . . ."

Writing in the *Washington Post,* Valentine estimated that prostitution is at least a $12 million a year industry, supporting 3,000 full-time and parttime streetwalkers, three to four dozen pimps and a network of rented rooms. He estimated that the numbers racket is a $150 million annual industry and that approximately $500,000 in bets is placed each day, six days a week, mostly by blacks. In addition, narcotics addicts, again primarily black, pay $109.5 million annually for their heroin supply. The District of Columbia Corrections Department estimates that there are 15,000 addicts in the city with an average daily habit of $25 each. This estimate is considered low.

Representative William Clay of Missouri expresses the view that some 15 percent of the gross income in American urban slums stems from criminal activity. He states that this estimate is based on federal economic data and his own experience as a one-time ghetto dweller. The bulk of the money generated by heroin traffic, he says, leaves the ghetto "and goes to the handful of guys at the top of the business . . . . But most other money from prostitution, numbers, liquor, things like that, stays in the community." Writing in the *Boston Globe,* Representative Clay argued that "a hustler can make up to $300 a day or more. To him, the square who gets up at 5 a.m., takes a bus across town, works eight hours and returns at 6 p.m. is not wise to the system."

The crime that seems so pervasive in Washington's inner city has spread an atmosphere of fear throughout the entire area. The number of taxi-cab drivers has dropped to less than 11,000 from 13,000 in two years. James E. Jewell, president of the Independent Taxi Owners Association, declares, "This is a very dangerous town to drive in. Many men won't work after the sun goes down."

Foreign embassies have also become targets of crime. During an independence day celebration at the Mexican Embassy, two guests were robbed. Female employees have been accosted. Vandals have struck repeatedly. All embassy doors are now kept locked and a fence has been erected around the property. "We live in fear," says a spokesman.

Among those victimized by crime in Washington have been Senator Frank Church of Idaho, White House Press Secretary Ronald Ziegler, the President's personal secretary Rose Mary Woods and Deputy Defense Secretary David Packard. Senate Majority Leader Mike Mansfield expressed outrage over the "senseless" slaying of a fellow Montanan and friend in the streets of Washington. He took the Senate floor to demand "new and better ways to fight crime to cut down the inordinate rate of violence."

Discussing the atmosphere of fear in the nation's capital, Monroe

W. Karmin, writing in the *Wall Street Journal,* notes: "Cruise through downtown Washington in a police car on a Saturday night and the mood can be felt. On F Street, the main downtown shopping street, merchants lock their doors at 6 p.m. Many put up iron grill-work nightly to protect their windows. Shoppers and employees hurry to the bus stops. Many employees who fear the lonely walk at the end of the bus ride wait in the stores until their spouses drive up to take them home. At 7 p.m. F Street is almost deserted."

Mr. Karmin continues: "The relatively small number of people out for an evening of entertainment arrive a bit later. Some go to the National Theatre, which now raises its curtain at 7:30 p.m. instead of 8:30 so patrons can get home early. Some head for downtown movie theatres . . . . Fashionable Georgetown, more than a mile from downtown, is still lively, as are some of the posh restaurants and clubs. But that's about it. Much of Washington is dark and scared . . . . 'Watch the people,' advises a seasoned policeman. 'See how they walk quickly and with a purpose. There's no casual strolling. People don't come into this town at night unless they have a specific destination in mind. They go straight to it and then go home as fast as possible.' "

Fear inhibits daytime activity as well. A survey taken by the Metropolitan Washington Council of Governments discovered that 65 percent of the city's largely white suburban residents visit the downtown area less than once a month, and 15 percent come downtown less than once a year. Asked their chief worry, the large majority of those surveyed responded: "Crime."

The National Presbyterian Church has moved from its 60-year-old location about a half mile from the White House to a new site three miles farther out. The Reverend Edward L. R. Elson calls the new location "the quietest zone in Washington," but vandalism is as bad at the new church as at the old one. According to Mr. Elson, the vandalism has included "obscenity on chapel pillars, destruction in the church hall and lights pilfered and broken."

In many instances, government programs which were meant to improve living conditions among blacks in the inner city and to reduce crime and violence have had precisely the opposite effect. This is particularly true with regard to urban renewal policies and the high-rise apartment buildings which have been constructed with public funds.

A three-year study by a New York University research team, issued in November 1972, has produced evidence of a major cause of the terror that afflicts public housing residents in many major cities: the higher the building, the higher the crime rate. The most dangerous type of public housing of all, the study found, is the high-rise elevator building with floor upon floor of "double-loaded corridors" serving so many apartments, ranging along both sides of the hall, that residents can't tell neighbors from strangers. The crime rate in such buildings is more than twice that in walk-up public housing.

In three-floor walk-up buildings, the study found, there were 30 serious crimes for every thousand families. In buildings of six or seven floors, there were 41 serious crimes. In high-rise buildings of 13 to 30 floors there were 68.

While the total serious crime rate was twice as high in tall buildings as in walk-ups, the rate of crime in public spaces in the high-rises was seven times higher. Why was this the case? The study, conducted by New York University's Institute of Planning and Housing and financed by research grants from federal and city agencies, offers this answer: "In a high-rise, double-loaded corridor apartment tower, the only defensible space is the interior of the apartment itself; everything else is a 'no man's land,' neither public nor private. Unlike the well-peopled and continually surveyed public streets, these interior areas are sparsely used and impossible to survey; they become a nether world of fear and crime."

"Van Dyke" and "Brownsville" are the names of two New York City public housing developments across the street from one another in Brooklyn. Almost identical in size, each houses approximately 6,000 people. Most residents are black, poor, often broken families, mostly on welfare and endowed with a large number of children. Van Dyke is a cluster of 14-story high-rise slabs, with a few three story buildings mixed in. The Brownsville project houses its residents in more closely spaced three- to six-story apartment houses of some diversity.

The high-rising Van Dyke project was found to have 66 percent more crime than the low-rise Brownsville houses—over two and one-half times more robberies and 60 percent more felonies, misdemeanors and other offenses. In addition, Van Dyke, though more recently constructed, requires a total of 72 percent more maintenance work than its older neighbor.

While most observers who consider these statistics conclude that public housing and urban renewal projects should, in the future, be constructed in a different manner, some have come to the more realistic conclusion that the concept of huge public housing projects must lead inevitably to the high crime situation we have faced, regardless of design.

Discussing the concept of urban renewal, Michael Harrington, in his volume *The Other America,* declares that "under the present setup it is the poor who are victimized by urban renewal. In 1959 Charles Abrams told a Senate Committee that the public housing program had become 'tattered, perverted and shrunk ... little more than an adjunct of the publicly subsidized private urban renewal program.' This urban renewal program too, while it does help the cities to get rid of slums, has developed into a device for displacing the poor from their foot-holds to make way for higher rental dwellings which those displaced cannot afford. Thus, the lowest income family remains the forgotten family."

Harrington points out that many public housing projects "have become low-income ghettos, centers for juvenile gangs, modern poor farms where social disintegration is institutionalized. In addition, the destruction of old slum neighborhoods has resulted in mass evictions. The new public housing did not provide enough units for those who had been driven out to make way for improvement. The projects thus created new slums and intensified the pressures within the old slums."

One example cited by Mr. Harrington is that which occurred in 1959 in the Mill Creek area of St. Louis, which was cleared as part of an urban renewal effort. In place of a Negro slum there rose a middle-income housing development. "Typically," he writes, "the majority of those evicted were forced to find housing within the existing and contracted Negro ghetto. In St. Louis, 50 percent of the families displaced disappeared from sight of the authorities altogether."

In December 1959, a grand jury investigation in St. Louis found that in the housing developments "the rates of crimes against the person—murder, rape, robbery, and aggravated assault—are approximately two and a half times higher than the city-wide average . . . based on testimony we have received, outside teenage hoodlums have used the project buildings for gambling, drinking, and all kinds of minor crimes . . . ."

A similarly critical view of urban renewal programs has come from Father Theodore Hesburgh, president of the University of Notre Dame and formerly chairman of the Civil Rights Commission. He noted that "these enormous federal programs . . . are coming in, supposedly to help the community. They want to rebuild society. What has happened in many cases is that people who are presently in the worst situation have their houses swept out from under them by bulldozers; they were given very little help in finding houses and they generally do worse than where they came from. This is immoral."

By forcing people out of their homes and neighborhoods, by placing them together in high-rise urban ghettos financed by the federal government, crime has been stimulated and one of the unique features of such crime in the inner city in the 1960s and 1970s has been the high-rise housing project. Crime within these projects has been aimed at poor, often defenseless black women, children and old people. This is, of course, not the kind of crime that excites the general society. It is, however, an unfortunate fact of life for untold numbers of black residents of the inner city.

Crime that does excite public concern—and which occurs both within the inner city and in outlying areas to which inner-city children have been bused to school—is crime and violence within our educational institutions. In many instances, schools have become battlegrounds, and in many cities policemen now patrol the hallways of each building, and teachers make certain that their classroom doors are locked before beginning the business of education.

In New York City, the number of reported acts of crime and violence in and around city schools increased from 333 in 1970 to 580 in 1971, according to Board of Education figures. These incidents involved assaults on teachers and students, including rapes, attempted rapes and molestations, robberies and purse snatchings, the setting off of smoke and fire bombs, and telephoned and written threats against school staff members. Among the incidents reported to school headquarters during the 1971 calendar year were 285 assaults on teachers and other school personnel.

The record of school incidents is compiled by a unit of the Office of Education Information Services at central headquarters. Each school day the office gives top officials a "Log of Untoward Incidents" reported by the schools. Among the incidents reported in the winter of 1972 were these:

• An English teacher at a Brooklyn junior high school was assaulted by two intruders he had encountered in the hall. They hit him on the head with a hammer and knocked him down a flight of steps. The teacher was taken semiconscious to a hospital.

• Students from a Bronx high school were attacked by a group of youths while waiting for buses. Several students were injured.

• Two students sitting in the lunchroom of a Manhattan high school were attacked by four unidentified assailants. Both youngsters suffered stab wounds of the back and other injuries.

• An eight-year-old boy, on his way back to class from the lavatory, was "accosted by a male intruder who dragged him to the fourth floor landing leading to the roof and sexually assaulted him."

The incidents reported to authorities are, it is estimated, only a small portion of those which occur. Albert Shanker, president of the teacher's union, said that many teachers, parents and students do not report incidents to local school officials because they "have no confidence in the school system's procedures for dealing with violence" and fear that a complaint could possibly lead to another assault.

In his column in the *Washington Post,* black journalist William Raspberry discussed a call he had received from a white parent whose daughter was a member of a minority of white students at one of the city's public schools.

"What am I supposed to do?" asked the mother. She was doubtful that her daughter would be able to finish out the school year, and was virtually certain that the girl's brother, who will soon enter high school, will not be attending the Washington public schools. "It's a question of physical safety," said the mother, herself a teacher.

"At first," wrote Raspberry, "it was only words, racial epithets, insulting remarks—threats no less menacing because they were followed by laughter. At this school, or at others in the city, it's considered sort of a hip thing for black kids to pick on white ones. The woman says her daughter had tried to ignore the taunts (for a long time she didn't even tell her parents what was happening) but the situation grew worse. Recently it became physical: a teenage boy struck her."

What are the choices, asks Raspberry: "What do you do? Arrange private transportation that you can't afford? Find a private school, perhaps with an inferior education program, that you can afford even less? Move out of the city? They are all intolerable choices, and to say that black people have been faced with equally intolerable choices hardly suffices as answer."

The situation in the nation's schools in the 1970s makes the "blackboard jungle" days of the 1950s seem mild by comparison. In November 1972, teachers at the predominantly black Thomas Jefferson High School in the East New York section of Brooklyn canceled classes and sent all 800 students home to protest "rampages" by youth gangs and other acts of violence at the school.

In what was believed to be the first such action in New York by teachers complaining of the growing violence in the schools, the 59 teachers called off classes and held a meeting with City Hall officials, representatives of the United Federation of Teachers, the police and members of the central Board of Education's school security office to discuss the problem.

"They felt a strong sense of frustration," said Mrs. Margaret Baird, the principal at Thomas Jefferson. "They feel that they're under siege, and basically it's a problem of not enough security."

Mrs. Baird said that the chain-link fences around the complex of four one-story buildings at Linden Boulevard and Vermont Street had been climbed repeatedly by members of such gangs as the Black Spades and the Tomahawks. The Tomahawks were also linked to an attack upon acting principal Stanley Lavnick of Brooklyn's Junior High School 166. In November 1972, from five to a dozen teenage boys beat the principal when he tried to stop them from assaulting a younger boy from his school. Lavnick was hit in the head several times.

District Superintendent Annete Goldman said that in the six weeks prior to the attack on Mr. Lavnick a number of teachers had been mugged in the district. "It's a little ridiculous to try to run an educational system under such a Damocles sword. It keeps dangling and swerving and swinging," she added.

Mrs. Goldman noted, "We call the Police Department and all they can do is send a couple of cars around the district, which is very vast.

We have 34 buildings in this district. They send two people down, but they can't be in every school. We've had many teachers leave the district because they feel unsafe. Teachers go out to their cars and there are no cars left. Tires are slashed, batteries taken, cars are wrecked, the entire morale is suffering. You tell me how you can concentrate on improving the reading when you have to worry about vandalism and theft."

If anything is standing in the way of black children learning to read and write and obtaining the tools necessary for success in the American society, it is these black gangs which perpetrate violence and produce fear within the entire inner city area. Too often, the response of allegedly "responsible" leaders, both white and black, is a conciliatory one toward those who have created disruption and fear, and not one that seeks to correct the problem.

Abraham H. Lass, a former high school teacher in Brooklyn, criticized this approach in an article in the *New York Times* published in November 1971. He noted that the leaders of the Board of Education "seem inclined to the current notion that the junkies are pushing dope, the rapists are raping, the molesters are molesting, the arsonists are setting fires in the schools, the vandals are smashing hundreds of thousands of school windows, the disoriented youngsters are running amok because they find their courses of study not relevant. So, give the curriculum more contemporary zing. Let the children take what they want. And the mayhem will cease."

Unfortunately, states Mr. Lass, this course is the course of disaster. He concludes his article by pointing out that "the parents and children who can are running from our city schools. They are not deceived by Chancellor Scribner's nor the Board of Education's panaceas. They know that the climate of fear that has settled over the schools has nothing whatever to do with the curriculum, the teachers, the principals, the presence or the absence of such experiments and innovations as street academies, mini-schools and mini-courses. They know the score better than the official ostriches at Livingston Street."

Nearly half of the high school students in New York City are more than occasional users of some "psychoactive drug," according to the report issued by the Fleischmann Commission in October 1972. The report estimated that in New York City, where the drug problem was most serious, 45 percent of the students in grades ten through 12 and 20 percent of those in grades seven through nine are "currently users of some psychoactive drug."

The growth in narcotics addiction and school violence in the inner cities of the nation's large metropolitan areas seems to be intrinsically linked with the rise in youth gangs, which are, in most instances, racially based and motivated.

Writing in the *New York Times* of November 27, 1972, Robert A.

Wright declares that "youthful assassins in three major American cities have committed more than 100 murders this year in what some police officials fear may be a resurgence of the street gang warfare that swept urban America in the 1950s. The cities are Los Angeles, where there have been 31 deaths caused by gangs; Philadelphia, where the total is 37, and New York, where there have been 30 gang killings in the Bronx alone, the borough with by far the highest gang toll."

Black gangs are, of course, not the only gangs involved in the increasing violence. In San Francisco, the Chinese community has been terrorized by gangs of youthful extortionists. The police arrested six members of the teenage gang, composed mostly of Filipino-Americans, and charged them with four armed robberies, including one in which a policeman was shot at. Similarly, American schools are not the only ones beset by youthful violence.

In England an investigation into school violence was commissioned in 1972 by the 56,000-member National Association of Schoolmasters and was carried out by Ludwig Lowenstein, senior educational psychologist for Hampshire. One in ten of the 622 schools reporting violence claimed attacks on staff, pupils and property were either "very frequent" or "frequent."

The English survey showed that schoolmasters reported 295 incidents of violence against property such as the tearing up of school books, destruction of other pupil's belongings, damage to toilets and the breaking of windows and furniture. The schoolmasters also told of 273 examples of violence against other pupils, including gang fighting, punching, hair-pulling, waiting for a child to leave school and then attacking him and "vicious attacks on other children with various weapons."

There were 205 incidents of bullying mentioned by the teachers, 178 cases of "violence against teachers," 56 scenes of "gang violence" and 47 examples of "extortion." Terry Casey, leader of the National Association of Schoolmasters, says in his introduction to the report that "solid facts support the view that violence and indiscipline have already reached intolerable levels in more than a few schools. Teachers take the gloomy but realistic view that the raising of the school-leaving age will inevitably exacerbate these difficulties."

The most violence, however, clearly occurs in the United States. In our country, moreover, it is clear that blacks are the predominant victims of violence as well as the primary perpetrators of it. Ron Bloomberg, an advertising executive, placed an advertisement in the *Philadelphia Bulletin* with the headline, "Say a Prayer for the Children of Philadelphia." It appeared over a photograph of a black boy sprawled on a street clutching his stomach, which had been blown open by a shotgun blast. The text asserted that the city had done nothing to alleviate gang violence, although city officials say they are spending $4 million a year in programs aimed at ending it. Mr. Bloomberg said in an interview that he found that "gang killings don't make the papers any more, especially if you're a black kid. Maybe they'll get a couple of lines on the back pages."

Los Angeles now has some 150 gangs, compared with about 75 in the 1950s. Police Lieutenant Appier notes that memberships are as small as eight or ten and as high as in the thousands. They range from 11 years of age to, usually, 18. Most are males, although increasing numbers of girls are admitted or formed into auxiliaries. He states that most gangs are black, with a sprinkling of Mexican-American groups.

Similarly, in New York police say that gangs more than doubled in 1972. A proliferation that started in the Bronx spread to Manhattan, Brooklyn and Queens, with a total of 285 distinct gangs identified by the police. Police Sergeant Collins says that gangs vary in size from 35 to 100 members. "We're dealing with 9,000 kids running around," he says. Most are black or Hispanic, but police note that white gangs have been formed in defense.

An example of the terror inflicted by black gangs in racially motivated violence may be seen in the case of John Keith Lunsford of Prince Georges County, Maryland, a Washington, D.C., suburb.

Lunsford was an eighth-grade student at Walker Mill Junior School. About a block away from his home in District Heights, Maryland, he was attacked by a large group of black youths, perhaps 20. The attack produced an emotional trauma and brain injury, but six months after it occurred the *Washington Post* reported that "the 17 youths charged in the attack have not been brought to trial, and there is a possibility that because of legal difficulties most of them will not be."

An assistant county prosecutor, Carmen Tidler, said that her investigation, which included questioning the suspects, showed that the attack by some of the youths "apparently started as a racial thing—because he was a white kid," but that others said later "they didn't know why . . . they were just beating him."

Keith remembers someone yelled, "Stop that white boy," as he walked down a path leading away from the school. Then he was tackled, beaten, kicked and struck with sticks. The fury lasted less than a minute; it left Keith with a blood clot on his brain, and he underwent surgery. To relieve the brain's swelling, a section of his skull was removed.

In the weeks that followed, doctors at Prince Georges General Hospital concluded that Keith had lost his left peripheral vision. His speech was slurred and his right eyelid hung a shade lower than his left. Dr. Gertrude Cotts, a psychiatrist at the Psychiatric Institute of Washington, said that Keith "retreated" into the safety of his early childhood. According to psychiatrists who have examined Keith, he apparently identified his savage treatment with his coming adulthood, then regressed to enter what he looked upon as an earlier, happier time.

After unsuccessful treatment Keith was finally admitted to a Washington mental hospital. Psychiatrists have said that Keith's regression has taken him back about ten years, and that he could be in an institution for years. Keith's daily costs at the institution total more than $100 a day.

Seventeen students at Walker Mill were arrested and charged in the attack. Two were charged with assault and intent to murder, and the others with assault and battery. All were released to the custody of their parents pending a trial, which six months later had not been scheduled.

Mrs. Tidler, the Prince Georges assistant prosecutor handling the case, said that she had several confessions, but that under Maryland law corroboration is required to convict juveniles. "A lot of kids saw it happen, but nobody wants to talk," Mrs. Tidler said. "These witnesses are scared to death. Apparently it was a bad group, because the witnesses are very afraid."

Walker Mill draws its students from an area along the Washington, D.C., boundary that is rapidly changing from white to black. Of the school's 872 students, 139—15.9 percent—are white. The school was opened in September 1970 to relieve overcrowding in neighboring schools. At its birth it was the scene of racial fighting, and the administrators said that racial tension has never been completely absent. Many white parents kept their children home for days after the beating.

Racial incidents such as this, multiplied many fold across the country, have led to a white exodus from the cities and the corresponding development of all-black schools within the cities. It is this exodus and that development which have led to government pressures for school busing across state and county lines to achieve an artificial racial balance, which in turn has led to the political controversy of recent years.

In Houston, Texas, white enrollment in the public schools declined 20 percent between 1970 and 1972, reflecting a nationwide white flight to the suburbs. Writing in the *New York Times*, Martin Waldron points out, "Many public officials around the country attribute the exodus partly to crime, congestion and pollution, but they say that the major cause is school integration." The fact may be that it is crime *within* the schools in the inner city which has been the prime factor in causing the recent suburban migration.

In Atlanta, whites began moving out of the city in the 1950s. By 1972, about 77 percent of that city's public school population was Negro, while many of the bedroom suburbs were practically all white. In New York City in 1958, some 85 percent of the students attending academic high schools in New York were white. In 1971, only 48 percent were white. An estimated total of two million whites moved from New York City in the 20 years from 1952 to 1972 and have been replaced by Negroes and Puerto Ricans.

While a great deal is said and written about the fact that Negroes are responsible for the majority of serious crimes in our urban areas, less is said about the fact that they are also the predominant victims —that the all-black inner city areas of New York, Chicago, Washington, Los Angeles and other cities are more dangerous than white areas within those cities, or in the surrounding suburbs. If white Americans fear crime and violence, that fear is even more overwhelming for black Americans, since most of them live in the midst of it.

The police in the District of Columbia keep a record by race of persons who complain of certain crimes. In its annual report for the fiscal year that ended June 30, 1971, the department reported that in certain categories of serious crime—such as murder, rape, robbery and aggravated assault—there were 6,651 white complainants and 14,386 black complainants.

Robbery and related crimes such as purse-snatchings accounted for 6,015 complaints from whites and 10,086 complaints from nonwhites. This means that in other categories—murder, rape, aggravated assault —the number of nonwhite complaints was 4,300 while white victims numbered 636.

In the categories of murder, manslaughter and negligent homicide, there were 27 complaints involving whites and 201 involving blacks. A total of 113 whites complained of rape and related crimes as against 348 nonwhites.

Writing in the *Washington Post,* J. Y. Smith points out that "blacks do not need the police department to tell them that many of them become the victims of crime. It is necessary only to walk around the city and see the number of businesses, owned by blacks and whites alike, that have heavy iron shutters that cover windows. Many store owners keep firearms on the premises. Many citizens keep guard dogs. All these are manifestations of an awareness of the crime problem in both the black and white communities."

District Superior Court Judge Harry T. Alexander, who has a reputation of ensuring that the rights of defendants are enforced, declares: "I'm in a position to know that black people abhor crime, just like white people. People who talk about crime fail to mention that the vast majority of black citizens are law-abiding. Crime in this city is perpetrated by a relatively small number of recidivists, which suggests that there may be a problem in our prison system."

Fear clearly prevails in the black inner city. Writing in *New York* magazine, black author Orde Coombs describes his own life in Harlem, and the lives of his family and friends. He writes, "In the past year the following incidents have occurred to black people close to me: a cousin, 70 years old and suffering from a lymphatic disorder, is knocked down and robbed of $10 by two young blacks at four o'clock in the afternoon on Decatur Street in Brooklyn. A girl friend, 26 years old, is dragged by her hair behind a hedge near the Clinton Avenue Apartments in Brooklyn. Her assailant is a black man in his early twenties and her muffled screams attract the attention of two old men who chase the ambusher away. A friend, male, 36 years old, is returning to his apartment on Central Park West when two black junkies pull a knife on him in his vestibule and relieve him of his money and his watch."

The author quotes a black woman who has been in Harlem politics for a quarter of a century, who states, "After Nixon, the person I fear most in the world is the ghetto black teenager." Her friend, a lawyer's wife who was determined to raise her children in Harlem, finally, after a series of incidents, gave up when her ten-year-old son was robbed of $3 on a sunny day in front of Harlem Hospital by two middle-aged black women. She declared: "There is no hope. I can stay here because I know how to fight, but I can't stand to look at the fright in my children's eyes."

The 5th Division of the New York City police force covers part of the Harlem area. It extends northward from 100th Street to the Harlem River. It is bounded by Manhattan Avenue on the east and the Hudson River on the west. The 6th Division covers the remainder. It extends northward from 110th Street to 160th Street and is bounded on the east by the Harlem River and on the west by Manhattan and St. Nicholas avenues. In the first six months of 1972, in this relatively small area, the following reported crimes took place: 8,600 robberies, 9,000 burglaries, 3,300 acts of criminal assault, 200 homicides. "Harlem," states Orde Coombs, "our community—has become one of the most dangerous places in the world."

A great deal has been said and written concerning police mistreatment of blacks and of members of other minority groups. There is no doubt that both in the South and in many large cities of the North police brutality has been a reality. Although indications are that it is diminishing, there are nevertheless disturbing examples of its continuation which no citizen of good will can ignore. The press gives much coverage to the criticism of the police presented by black spokesmen, often militants who appear to be as much against the concept of law itself as they are against its abuse in individual instances. The general impression in the white society is, quite understandably, that the majority of Negroes view the police as the enemy, and are themselves unconcerned with the mounting problem of crime. This is far from the truth.

While there is a justified concern over police abuse, and this concern is also prevalent in the white society as is indicated by the investigations of police corruption in New York and other large cities, the fact is that the single most important attitude expressed by blacks concerning the police is that they want more and better police protection of their own inner city communities.

George Sternlieb's Center for Urban Policy Research conducted a poll to determine the chief concerns of people on welfare in New York. "It was law and order all the way," says Sternlieb. "These people live in fear—physical fear—all the time."

In Los Angeles, a study was conducted by the community relations section of the office of Police Chief Edward Davis. The study showed that a majority of blacks liked the police and wanted more police patrols in their neighborhoods.

Expressing the anguish of black neighborhoods in need of effective law enforcement, Orde Coombs stated, "We can no longer excuse crime because of society's inequities, for we will not live to see the end of those injustices. We stand menaced by our kith and kin. All our nobility and all our endurance, which have brought us to this place, will be corroded by the unremitting fear of the muggers who hide behind every lamppost. It is inconceivable to me that we who prevailed in spite of the barbarism of white people should, in the last quarter of the 20th century, stand as mute spectators to our doom."

Speaking for residents of the inner city, Louis S. Campbell, a resident of the Bedford-Stuyvesant section of Brooklyn, discussed the fear felt by himself and others in the area. He states, "One of these nights I will not be coming home to my wife and four-year-old son. I will have been the victim of one of the numerous packs of muggers that have turned the streets of Bedford-Stuyvesant and Williamsburg into an asphalt jungle filled with terror and violence for my fellow black and Puerto Rican neighbors and myself and my family."

Campbell, a black Puerto Rican, grew up in Harlem and East Harlem. He noted that "as a young man I would come home late at night from evening college after working during the day. During all my previous 39 years I never really felt afraid for my own safety. I have been afraid for my mother, my son, my wife and other loved relatives, but never for myself. Now I'm afraid, really afraid, because I can see my number coming up, and feel absolutely helpless."

Expressing the feeling of many black inner city residents, Campbell states that "I want to see my son grow up into a happy, successful and honorable person. What is most terrifying is the knowledge that the odds are now definitely against that happening. So many of my friends, neighbors and relatives are getting mugged, stabbed, assaulted and robbed that I know it is just a matter of days or merely hours before my turn will come."

While black militants argue against law enforcement and urge racially motivated violence, Louis Campbell speaks eloquently for what has been, until recently, a black silent majority. He urges action to correct the trend toward decay and barbarity: "I pray that the people and our leaders wake up, organize and stamp out illicit drugs, permissiveness and loss of respect for authority, which I know are the causes of this tremendous increase in violent crime. Then we will be able to save the lives of our children and of countless other people who deserve a life free from fear of a violent death or even a violent mugging. Then people will be able to concentrate on living life to its fullest, on being happy, bright-eyed and filled with a love for humanity that is reciprocated by their fellow human beings."

If any single problem looms large in the inner city areas of the nation's cities it is that of increased narcotics addiction leading to increased crime in order to pay for the habit. The extent of the increase in addiction may be seen not only by testimony of police and narcotics officers, but by figures on deaths attributed to heroin. Between 1967 and 1971, the number of deaths in Los Angeles County attributed to heroin use more than tripled. A Harvard student task force has used several techniques to estimate the size of the heroin-using population in Boston, and concludes that there was a tenfold increase in the decade of the 1960s. A group at the University of Southern California estimated that there are at least 50,000 addicts in Los Angeles; the Harvard group estimated that there are 6,000 in Boston; various sources refer to 100,000 addicts in New York.

In a discussion of the problem of heroin in *The Public Interest* of Fall 1972, James Q. Wilson, Mark H. Moore and I. David Wheat, Jr., note that "black males living in low-income neighborhoods, coming from broken or rejecting families, and involved in 'street life' have much higher chances of addiction than upper middle-class whites in stable families and 'normal' occupations . . . . It is easy to argue that heroin use occurs only among people who have serious problems (and thus to argue that the way to end addiction is to solve the underlying problems), but in fact many heavy users seem to have no major problems at all. Isidor Chein and his co-workers in their leading study of addiction in New York (*The Road to H*) found that between a quarter and a third of addicts seemed to have no problems for which heroin use was a compensation . . . . When asked how they got started on heroin, addicts almost universally give the same answer: They were offered some by a friend. They tried it, often in a group setting, and found they liked it . . . . Heroin use grows through peer group contacts, and those peer groups most vulnerable to experimenting with it are those that include a person who himself has recently tried it and whose enthusiasm for it is contagious."

A study done at American University found that the average age at which identifiable addicts in Washington, D.C., began using heroin was under 19. Though stories of youngsters under 15 becoming addicts are heard more and more often, most studies place the beginning of heavy use between the ages of 17 and 19. It is persons in this age group who are most exposed to the contagion, and most particularly in the black inner city.

The Public Interest article states of these young people, "They are intensely involved in peer groups; many have begun to become part of 'street society,' because they had either dropped out of or graduated from schools; and they are most likely to suffer from boredom and a desire to 'prove themselves.' It is claimed that many of those who become serious addicts 'mature out' of their heroin use sometime in their thirties, in much the same way that many juvenile delinquents spontaneously cease committing criminal acts when they become older. Unfortunately, not much is known about 'maturing out,' and it is even possible that it is a less common cause of ending heroin use than death or imprisonment."

Estimates of the proportion of all property crime committed by addicts range from 25 to 67 percent. The kinds of crimes committed by addicts are well-known. Selling heroin is one of the most important of these. The Hudson Institute estimated that almost half of the annual heroin consumption in New York is financed by selling heroin and related services (such as selling or renting the equipment needed for injecting heroin). Of the nondrug crimes, shoplifting, burglary and prostitution account for the largest proportion of addict income used for drug purchases—perhaps 40 to 50 percent. Muggings and armed robberies are also committed regularly by addicts, and even in burglary violence may result. Thus, the correlation between crimes of violence as well as crimes against property and narcotics addiction is significant.

Estimates in New York City of the amount of property taken annually by narcotics addicts range from a high into the billions of dollars to a low of more than $500 million. It is clear, state *The Public Interest* authors, "that addiction produces a significant increase in criminality of two kinds—stealing from innocent victims and selling heroin illegally to willing consumers. More accurately, the heroin black market provides incentives for at least two kinds of antisocial acts—theft (with its attendant fear) and further spreading the use of heroin."

The black community is far more concerned about the rise in narcotics addiction than any other segment of society, although that concern is not publicized and black opponents of the narcotics traffic often remain mute voices in a media-dominated society which gives more of its attention to the flamboyant rhetoric of radicalism than to the serious concerns of the majority of inner city residents.

This incident, as recorded in the black weekly magazine *Jet,* is

49

typical: "Late on a Friday evening, a 13-year-old black boy named John tightly strapped his forearm with a rubber tube. Beads of sweat glistened on his skin as he clenched his fist and anxiously plunged a hypodermic needle deep into the vein that bulged in his arm. For a moment, John's head exploded. Then his senses mellowed and seemed to drift gently, high above the misery of his life, making him forget the things left behind; the pain, the anger and hopelessness . . . . John's eyes were lost behind a blur; he could not see his shadowed childhood dreams. He nodded for a time and then he grew limp as the heroin jellied the muscles of his back and legs. He began whispering words that no one could hear. Later that Friday night, John, 13, died, the needle still sunk deep into the vein of his paralyzed arm."

Today, in New York City, narcotics addiction is the greatest single cause of death of adolescents and young adults from 15 to 35, exceeding deaths from any other single cause—accident, suicide, homicide or natural disease.

The manufacture and distribution of narcotics is big business, and, as *Jet* points out, "the people who profit from the manufacture and sale of dope care less, if anything, about how many black lives dope claims." This point is graphically made in the film "The Godfather," when one Mafia leader states, "In my city, I would like to keep the traffic in the dark people, the colored. They are the best customers, the least troublesome and they are animals anyway. They have no respect for their wives or families or for themselves. Let them lose their souls with drugs."

In 1971, at least 3,164 blacks are estimated to have died from heroin alone. Federal officials state that this figure "is very scanty and incomplete" and does not include blacks who committed suicide or were cut down while attempting to commit a crime to support a habit.

The Federal Bureau of Narcotics and Dangerous Drugs has estimated that there are about 270,000 black heroin addicts in the United States. At least 264,000 of these addicts turn to crime to support their habit, which can run as high as $190 a day or more.

Most black drug addicts steal from the other inhabitants of the black inner city to obtain the funds with which to purchase narcotics. Representative Charles Rangel, whose district includes Harlem, notes that "an addict steals a television set from a brother at one end of the block and sells it to another one at the other end of the same block." On a yearly basis this addict must steal over $73,000 which, according to *Jet,* "means that drug abuse possibly costs the black community more than $10 billion annually."

Jet expresses the view that "while it is difficult to estimate accurately the amount of heroin the average addict needs daily to maintain his 'high,' it cannot be denied that more than 50 percent of the crimes committed in black communities are drug related."

Newark, New Jersey, a city with 20,000 "hard core" heroin addicts out of a predominantly black population of approximately 382,000, held hearings on the drug problem chaired by black Mayor Kenneth Gibson. These statistics emerged: A minimum of 50 to 75 percent of "person to person" crimes in Newark, New Jersey's largest city, are committed by drug addicts; the addicts, in illegal activities to gain money to buy drugs and in illegal drug purchases, cost the city $1 million a day; the city school board has estimated that "approximately 50 percent" of all high school students have experimented with or are addicted to some narcotic drug.

The black community is so concerned about the rise in narcotics addiction that there is the feeling that government has paid less attention to this question than it would have if white youngsters were involved. Congressman Rangel, for example, has often criticized the federal government for not cutting off foreign aid to those nations which traffic and manufacture heroin. The government refuses even to discuss the mounting evidence concerning Communist China's involvement in the narcotics traffic. "If the drug problem had hit communities other than black or Puerto Rican, the government would have hurried up and done something about it," Rangel said.

It is easy for anyone with sufficient money to purchase heroin on the streets of Harlem or other predominantly black inner city areas. "We've been trying to get this junk out of Harlem for the longest time," reflects Mrs. Martha Davis, director of the United Harlem Drugfighters. "But sometimes I really wonder if our best ain't good enough. It's still so easy, too easy, for somebody to get a hold of drugs here in Harlem."

Mrs. Davis showed *Jet* reporters how addicts "cop" heroin. She gave a 10-year-old a $10 bill and sent him to a corner drugstore. In less than five minutes, the youth returned with a "dime" bag of heroin. The question of inner city residents is not why police are so strenuous in fulfilling their responsibilities in that area, but why they have been so ineffective and inefficient in fighting the growing threat of narcotics addiction.

The damage which drug addiction has done to the black community cannot be exaggerated. Dr. Beny J. Primm, a co-chairman of President Nixon's National Methadone Program, states that "family structure and healthy interpersonal relationships are intensely disturbed by addiction. Children steal from parents; parental love turns into fear, disgust and hate. Husbands and wives are separated and children neglected by the debilitating effect drug abuse has on the ability to meet family responsibilities. How does one calculate the loss of life—especially the needless deaths of the young? Whether they are national idols of many of the young, like . . . Jimi Hendrix, or the thousands of anonymous black, Puerto Rican . . . youths dying annually of overdose—they are *our* children and no one can count the loss . . . the loss of future leadership and possibly important contributions to society."

In her autobiography, *Lady Sings the Blues,* Billie Holiday warns of the crippling effects drugs can have on black men, women and children: "All dope can do for you is kill you—and kill you the long, slow, hard way. And it can kill the people you love right along with you. And that's the truth, the whole truth, and nothing but."

The link between drugs and crime is only now being completely understood. Both plague the black inner city to a far greater degree than they do any other area of American society, and black Americans remain the most victimized segment of that society with regard to crime and violence. Blacks, accordingly, have a greater interest than others in stemming the crime rate, in supporting effective law enforcement and in fighting the narcotics traffic. This misperception of many Americans—leading them to believe that blacks encourage crime, violence and addiction—is largely the responsibility of the media which have, for a long period of time, ignored responsible black opinion and publicized only the excessive rhetoric of nonrepresentative radical and militant spokesmen. As a result, the real concerns and fears of black Americans have largely gone unrecorded.

In its issue of December 9, 1972, for example, the *Washington Afro American,* the weekly newspaper of the black community, had an editorial entitled "Time to Halt Crime." It stated:

"This is the season to be jolly, but to hundreds of District residents it has become a period of fear and apprehension, and in some instances, grave sorrow. Crime is the cause of the dilemma, and it is time responsible citizens began to look at their own city and its criminal growth in proper perspective.

"The exceedingly high incidence of housebreakings, pocketbook snatchings, robberies, shoplifting cases and shootings are not simply the outgrowth of bad social conditions. It is time to recognize that basic honesty has a lot to do with it. Honesty begins at home, and it makes little difference whether or not you are poor, unemployed and whatsoever."

Echoing the views of large numbers of residents of the black inner city, the *Afro American* declared:

"It is also time that we stop blaming everybody else for the criminal acts which occur in our neighborhoods. The victims of most of these criminal acts are black, and the instances are by no means racially motivated. A glance at the crime record discloses that the vast majority of these acts are caused by black people, and in the end the whole city, which prides itself on being a Black City (more than 70 percent in population) suffers. How to check crime should be the priority topic for District Citizens, and unless something is done soon what is normally a season of good cheer and joviality is going to be just the opposite for many more."

Underscoring the concern of those in the inner city with more effective law enforcement is the fact that a poll released in March 1972 by a consultant for the Washington, D.C., office of criminal analysis discovered that more than 38 percent of Washington's inner city residents believe that local police are "not tough enough." The percentage of inner city residents holding that view exceeded the percentage of persons in the rest of the city and in suburban areas with a similar belief. In those areas, "not tough enough" was the answer by 29.4 and 33.7 percent of those questioned, respectively.

The question concerning police behavior was: "In carrying out their duties, do you think the police in the District of Columbia generally are (a) too tough? (b) all right? (c) not tough enough? or (d) no opinions?"

The study also found that a majority of residents believe that courts in the District are not severe enough. In the suburbs, 65 percent of the persons sampled held that view. In the inner city area 52 percent felt the same way and in the rest of the city 48 percent offered the same opinion.

The survey found that within the previous several years, two of every five Washington area residents had taken safety measures to make their homes more secure from crime. The most common action was to purchase new locks for doors or windows, although one percent of the persons surveyed had obtained watchdogs. Inner city residents were more likely than residents of the remainder of the city or suburbanites to cite crime as "the most serious" national issue although crime had a high priority in all areas. Washington residents generally favored more policemen on foot as the best way to combat crime. This survey, taken during a seven-month period in 1971 and directed by Stanley Turner, a professor in the sociology department at the University of Delaware, leaves little doubt about the real concern which black inner city residents have for their own safety. Crime, for them, is a far more real threat than it is for those living in other parts of any metropolitan area.

Blacks in Pittsburgh have been so troubled with crime in their own neighborhoods that in August 1972 they began efforts to reduce personal crimes by blacks against black businessmen and residents of two inner city areas. Additional plainclothesmen were posted in the Hill district, the city's largest black area, in a campaign to force narcotics pushers and addicts off the streets. The additional policemen were posted in a four-block area where, Police Superintendent Robert Colville estimated, there were up to 2,000 pushers and addicts.

In the Manchester area of the North Side, black businessmen

opened a drive against blacks who, they said, were menacing them and preying upon residents. The businessmen announced plans to battle the criminal elements and formed a group called Black Businessmen of the North Side.

George A. Wilson, a black constable and spokesman for the organization, said that with the emergence of black power, blacks believed that the white man was their greatest menace. "I say that the greatest menace to the blacks in Manchester are blacks who prey upon other blacks," Mr. Wilson said. "We are not being menaced from the outside; we are being menaced from within. We are not being menaced by the so-called enemy—'whitey.' " He pointed out that black businesses were being broken into and homes burglarized by blacks, not whites.

On the first day of the drive, 58 persons were arrested on a number of charges, including loitering. Matthew Moore, a state coordinator of the National Association for the Advancement of Colored People, said that the sweep was a dramatic success. The home of Mr. Moore, a Hill resident, was burglarized three times within a year, "presumably by junkies," he said.

Until the police action, Mr. Moore said, sidewalks were blocked by loiterers harassing residents. But after the drive started, he noted that "the Hill district streets give us the same freedom to walk around as there is anywhere in the city."

The impression that black citizens are apathetic about crime, or are simply its perpetrators rather than its primary victims, is a view which seems to be prevalent in white society. Those who hold this opinion completely misunderstand the difficulty of life in the inner city and have accepted the stereotype of the guilt-ridden news media, manned primarily by well-educated white journalists whose knowledge of crime and violence in the inner city is based upon certain ideological preconceptions rather than upon the harsh realities.

One black police chief, Charles Boone of Gary, Indiana, has said what has to be said if crime by blacks is to decrease and city life is to be made tolerable for citizens of both races. Chief Boone accused two judges of leniency in cases of black burglars and of giving Negro criminals "license to steal." A study of his department showed that 90 percent of the Negroes charged with robbery and other crimes in his county are "back on the streets committing the same crimes they were arrested for."

Criticizing those Negroes who have not spoken out against crime, Roy Wilkins, executive director of the NAACP, declared that "except for a few voices, Negro citizens have given consent to robbery, muggings, assaults and murder by their silence. They have been intimidated by a curious twisting of the 'us blacks together' philosophy which holds that complaining of black criminals is somehow 'betraying the race.' This is nonsense. One can be proud of being black without embracing every black mugger, rapist and auto thief."

Wilkins stated that "Negro communities need to speak out and act against Negro criminals. They need to cease trotting out the same old excuses for black wrongdoings: 'broken homes,' 'prejudice,' 'inferior schools,' 'joblessness,' ad infinitum. Negro Americans should not cease fighting against those evils, but they should cease using them to excuse criminality."

It is equally necessary for the white community to understand the reality of what has been happening—and is happening today—in the black inner city. Nothing but increased racial strife based on false information and misunderstanding of reality lies in the path of our current situation. As whites flee from the center cities to the suburbs, as they hold the view that Negroes are responsible for crime and violence and that it is necessary to be as far away from centers of black population as possible in order to live safe and normal lives, we set the stage for a segregation more real than any we have endured in the past.

None of this needs to happen, however, for the fact is that blacks in the inner city, far from being advocates of crime and disorder, are its primary victims. In too many instances, they have not spoken out, often because of a pervasive fear. More than this, however, they have been as victimized as the white population by hearing radical and militant black spokesmen in the mass media being hailed as "representative" black voices and, more and more, as black "leaders." If these are our "leaders," some conclude, "then we must follow their counsel."

If crime is mounting in our urban areas generally, which it is, the rate of increase is most dramatic in the black inner city. Perhaps when the society as a whole views blacks as victims as much as perpetrators of violence it will come closer to understanding the reality which can only be altered when it is properly perceived.

Chapter 3

Modern American Society:
Seedbed for Crime

In discussing the causes of crime many who propose solutions to the problem tend to portray those causes in such a way that their own "solutions" will fulfill society's needs in this area. Thus, advocates of increasing governmental involvement in the economy and in the redistribution of wealth argue that crime is caused by poverty. If poverty is eliminated, they tell us, crime will be eliminated as well.

It would be helpful if serious and complex problems did, in fact, have simple and single causes which could be corrected by simple and single solutions. If crime was caused by poverty it would certainly be within our range to correct, for ours is, after all, the most affluent society in the world.

So committed are many within our political arena to this line of argument that it has been codified in many ways. Both the President's Crime Commission Report in 1966 and the 1968 report of the Riot Commission came to the same conclusion: violence, whether in the form of criminal acts or in the form of civil disturbances, is caused by economic factors.

At the time of the Crime Commission's findings, then Attorney General Nicholas Katzenbach expressed the view that responsibility for riots rested not with individuals but with "disease and despair, joblessness, rat-infested housing and long impacted cynicism."

According to the 1968 report, riots were caused by everyone but those who had, in fact, perpetrated them. The blame was spread over a wide range. Government was to blame, for its programs had not effectively reached the people. Judges and police were to blame, for they were often too harsh and disrespectful. The press was to blame, for it exhibited lack of understanding. The real cause, according to the Commission, was "white racism."

The Commission stated that "our nation is moving toward two societies, one black, one white, separate and unequal." This was even too much for then Vice President Hubert Humphrey. He noted that the Commission did not take adequate account of the rising repudiation of racism throughout the white community over the previous 20 years. It ignored, he said, "a solid platform of laws, programs and experience on which to build."

The approach taken by the Commission was characterized this way by columnist Joseph Kraft: "It is based on the notion—the Marxian notion—that economic deprivation is the root of social unrest. It thus prescribes elaborate programs to improve economic opportunity through welfare payments, public housing and educational subsidies . . . . The result of that approach, alas, has been what might be called reservationism . . . the herding of Negroes into core cities, guarded by the police, and the monthly handouts of whiskey and blankets in the form of federal programs."

Kraft noted that the Commission took into account the noneconomic causes of the riots, and that the Commission itself showed that rioters did not emerge from a background of hopeless poverty. Still, its recommendations were all based on the fallacious economic theory.

The economic theory has been shown to be completely invalid. Irving J. Rubin, head of the University of Michigan Center for Urban Studies, made a survey of those who had been arrested for rioting in Detroit. He stated that "solutions based primarily on improving schools, housing and employment for urban Negroes are not responsive to the deeper needs behind the violence. They are comfortable solutions, things our society knows how to do best . . . but they are not what the riots are all about."

In the main riot areas of Detroit, according to the University of Michigan Survey, the median annual income of Negro households was $6,200. This is only slightly lower than the figure for all Negro households in Detroit, $6,400, and not far below the median white household income of $6,800.

Educational attainment of Negro household heads—45 percent were high-school graduates or better—was higher in the riot area than throughout the city.

Seventy percent of Negro households in the riot area had automobiles available, and "Negroes living within the riot area are substantially better off in every respect than Negroes who live inside the deep core. They are also somewhat better off than the whites who live in the riot neighborhoods."

Of those arrested, Detroit Police Department arrest records showed that only 10 percent of the Negroes were juveniles; 18 percent were between 17 and 19 years old, 24 percent were between 20 and 24, 17 percent between 25 and 29, and 31 percent over 30.

The Urban Law Center's survey of 1,200 nonjuvenile male arrestees shows that 83 percent were employed, 40 percent of them by the three major automobile companies and an equal percentage by other large employers. No income data was gathered, but annual wages of $6,000 and more can be assumed. The conclusion of Professor Rubin was that "if we deal only with housing, education and jobs, we are sowing the seeds of even greater trouble."

The records of crime statistics show that there was much less crime in America during the Depression than in today's affluent society. In 1933, total reported crimes against the person stood at about 150 per 100,000 population. This figure dropped steadily throughout the continuing years of the Depression and the enforced scarcity of World War II. As the war came to an end and prosperity returned, the line turned sharply upward and has continued to climb ever since. In 1965, for example, the figure stood at more than 180.

Judge David Pine states that "during the dark days of the Great Depression in the early 1930s there existed all over the land abject poverty, distress and misery, but I do not recall at that time there was a vast upsurge in crime ... from 1931 to 1935, while the nation's population grew by better than three million persons, the number of robberies and auto thefts decreased 35.2 percent, burglaries decreased 8.9 percent, and aggravated assault and larceny remained relatively constant."

In 1938, Attorney General Homer S. Cummings announced that the preceding year had seen "nearly 1,500,000 crimes committed"—a number he felt, quite properly, to be enormous. The population of the United States was then estimated at 130,320,000. In 1964, no less than 2,729,659 major crimes were committed—an increase of better than 1.2 million. The population was then approximately 191,372,000. Crime in the United States between Depression year 1938 and boom year 1964 had increased by 80 percent; population had increased by only 47 percent.

It seems clear that it is not economic deprivation which has caused our dramatic increase in crime, for as income has risen, so have crime statistics. While many insist, as the Riot Commission did, that poverty creates crime, and that if you spend enough money to combat poverty you will end violence, the fact is that suburban crime is rising at an even more rapid rate than is crime in the inner city. In Nassau County, New York, major crimes jumped from 698 to 854 per 100,000 population in three years' time. The police chief of Evanston, Illinois, says, "It's been a steady increase. That's what's alarming."

Professor Ernest van den Haag concludes that "the countries with the lowest living standards usually have very low suicide and homicide rates." Sweden, for example, has a far more advanced welfare state than does the United States. The result: crime is increasing at an even more rapid pace. In Sweden, known offenses against the penal code have risen from 172,000 in 1950 to 373,000 in 1965. The crime rate per 100,000 population has gone up 97 percent in 15 years. Crime has increased from 250,000 cases in Sweden in 1960 to 500,000 in 1970. During 1969–70 there was a 20 percent increase in thefts, 16 percent in robberies, and 62 percent in check passing, and violent crimes increased by 40 percent in 1969. Seventy-five percent of crimes in Sweden are committed by children and youths between the ages of ten and 25. Despite "sexual liberation," rape increased by 65.2 percent between 1963 and 1967. In addition, Sweden is one of the nations with the fastest rising rate of narcotics users among its young people. Its suicide rate is one of the highest in the world.

In considering statistics concerning suicide, homicide and alcoholism in Europe, Erich Fromm points out that "the countries in Europe which are among the most democratic, peaceful and prosperous ones, and the United States, the most prosperous country in the world, show the most severe symptoms of mental disturbance. The aim of the whole socioeconomic development of the Western world is that of the materially comfortable life, relatively equal distribution of wealth, stable democracy and peace, and the very countries which have come closest to this aim show the most severe signs of mental unbalance." The fact is that the countries with the lowest living standards more often have very low crime rates.

In his volume *Kids, Crime and Chaos,* Roul Tunley notes, "Progress . . . was recognized as a major factor in delinquency in almost every country I have visited." He quotes a government official in India as saying relative poverty and backwardness are deterrents to juvenile crime and reports the statement of a British authority on delinquency who states that "20 years ago people in Great Britain said that if you could do away with poverty slums, it would help do away with delinquency. But we've done away with lots of poverty and we've improved housing, and it's worse than ever."

Tunley points out that in Sweden the most advanced welfare measures have been used to eliminate poverty, yet the crime rate continues to soar. He writes, "If the theory of most of our prevailing experts were correct, namely, that juvenile crime springs from underprivileged status, Sweden should be a country with little or no delinquency. Yet we know it has one of the highest rates, if not the highest, in the world."

William S. Schlamm, in his book *Germany and the East-West Crisis,* makes a similar assessment with regard to crime in West Germany. He writes, "The socioeconomic explanation of the phenomenon —poverty of the parents, slum conditions—must be discarded. In Germany this young generation started its bizarre conduct while all of Germany was going through the greatest economic uplift in its history."

One study of 794 German young people arrested for rioting, Schlamm points out, discovered that they were "by no means primarily children of lower-class families or broken-up homes; every element of German society, the whole scale up and down, was represented. Nor are the *Halbstarken* [the "half-strong" delinquent youth] financially starved: on the average the investigated *Halbstarken* earn or administer DM 235 a month—more than one half of the adult German's average income."

A United Nations report similarly concluded, "The existing data suggest that improvement of living conditions—what is called a better standard of living—does not necessarily . . . reduce juvenile delinquency . . . . Although statistical data are incomplete, it would seem . . . that juvenile delinquency is not caused by poverty or poor economic conditions alone."

If crime is, in fact, not caused by economic deprivation, why have so many in our political process, in the press, and in the academic world, continued to argue that it is, and that it can be lessened by implementing a variety of legislative formulas—wars on poverty, job corps training camps, guaranteed annual incomes and prison reforms? The unfortunate fact is that whenever a problem is discussed in political terms, the goal is the finding of an "answer" which may be implemented in specific legislation, implying that every problem has a legislative remedy and that government, in effect, can successfully involve itself in all areas of concern.

For too many Americans, government has become the source of all good and all evil to be found in the contemporary world. If there is too much crime, if the highways are overcrowded, if programming on television is mediocre, if jobs are unsatisfying and marriages are unrewarding, if children seem indifferent, and a sense of community seems less and less evident, then what we need, it is said, is a change in administration, a new party in power or, to radicals, a revolutionary upheaval.

Somehow we have come to believe that we do not have responsibility for our own lives but that established political authority is responsible for the good, the evil, even the ambivalence of the modern world. Where men and women once turned to the church and to the family for the inner meaning of life and the fulfillment of emotional needs, they now seek such answers from the political process. Unfortunately, politics cannot provide such answers.

Discussing the faith which modern man has placed in politics, and the futility of such an approach to life, the Russian poet Joseph Brodsky, now poet-in-residence at the University of Michigan, has provided an analysis worthy of consideration.

Brodsky declared, "I do not believe in political movements, I believe in personal movement, that movement of the soul when a man who looks at himself is so ashamed that he tries to make some sort of change —within himself, not on the outside. In place of this we are offered a cheap and extremely dangerous surrogate for the internal human disposition toward change: political movements of one sort or another —dangerous psychologically more than physically. Because every political movement is a way to avoid personal responsibility for what is happening . . . . As a rule communality in the sphere of ideas has not led to anything particularly good."

What, then, is to be said of political ideas? Often we are told by politicians, such as those who argue that crime can be reduced by the redistribution of wealth or by the complete alteration of our social and economic systems, that "the world is bad, it has to be changed."

To this, Brodsky replies: "The world is precisely *not* bad; one could even say the world is good. What is true is that it has been spoiled by its inhabitants. And if it is necessary to change something, it is not the details of the landscape, but our own selves. What is bad about political movements is that they depart too much from their own origins, that on occasion their results so disfigure the world that it really can be called bad, purely visually; that they lead human thoughts into a dead end. The intensity of political passions is directly proportional to their distance from the true source of the problem."

Underneath the rhetoric, what those who seek political solutions for all social and personal problems are saying is that such solutions do exist, and that, in effect, all of our difficulties can be corrected, if only *they* are given a chance to do it. Joseph Brodsky, who emerged in 1972 from a Communist society which tells us that *it* has all the answers to such problems, stated that "there is something offensive to the human soul about preaching paradise on earth. Replacing metaphysical categories with pragmatic ethical or social categories is somehow a debasement of human consciousness."

The conception of government believed in by the Founding Fathers of our own country was that all the political process could or should do was to provide order and an atmosphere of freedom within which each man could go as far as his own ability would take him. A political process which attempted to do more than this, to provide equality of condition rather than of opportunity, would inevitably end in tyranny. While many today tell us that all domestic social ills may be corrected by programs which call for economic and environmental solutions, there was no doubt at the beginning of our country that government has to be severely limited and that the political process should not deal with a wide range of societal and personal problems but should deal only with certain carefully and clearly defined areas of concern.

The *Federalist Papers* (Number 47) declare: "What is government itself but the greatest of all reflections on human nature? If men were angels, no government would be necessary . . . . In framing a government which is to be administered by men over men, the great difficulty lies in this: you must first enable the government to control the governed; and in the next place oblige it to control itself. A dependence upon the people is, no doubt, the primary control on the government, but experience has taught mankind the necessity of auxiliary precautions."

Given the fact that economic factors are demonstrably not the cause of the increase in crime which we have witnessed in recent years, and that the solutions proposed within the political process are the kinds of solutions government is able to implement but precisely the approaches which have no relevance to the real problems we face, the valid questions before us remain to be answered. If economic deprivation is not the cause of the increase in crime, what is? More particularly, if poverty is not the cause of the dramatic increase in crime among Negroes in the inner city, what is?

To think that complex problems have either simple solutions or simple explanations is to misunderstand the nature of such problems. It is because our political system has a vested interest in misunderstanding such problems, that they are permitted to deteriorate still further. To argue that crime is not caused by economic deprivation, and that, as a result, programs such as the War on Poverty and the Job Corps are not the way to correct the problem, is to attack today's conventional wisdom.

Before examining the real causes of the complex crime problem we face, it is important to understand why irrelevant concepts and irrelevant programs are considered politically appropriate, while facing reality is not. The same is true with regard to inflation, housing, agriculture and a host of other questions.

One of the most frequent responses to any suggestion that perhaps real problems can best be solved by discovering their cause and attempting to deal with it is that such a course would be "politically impossible."

Thus, it is well-known by economists that we have inflation because of an increase in the money supply by the Federal Reserve Board, because of the overwhelming and coercive power of labor unions which results in wage settlements bearing little if any relationship to worker productivity, and as a result of continuous deficit spending by government. Yet when "solutions" are sought for inflation, our political leaders never suggest that inflation might be brought to an end by ceasing to increase the money supply by arbitrary government decision-making, by ending the coercive power possessed by labor unions or by balancing the federal budget. Such approaches, we are told, are "politically impossible."

What compounds the problem—which is the same with regard to crime and violence, alienation of the young, welfare, farm prices and a host of other public ills—is that it is not only the politicians who reject real solutions because of their "political impossibility." Those to whom they go for advice—intellectuals and academicians—themselves have tended to present only those approaches they felt would be accepted "politically." As a result, no one has really told the American people the truth about any of the major problems facing the country.

When Professor W. H. Hutt set out to write his small volume, *Politically Impossible* (a product of the Institute of Economic Affairs of London), he told a leading American economist that he was preparing a work on the subject. The American at once suggested a definition of the idea: "All the reforms which would be really worthwhile undertaking."

His reaction, notes Professor Hutt, "was not entirely facetious. It reflects a frustration felt by many. If wise changes are indeed ruled out by 'politics' it is a damning criticism of the contemporary working of democracy. The problem is one of the most serious confronting the inheritors of Western civilization today."

Important public proposals are said to be "politically impossible" not because of their intrinsic demerits but, as Dr. Hutt points out, because "it is often said to be 'impossible' to enlighten electorates on policies which, it is implied, would be profoundly for their benefit. The notion then is that it would be absurd to make the attempt . . . . A policy may be economically wise, sociologically beneficial, morally desirable, fiscally feasible and organizationally practicable yet supposedly incapable of statement in an electorate-satisfying manner."

In 1953, Professor Milton Friedman declared that "the role of the economist in discussions of public policy seems to me to prescribe what should be done in the light of what can be done, politics aside, and not predict what is 'politically feasible' and then recommend it."

In his book, Dr. Hutt has some limited hope for the future. "We must never," he writes, "regard the opinions of voters on any issue important to their well-being unalterable."

In discussing crime we must look at the American society in which the rate of crime has notably increased and discover what changing standards and values have contributed to what appears to be a breakdown of traditional patterns of living. We must, in addition, consider the changing attitude toward law itself, and toward the idea of what a citizen's responsibility is with regard to obeying the law.

More than this, we must examine the nature of family and community life, and with regard to Negroes we must consider the effects of rapid urbanization, increasing transience and a general deterioration of the quality of life in the inner city. These clearly are all complex problems. They are all intrinsically part of the crime problem we face.

In its issue of November 13, 1967, *Newsweek* magazine featured a cover story on "The Permissive Society." It declared, "The old taboos are dead or dying. A new, more permissive society is taking shape. Its outlines are etched most prominently in the arts—in the increasing nudity and frankness of today's films, in the blunt, often obscene language seemingly endemic in American novels and plays, in the candid lyrics of pop songs and the undress of the avant-garde ballet, in erotic art and television talk shows, in freer fashions and franker advertising. And behind this expanding permissiveness in the arts stands a society in transition, a society that has lost its consensus on such crucial issues as premarital sex and clerical celibacy, marriage, birth control and sex education; a society that cannot agree on standards of conduct, language and manners, on what can be seen and heard."

The permissive society is seen by many observers as a mark of social breakdown and decay. British author and commentator Malcolm Muggeridge notes that "it is the inevitable mark of decadence in our society. As our vitality ebbs, people reach out for vicarious excitement, like the current sex mania in pop songs and the popular press. At the decline and fall of the Roman Empire, the works of Sappho, Catullus and Ovid were celebrated. There is an analogy in that for us."

Discussing a period in which men no longer have a clear understanding of what is right and what is wrong, Father Walter J. Ong, the Jesuit theologian and author of *The Presence of the World,* states that "we're going to have to live with a degree of freedom much greater than anything we've known in the past. Man can't just say anything goes and hope to get by. We're going to have to employ our minds and morals in determining that some things go and other things don't. We're going to have to constantly reassess the situation because the situation will always be changing."

With regard to the disintegration of the moral consensus in America, novelist Norman Mailer argues that "we're in a time that's divorced from the past. There's utterly no tradition any more. It's a time when our nervous systems are being remade. There's an extraordinary amount of obscenity around—and it's in my new book. I had to write it that way despite the fact that I hate to add to all that obscenity."

64

One of the direct impacts of the new era of permissiveness upon crime and violence is the increasing portrayal of violence on television and in the movies as an acceptable and natural phenomenon.

Based on the extensive surveys by Professor George Gerbner and his associates at the Annenburg School of Communications, it seems clear that what children are shown on contemporary television is heavily saturated with violence. In 1972, Professor Gerbner reported that the frequency of overt physical violence during prime time and Saturday morning network programs during the fall of 1969 was such that eight in ten plays contained violence with the frequency of violent episodes running about eight per program hour. Children's cartoons, which have long been the most violent of programs, actually increased their lead in violence portrayals from 1967 to 1969.

Do children actually learn violent and aggressive behavior from watching television? Professor Albert Bandura of Stanford University declared that "there is little doubt that, by displaying forms of aggression or modes of criminal and violent behavior, the media are 'teaching' and people are 'learning.' "

If children can learn aggressive behavior from watching television, does that mean that such learning will, in turn, lead to the instigation of a greater willingness actually to behave aggressively? An investigation conducted by Faye Steuer, James Applefield and Rodney Smith was published in the *Journal of Experimental Child Psychology*. Designed to show the absolute degree of control which television violence can have on naturally occurring aggressive behavior, this study involved ten normal youngsters, enrolled in the preschool of the University of North Carolina's Child Development Center.

The children, boys and girls, comprised a racially and socioeconomically mixed group who knew each other before the study began. First, they were matched into pairs on the basis of the amount of time they spent watching television at home. Next, to establish the degree to which aggressive behavior occurred among these youngsters before any modification of their television diets, each was carefully observed for ten sessions, in play with other children, and the frequency of aggressive responses recorded.

Steuer and her associates used a measure of physical interpersonal aggression, including: (a) hitting or pushing another child, (b) kicking another child, (c) assaultive contact with another child which included squeezing, choking or holding down, and (d) throwing an object at another child from a distance of at least one foot. Only these severe acts of physical aggression were recorded. The baseline established a significant degree of consistency within each pair, prior to the modification of television diet.

Next, Steuer and her associates asked about the effect of television. One child in each pair observed, on 11 different days, a single aggressive television program taken directly from Saturday morning program offerings, while the other member of the pair observed a non-aggressive television program. Subsequent observations of the children at play provided continuous measures of interpersonal physical aggressive behavior by each child. Changes from the original measures, if any, would have to be caused by TV effects.

By the end of the 11 sessions, the two groups had departed significantly from one another in terms of the frequency of interpersonal aggression. In fact, for every pair, the child who observed aggressive television programming had become more aggressive than his mate who watched neutral fare. In most of the cases, these changes were striking.

Based on more than 30 other studies involving thousands of normal children, the committee appointed by the Surgeon General to investigate television violence in 1972 reported that "as matters now stand, the weight of the experimental evidence from the present series of studies, as well as from prior research, suggests that viewing filmed violence had an observable effect on some children in the direction of increasing their aggressive behavior."

It was further noted in the Committee's summary statement that "there is a convergence of the fairly substantial experimental evidence for short-run causation of aggression among some children by viewing violence on the screen and . . . from field studies that extensive violence viewing precedes some long-run manifestations of aggressive behavior."

Even more outspoken on the subject of television violence was the report of the National Commission on the Causes and Prevention of Violence issued December 10, 1969. That commission assigned social scientists to undertake research studies and one of its major by-products was a 614-page staff report entitled *Violence and the Media.* From the studies, the commission concluded: "The preponderance of the available research evidence strongly suggests . . . that violence in television programs can and does have adverse effects upon audiences —particularly child audiences. Television enters powerfully into the learning process of children and teaches them a set of moral and social values about violence which are inconsistent with the standards of civilized society."

In her study *Violence in the Media,* Helen B. Shaffer points out that "two key factors pertain to violence in the media today as it affects the character of modern life differently than in the past. One is the very existence of the mass media; the other is the way violence is presented. Man in the past heard tales of woe or witnessed the comic mayhem of a Punch and Judy show only on special occasions. Man in modern urbanized society is almost constantly bombarded with a multitude of impressions from the media, all laced with accounts or picturizations of violence."

The Crime Commission study estimated that in a typical weekday, 82 percent of adults watch television for an average of two hours, and two thirds of America's adults listen to the radio more than an hour a day. More than nine out of ten adults read a magazine sometime during the month and approximately three-fourths of the adult population read one or more newspapers. A third of the adult population sees at least one film in a typical month.

Studies of network drama on prime evening hours and of programs on Saturday mornings over the period 1967–69 showed the rate of violent episodes remained constant at about eight per hour. The most violent of all programs were children's cartoons. A study of Saturday morning network programs in 1971 found three of every ten dramatic segments saturated with violence; a total of 71 had at least one instance of human violence. By the time the average American child reaches the age of 15, he has witnessed at least 18,000 individual murders on the television set, not including beatings, stabbings, muggings, rapes and other forms of mayhem.

In its final report to Surgeon General Jesse Steinfeld, a group of experts that included psychiatrists, psychologists, sociologists, anthropologists and statisticians concluded the following:

• Violence is used early to attract the viewer and is used to hold his attention, as when a violent sequence is interrupted for commercial messages.

• Violence is used mostly to provide a simple solution to what are complex or otherwise insoluble problems.

• Violence on television has become sanitized—individuals are killed cleanly, quickly and with no bloodshed, no pain, no family grief and no obvious consequences for the aggressor or the victim's family or friends.

• Cartoons for the very young are the most violent of all television programming.

• Young children are unable to distinguish reality from fantasy; they view each violent episode as a concrete, separate event isolated from its context.

• By the age of five or six, children have chosen favorite programs.

• Youngsters spend 20 percent of their television time watching children's programs and 80 percent watching adult television fare.

• For some children at some time, viewing television leads to subsequent antisocial behavior.

• When adults watch programs with children and interpret the action and its consequences, the child's behavior patterns are considerably modified.

If the mass media have a negative effect upon children in general with regard to spreading ideas of violence and other forms of antisocial and criminal behavior, the Negro community is affected in an even more dangerous way by the manner in which advocates of racial violence are portrayed.

"Outside agitators" were widely blamed for the rioting which occurred in the 1960s in cities such as New York, Los Angeles, Newark, Detroit and Cincinnati. In fact, the House of Representatives passed a bill making it a crime to cross state lines for the purpose of inciting such disorders. Significant evidence, however, suggests that if outside agitators were involved, their names may be ABC, NBC and CBS.

Toledo Mayor John W. Potter cited television coverage of other riots as a major cause of his city's troubles: "The Detroit situation had much to do with starting it. It was young people who felt they wanted to get into the act. They saw on television how Detroit police just monitored without stopping looting."

In Newark, Donald Malafronte, administrative aide to the mayor, said that a key reason for the riots was the press and television coverage which had given too much attention to the militant demands of black nationalist groups, demands which, he said, the city government "did not give weight to."

Mayor Richard J. Daley of Chicago referred to the difficulties in Chicago when he noted that "in disturbances resulting from protest marches, the television cameras didn't seek the violence, the violence sought the camera."

New York's Mayor John Lindsay referred to the rioting as a "fever" and said that "fevers can spread . . . there are aspects of contagion here." Television may have been one of the prime carriers of the disease.

This has all been reminiscent of the famed Orson Welles broadcast on Halloween weekend, 1938. At that time a small company of radio actors broadcast in semi-news style a dramatized version of H. G. Wells' fictional account of a Martian invasion of earth. Though clear announcements that the production was purely fictional punctuated the program, many listeners by some mental process simply tuned this qualification out. Thousands literally believed that a mysterious interplanetary cylinder had landed in New Jersey, disgorging giant machines that were soon wading across the Hudson River and blasting Manhattan with invincible death rays. Widespread panic ensued. People rushed from their homes in tears and prayed in the streets. Several died of heart attacks. Hardier souls grabbed shotguns and prepared to fight for their lives, or fled to the woods and hills.

If radio can convince people the Martians are coming and send them into the streets with shotguns, is it so surprising that television broadcasting the inflammatory speeches of Stokely Carmichael and Rap Brown could convince people that they are being exploited by a "brutal colonial welfare system" and "mad dog president" and "white power structure" and send them into the streets to "shoot these honkie cops" and "burn America down?"

Representative Durward Hall of Missouri stated that "a Stokely Carmichael calling for insurrection on a street-corner soapbox is a curiosity—a hippie talking to a few other hippies. But a Stokely Carmichael talking face to face to millions of people (via television) is immediately transformed from an oddball to a national figure." Representative Hall suggested that the riot bill which had been recently passed by the House be applied to television networks, "which transmit 'hate messages' over their interstate facilities."

There is, of course, nothing new about psychological epidemics. They have occurred throughout history. But the combination of electronic communication and mass urbanization has loosed some dynamics totally unprecedented in the history of civilization. The news of the Declaration of Independence required a month to travel from Philadelphia to Georgia. In 1960, however, 70 million people watched the Kennedy-Nixon debate. In addition, television's reach is far greater than that of the printed media for it influences those who either cannot or do not read.

The world of television news is a great deal different from the world of the printed word. Henry Fairlie, Washington correspondent for the *London Express,* notes that "not only is the core of television the public and the spectacular, but there is an important sense in which television has a vested interest in disaster. From the point of view of a good story, both newspapers and television prefer covering a major strike to covering negotiations which prevent a strike. But what can television do with negotiations? . . . Violence, movement—that is the stuff of television, something it cannot help emphasizing." Yet, "as television cameramen and reporters move into the streets literally looking for trouble, they add an external provocation. The crowds begin to play up to them. Television, merely by its presence, helps to create incidents."

An NBC television newsman tells how the civil rights demonstrators in Cambridge, Maryland, conferred with the assembled broadcast cameramen and moved their demonstrations back from 8 to 6 p.m. so that the cameramen would have time to get their film flown to New York for the 11 p.m. news roundups. Yet the public was given the impression that they were seeing largely "spontaneous crowds of protestors." In many cases, there were more newsmen on the scene than demonstrators, as in a California episode where some 400 reporters and photographers showed up to cover only a handful of Klansmen holding a rally.

Concerning journalism's ethical role, Eugene Methvin of the *Reader's Digest,* a member of the national board of Sigma Delta Chi, the professional journalistic society, points out that "American journalism has a great tradition that the newsman's role is to 'report the news without fear or favor.' But interpreted too simply this injunction might lead to some evil results in today's complex world . . . . Do the media have a positive peace-keeping role? A duty to help preserve parliamentary due process and a climate of democratic decorum essential to compromise and settlement of conflict?" Mr. Methvin answers in the affirmative.

Also affirmative was a code of ethics for newsmen prepared by Dr. Kenneth Harwood, chairman of the Department of Telecommunications at the University of Southern California and Dr. Theodore Kruglack, Director of the School of Journalism at the University of Southern California. This code calls for avoiding an emphasis on stories on public tensions while they are developing and urges great care by crews at the site of public disorders. It urges reporters to avoid interviews with obvious "inciters" as well as scare bulletins and headlines. This code was adopted by the Radio and Television News Association of Southern California and by many stations elsewhere in the country.

A somewhat different view was expressed in a statement to viewers who criticized the emphasis placed on coverage of extremists, by Richard S. Salant, President of CBS News. He stated, "It is our job to follow the news, wherever it is and whoever makes it. We cannot allow ourselves the luxury of deciding that there are some people whom we dislike or with whose views we strongly disagree and then, for news purposes, pretend that they do not exist."

This brings up the important question of what is news? Is it only news when an extremist calls for violence, or is it also news when men of good will seek valid solutions to real problems? The late Whitney Young, who served for many years as executive director of the Urban League, often criticized the stress placed on extremists and said that "the press lacks sophistication. They ought to be covering where Negroes move in and whites don't move out. At CORE's convention in Baltimore there was a tiny number of delegates but almost twice as many reporters. At the Urban League convention in August there were 1,500 delegates and less than 30 reporters."

There is something radically wrong with news coverage which makes the average American aware of a Rap Brown and not a Whitney Young. It has created two wrong impressions. One is that men such as Brown are truly Negro leaders and that responsible spokesmen do not exist. The other is the one fostered among Negroes that the white community views such extremists as being true representatives.

At the same time violence is portrayed on television, in the movies, on the stage and in other forms of mass entertainment in the terms we have discussed, we face a parallel situation in which violence and disrespect for law and for all authority have been advocated as political tactics by a wide variety of spokesmen, both white and black, both radical and, in some instances, well-known churchmen and political figures. Thus, violence and violation of the law have, in the eyes of many, become "respectable" and "legitimate."

The unfortunate fact is that violence, in a short period of time, has moved from an occasional aberration and disturbance to a political tactic, endorsed by many leaders of the New Left, by leaders of the new black nationalist movement, and by others who, for a variety of reasons, feel disaffected and disillusioned.

This tactic has resulted in many overt and covert acts, the full importance of which is yet to be understood and assimilated. There are, of course, the major incidents, such as the takeover of Columbia University and the disorder which was precipitated at the Democratic Convention in Chicago in 1968. These bear careful analysis. But there are many, often unreported, incidents, of what their perpetrators term "sabotage."

The Institute of Science and Technology at the University of Michigan was rocked by an explosion on October 14, 1968. The bombing was the thirteenth to hit the Detroit area since the previous August and came only two weeks after extensive damage forced the closing of a semi-secret CIA recruiting office in a downtown Ann Arbor office building.

Ann Arbor Police Chief Walter Krasny claimed the series of bombings may have been the work of "antiestablishment militants" at the University of Michigan, while Detroit officials blame "hippies" for the explosions. The *National Guardian*, a far-left newspaper, reported that "reaction to the bombings in the Ann Arbor radical community has ranged from quiet amusement to fantasy to increased discussion regarding the nature and timing of revolutionary chaos and terrorism and their possible relation to politicization of young people and/or mass repression of the radical movement. While some feel that such violence will help increase the consciousness of students, others feel that the level of awareness is now so low that the bombing will do little . . . ."

Much violence that occurs in the nation's black communities appears to be spontaneous or, as liberal commentators argue, the result of poverty and discrimination. This, however, seems to be less important as a cause than planning and organization by those who, for their own reasons, are committed to an increase in lawlessness.

The Cleveland riots of July 1968, for example, were, according to federal investigators, the product of a black nationalist conspiracy. Key figure in the conspiracy, the experts say, was Fred "Ahmed" Evans, a local black power leader who has been linked with the pro-Peking Revolutionary Action Movement. In May 1967, Detective Sergeant John Ungvary, head of the Cleveland police department's subversive squad, said that terrorists under Evans' direction were plotting a "black revolution" to coincide with "a war between Red China and the United States."

Evans, who was arrested during the riots, was charged with shooting to kill. "If my carbine hadn't jammed I would have killed you three," police quoted him as saying. "I had you in my sights when my rifle jammed." Evans told police that he and 17 others had organized the sniper attacks that resulted in the deaths of three policemen. Told that three of his snipers had been slain, Evans said, "They died for a worthy cause." Phil Hutchings, militant head of the Student Non-Violent Coordinating Committee, told newsmen that the Cleveland outbreaks were "the first stage of revolutionary armed violence."

This was confirmed by Negro Mayor Carl Stokes who viewed the violence this way: " . . . it was not at all related to any kind of honest reaction to an environment, not at all. This was a planned, deliberate and previously contrived plot to damage . . . . The acts of the people the other night were just deliberately contrived lawlessness and determination to commit violence among this small group."

Violence is often proclaimed as the only means by which society can truly be cleansed. The Reverend William Sloane Coffin, already having been convicted of conspiring to violate draft laws, delivered his first sermon of the 1968 academic year at Yale University in praise of change, even if change comes in violent ways. He told 300 persons, mostly students, that "life is change, growth, love and readiness to suffer." Reverend Coffin warned that the condemnation of violence by the nation's political leaders might also be condemnation of change. He stated: "Jesus, when he threw the money changers out of the temple, was no more violent than [Columbia radical student leader] Mark Rudd."

The day before the 1968 election about 300 white and black students seized the Administration Building at San Fernando Valley College for about four hours. Several youths with knives held prisoner about 35 administrators, including the college president. Shortly after the elections, plainclothes police halted a brief outbreak of violence at San Francisco State College. Two arrests were made after members of a small gang wearing stockings over their heads ransacked offices and set small fires in the restrooms of several buildings. A strike by an extremist minority of the 18,000 students closed down the campus as a protest against suspension of Black Panther George Murray, English Department instructor, who had called on black students to carry guns on campus.

Courses in how to stage community demonstrations and how past revolutions have been planned and carried out were listed in the curriculum of evening adult education classes advertised for Junior High School 271 in the controversial Ocean Hill-Brownsville school district of New York. Among the teachers listed for the courses was Herman B. Ferguson, who was in jail awaiting appeal of a prison sentence for conspiring to murder moderate civil rights leaders. Another instructor was Robert Carson, head of the Brooklyn Chapter of the Congress of Racial Equality. He withdrew the chapter from the national CORE because he considered the parent group insufficiently militant.

Student protestors in the latter half of the 1960s, emulating black power militants, turned from nonviolent demonstrations to "Che Guevara-like tactics of organized guerrilla warfare," Dr. Edward E. Sampson, associate professor of psychiatry at the University of California campus at Berkeley, told a national symposium on violence. He said that on college campuses as well as in the ghetto, militant leaders were turning from the spontaneous violence of previous years to the use of violence as a carefully planned political tactic. He stated: "The tactics here are to force police or the national guard into an area ostensibly in order to prevent violence. What actually occurs, of course, is that their presence easily provokes spontaneous violence."

Following the teachings of Mao Tse-tung and Guevara, the militants found in violence "a radicalizing effect on predisposed but otherwise as yet uncommitted or barely committed people." Guerrilla warfare had already started on college campuses. "Several burnings have taken place at Stanford University and at Berkeley. These may be the work of small bands of organized protestors. This move to more secretive hit-and-run guerrilla warfare is definitely the future direction of protest in this country. Things are going to get much worse before they become any better."

All during the latter part of the 1960s black extremists urged a Castro-like revolution in America. Castro's newspaper, *Granma,* quoted Stokely Carmichael as saying, "Brothers, we see our fight connected with the patriotic struggle of the peoples of Africa, Asia and Latin America against foreign oppression, especially United States oppression." *Granma* published an interview with Carmichael in which he said that "Fidel Castro is a source of inspiration" and that Cuban communism has a special importance "because it is the nearest system." Carmichael said, "We are moving toward urban guerrilla warfare within the United States," and linked the purposes of his guerrilla warfare to Communist objectives: "When the United States has 50 Vietnams inside and 50 outside, this will mean the death of imperialism."

A long distance call between H. Rap Brown in New York City and a Castro functionary in Havana was broadcast throughout Latin America on August 13, 1967. Brown told Havana, "Our rebellion is against the power and structure of white America." He bragged that black power was then proficient in the terrorist urban tactics of the Viet

Cong and said of the summer: "Each city in America which has a large Negro population can predict with confidence that it will have a rebellion . . . . We live in the stomach of a monster and we can destroy him from within."

Ex-convict Eldridge Cleaver, the 1968 presidential candidate of the Peace and Freedom Party, did not hesitate to state that violence was his goal. In a talk before a group of San Francisco lawyers he stated: " . . . you're all chasing dollars, but there are other people who are chasing dollars to buy guns, to kill judges and police and corporation lawyers . . . . We need lawyers today who have a lawbook in one hand and a gun in the other . . . so that if he goes to court and the case doesn't come out right, he can pull out his gun and start shooting . . . . I hope you'll take your guns and shoot judges and police. Kill some white people or make them act in a prescribed manner."

The fact is that all through the 1960s, the atmosphere in America became one in which violence became commonplace. The media have repeatedly been singled out as one of the major culprits in the spreading of this atmosphere of violence. Dr. Kenneth Keniston, psychologist at the Yale Medical Center, stated, "My view is that we do live in an era of highly publicized violence. The basic impulse to violence does not originate in the media, but given an individual with that impulse, the widespread publicity provides a channel through which psychotic impulses are expressed."

Patricia Roberts Harris, former U.S. Ambassador to Luxembourg, and the only woman appointed to President Johnson's commission on violence, said this of the mass media: "There is no reality to life and death on the television screen. When a life is taken there are only cardboard figures dying on the screen. They don't hurt when the bullet goes in. The body doesn't jerk. No family weeps for them." Thus, the public becomes inured to violence, and death itself becomes meaningless.

The atmosphere of violence which steadily grew during the 1960s is far too complex, however, to be simply attributed to the media. Reed Irvine, a close observer of political thinking, points out, "Human beings are conditioned or 'programmed' to act in certain ways, but unlike guinea pigs or computers the main programming device is articulated ideas. This is much less easy to control than is the programming of a computer or the conditioning of a guinea pig with electric shocks, since there are many conflicting ideas that are constantly impinging upon our consciousness which may neutralize each other. In addition, we are all equipped, by the time we reach maturity, with what I call a mental mesh which screens out many of the ideas that are thrown at us."

Our rhetoric has escalated to a point where violence is almost routinely threatened if particular political aims are not achieved.

George Wiley, the militant black leader of the National Welfare Rights Organization, once declared, standing in front of the Congressional office of Representative Wilbur Mills, chairman of the House Ways and Means Committee, that if Mr. Mills would not see him, "the cities of America would burn." Incidents of this kind have become increasingly frequent on Capitol Hill.

We live in a society in which, more and more, anything goes. The churches preach "situation ethics," telling individuals that "right" and "wrong" are relative concepts, and that each man must judge for himself what is correct. In an atmosphere of an escalating political rhetoric, when draft-card burners compare America with Nazi Germany and Dr. Spock and others say that we have killed a million children in Vietnam, a country that does not have a fraction of that number of total casualties, when the General Board of the National Council of Churches approves civil disobedience as a "valid instrument" for those who seek to correct injustice, we must expect the deteriorating situation we have been observing.

The problem today is not so much that men are immoral, as that they do not recognize the existence of any moral standard at all. Men have always lied, cheated and killed. It dates back to the Garden of Eden and to Cain and Abel. Yet, they never argued that this was proper, or that they had a moral right to do it.

This point has been made by Professor Will Herberg, theologian and author of the well-known volume *Protestant, Catholic, Jew*. He stated: " . . . the really serious threat to morality in our time consists not in the multiplying violations of an accepted moral code, but in the fact that the very notion of morality or a moral code seems to be itself losing its meaning . . . . It is here that we find a breakdown of morality in a radical sense, in a sense almost without precedent in our Western society."

Student demonstrators have felt no hesitation in invading the office of the president of the university and removing his private papers. Their impulse says "Do it!" and the only evil in the kind of society toward which we are moving is to resist your impulse. In the violence at Columbia University, private papers representing ten years of research were taken from the files of Orest A. Ranum, an assistant professor of modern history, and burned. The reason: he had issued a paper opposing the student position early in the crisis when some buildings were occupied by student demonstrators. Of the burned papers, Mr. Ranum said: "All of this is personally irreplaceable."

At a time when American young people are being inflicted with heavy doses of violence and the advocacy of violence and disrespect for law—and are witnessing a growing permissiveness and breakdown of traditional morality—we find them particularly vulnerable to such appeals. Part of the reason is the increasing transience of the American society and accompanying breakdown of community and family life.

In his important book *Future Shock,* Alvin Toffler points out that "we are witnessing a historic decline in the significance of place to human life. We are breeding a new race of nomads, and few suspect quite how massive, widespread and significant their migrations are . . . . Between March 1967 and March 1968—in a single year—36,600,000 Americans (not counting children less than one year old) changed their place of residence. This is more than the total population of Cambodia, Ghana, Guatemala, Honduras, Iraq, Israel, Mongolia, Nicaragua and Tunisia combined. It is as if the entire population of all these countries had suddenly been relocated. And movement on this massive scale occurs every year in the United States. In each year since 1948 one out of five Americans changed his address, picking up his children, some household effects and starting life anew at a fresh place. Even the great migrations of history, the Mongol hordes, the westward movement of Europeans in the 19th century, seem puny by statistical comparison."

Discussing the growing transience of American life, novelist Louis Auchincloss complains that "the horror of living in New York is living in a city without a history . . . . All eight of my great-grandparents lived in the city . . . and only one of the houses they lived in . . . is still standing. That's what I mean by the vanishing past."

Another sign of the lack of permanence in current American life is the fact that as late as 1955, apartments accounted for only 8 percent of new housing starts. By 1961 this had reached 24 percent and by 1969, for the first time in the United States, more building permits were being issued for apartment construction than for private homes. Apartment living, it seems, is very much in vogue. It is particularly popular among young people who, in the words of MIT Professor Burnham Kelly, want "minimum involvement housing."

Of the 885,000 listings in the Washington D.C., telephone book in 1969, over half were different from the year before. Within a single recent year fully one third of the members of the National Society for Programmed Instruction, an organization of educational researchers, changed their addresses.

People who make such frequent changes of location, writes Toffler, "are no longer the same as before, for any relocation, of necessity, destroys a complex web-work of old relationships and establishes a set of new ones. It is this disruption that, especially if repeated more than once, breeds the 'loss of commitment' that many writers have noted among high mobiles. The man on the move is ordinarily in too much of a hurry to put down roots in any one place. Thus an airline executive is quoted as saying he avoids involvement in the political life of his community because 'in a few years I won't be living here. You plant a tree and you never see it grow.' "

During eight recent years while the population of the United States was increasing by 7 percent, the use of moving vans increased 58 percent. The migratory American is moving increasingly greater distances. United Van Lines reports that every year for nine recent consecutive years the average distance a client-family moves has been increasing. From 1960 to 1968 the increase in distance clients moved rose from an average of 403 miles to 529 miles.

High mobility and transience have a marked effect on the way people act. "Once they arrive in California, hardly anyone 'settles'—no familial or community relations bind them. That's why we have so many nuts out here," says Los Angeles pollster Don Muchmore. "People come and do things they wouldn't normally do back home because such behavior is unacceptable."

Commenting upon this situation in his volume *A Nation of Strangers,* Vance Packard points out that "for one thing personal bankruptcies, in which others get hurt, tripled during a recent ten-year period. What is most noteworthy is the increasing casualness with which people take this move that once represented an ultimate in humiliation. Two possible contributing explanations are that high mobile people may be more prone to take chances on thin ice; and instant credit cards issued through anonymous, computerized credit card companies tend to depersonalize one's mounting indebtedness to individual creditors."

Discussing patterns of crime in the United States, Packard notes, "There are many causes for the soaring U.S. crime rates involving dishonesty and stealing; but certainly a major cause is the depersonalization of metropolitan life. People are far more willing to steal from strangers and institutions than from personal acquaintances: witness the contrast between life in small towns where doors frequently are left unlocked and life in big cities where residents often have three or four locks on a door."

Kenneth Watt of the University of California at Davis has assembled statistics concerning the question of aggression and anonymity. He found that as the population of an American city increases, the number of crimes per 100,000 citizens consistently increases as well. Consider the crime of assault: In cities with less than 10,000 population the annual assault rate per 100,000 population is 29. In cities of 100,000 to 250,000 population, the rate is 83. In cities of over 250,000 the rate is 154. A person living in a city of over 250,000 is four and a half times as likely to be assaulted as a person living in a town of 15,000. He is seven and a half times as likely to be robbed and three times as likely to be murdered. Women are four times as likely to be raped. Vance Packard points out, "All this happens despite the fact that as the size of cities grows the amount you, as an individual resident, must pay in taxes for police protection consistently increases, at least in cities above 90,000 in population. In a big metropolitan area you are likely to pay nearly twice as much in taxes for police protection as you do in a city of under 100,000."

A Stanford University research psychologist, Philip G. Zimbardo, has made an extensive study of the association between anonymity and aggression. In a test of vandalism he and a colleague left a car, seemingly in need of mechanical repair, on a street of a small city, Palo Alto, California, and another on the street of a big city, the Bronx area of New York City. In each case he had raised the hood and removed the license plates as possible "release" stimuli. In each case the car was in a white, middle-class neighborhood and across the street from a large college campus.

In Palo Alto, the car was left untouched for more than a week, except that when it rained a passer-by lowered the hood so the motor would not get wet. In the Bronx, within a matter of hours and in broad daylight, clean-cut adults and young men began stripping the car of its usable or salable parts, often within eyesight of others. There was no observable evidence that anyone cared or disapproved. There seemed to be a diffusion of individual responsibility for social acts.

At first, younger children began to smash the front and rear windows. Then over the next days well-dressed, "responsible-looking" white adults broke, bent, or ripped all easily detachable parts. Next they smashed the remainder of the car with rocks, pipes and hammers. In less than three days "what remained was a battered, useless hunk of metal, the result of 23 incidents of destructive contact." On a more recent visit to New York, Zimbardo learned that cars are now apt to be stripped if left for a day or two, even without any visible "release" clues that suggest the car has been abandoned, stolen, or is seriously ailing, such as cars in distress left on the Long Island Expressway and other highways.

In another test of anonymity and aggression, Professor Zimbardo arranged for a series of laboratory experiments in which coeds were permitted to apply a painful electric shock to two girls. They could see the victims but the victims could not see them. One "victim" was depicted as sweet and altruistic, the other as an obnoxious transfer student. The victims were presented one at a time to the group.

The coeds in charge of the shock machines were, on signal, to apply shocks to the victims as they tried to perform a learning task, just to see how the victims would react and to study to what degree the "shockers" identified with the situations of the victims. The girls who were to apply the shocks were divided into two groups. Professor Zimbardo made a significant effort to provide one group with a sense of anonymity and to deindividualize members. They had hoods over their heads and operated in the dark. No names were ever used. For the other group the individuality and identifiability of the girls was stressed and they could see one another's faces when they were assembled.

During the experiment the anonymous girls, on the average, continued to press the shock button twice as long as the individualized girls. In addition, as time passed, the anonymous girls gradually showed less and less discrimination. They applied pain to the obnoxious girl and the nice girl almost equally. Some pressed the pain button as long as they were allowed to do so.

Professor Zimbardo observed that, where social conditions of life destroy individual identity by making people feel anonymous, what will follow is what he saw in the laboratory. This led him to conclude that assaultive aggression, senseless acts of destruction, motiveless murders and great expenditures of energy directed toward shattering traditional forms and institutions are likely to be associated with a feeling of anonymity on the part of the aggressors. In his view, anonymity and deindividualization cause us to change our perception of ourselves and of others. The result is a "lowered threshold of normally restrained behavior." He suspects that this may be an important factor in the upsurge of social disorder of recent years. "What we are observing all about us," he states, "is a sudden change in the restraints which normally control the expression of our drives, impulses and emotions."

The growing anonymity of American life, suggests Professor Zimbardo, comes not only from the growth of vast cities but from the feeling of powerlessness in the face of large institutions, the renting of apartments instead of owning homes, and the immense mobility of Americans. He suggests that one best hope for change from all this is somehow to recapture our dwindling sense of identity within a meaningful social community.

Yale psychologist Kenneth Kenniston, in his study of the alienation of modern youth, said that whatever the gains of our technological age, many Americans are left with an inarticulate sense of loss, unrelatedness and lack of connection. Many of these people who lose a sense of relatedness begin to find life meaningless and become indifferent to the troubles of and the assaults against their fellow men. They become callous.

Writer Nat Hentoff cites an encounter with a district attorney in Queens, New York, who was bemoaning evidences of public apathy in his vast metropolitan area. The official complained: "They talk about an Affluent Society, a Great Society, a Free Society. You know what we really are, chum? We're a Cold Society."

Today, according to Daniel P. Moynihan, the United States "exhibits the qualities of an individual going through a nervous breakdown." Peter Weiss, in his play, "Marat/Sade," portrays a turbulent world as seen through the eyes of the inmates of Charenton asylum. Movies like "Morgan" portray life within a mental institution as superior to that of the outside world. In "Blow-Up," the climax comes when the hero joins in a tennis game in which players hit a nonexistent ball back and forth over the net. It is his symbolic acceptance of the unreal and irrational; he can no longer distinguish between illusion and reality. Millions of viewers identified with the hero in that movie.

Observing the dramatic changes which are occurring in American society, it is easy to see why politicians continue to insist that the problem of crime can best be solved by more government programs, such as job training and wealth-redistribution initiatives. If they look at the problem as it really is—if they consider the increasing transience of the American society, the breakdown of family life, the continual display of violence in movies, on television, and in books, the turning away from religion, and the turning of many churches toward a morality of permissiveness, the increasingly violent rhetoric of political extremists and their prominent display in the media—if they consider all these elements of the problem, their only conclusion would be that political "solutions" for such a situation do not, in reality, exist.

On what basis could such men offer themselves to the people for election, then, if they were to admit that they did not have a "plan" to eliminate crime and violence? The answer is that they could not so offer themselves. As a result, they continue the irrelevant exercise of advocating "plans" that bear no relationship to the problem. Society, accordingly, does not do the things that could be done to alter the atmosphere which has produced such a harmful situation. Society is itself the seedbed of crime and violence, and politicians cannot simply appropriate funds and employ bureaucrats to change it.

There is, in addition to all of the societal problems we have considered, still another serious contributing factor to the crime and violence we have observed. That is the fact that Americans are slowly coming to the view that, rather than the old maxim that "crime does not pay," crime can, in fact, pay very well. The guilty, more and more now believe, do not have to pay for their crimes. Thus, they can violate the law with impunity. Unfortunately, this view is based upon an all too realistic appraisal of our current legal system.

In Manhattan, for example, only 3 percent of the 13,555 persons indicted between July, 1963, and July, 1966, were convicted after a trial; almost 80 percent pleaded guilty. Even in one middle-sized nonmetropolitan county in Wisconsin, 94 percent of the convictions were the result of a plea of guilty, and it made little difference whether the offender had a lawyer or not.

Professor Martin A. Levin of Brandeis University found in a study of the Pittsburgh Common Pleas Court in 1966 that well over half of the white males convicted of burglary, grand larceny, indecent assault or possession of narcotics, and who had a prior record, were placed on probation; nearly half of the two-time losers convicted of aggravated assault were placed on probation, as were more than one-fourth of those convicted of robbery.

In Wisconsin, Dean V. Babst and John W. Mannering found that 63 percent of the adult males convicted of a felony during 1954-59 who had previously been convicted of another felony were placed on probation, and 41 percent of those with two or more felony convictions were given probation for the subsequent offense.

Between 1963 and 1969, the number of persons arrested in New York State on felony narcotics charges (usually dealers, rather than users) increased by more than 700 percent and the number convicted more than tripled. Yet, the number going to state prison remained unchanged and thus the proportion fell from 68 percent of those convicted to less than 23 percent.

In Boston, the average penalty in heroin cases fell during the 1960s, at the time when heroin abuse was rising. Between 1963 and 1970, the proportion of heroin cases before the Suffolk County (Boston) district and superior courts resulting in prison sentences fell from almost half to about one tenth; meanwhile, the estimated number of heroin users rose from fewer than 1,000 to almost 6,000.

Why, to cite this example, was this the case in Boston? Discussing the meaning of the situation, Professor James Q. Wilson of Harvard University writes that "this pattern of sentencing can be explained by neither a deterrence nor a rehabilitation philosophy: Obviously the decrease in penalties did not deter heroin dealers, and the absence during most of this time of any treatment-alternative to prison for heroin users meant that rehabilitation, if it were to occur at all, would have to occur spontaneously (which, of course, it did not)."

Professor Wilson notes, "The reasons for the sentencing patterns in many courts have little or nothing to do with achieving some general social objective, but a great deal to do with the immediate problems and idiosyncratic beliefs of the judges. A few sentences can be explained by corruption, many more by the growing belief among some judges that since prisons do not rehabilitate, it is wrong to send criminals to them, and most of all by the overwhelming need in busy jurisdictions to clear crowded court dockets."

When thousands of felony cases must be settled each year in a court, writes Professor Wilson, "there are overpowering pressures to settle them on the basis of plea bargaining in order to avoid the time and expense of a trial. The defendant is offered a reduced charge or a lighter sentence in exchange for a plea of guilty. Though congested dockets are not the only reason for this practice, an increase in congestion increases the incentives for such bargaining and thus may increase the proportion of lighter sentences. For those who believe in the deterrence theory of sentencing it is a grim irony: The more crime increases, the more the pressure on court calendars, and the greater the chances that the response to the crime increase will be a sentence decrease."

Those criminals and potential criminals who believe that they have a good chance to avoid punishment for their crimes are quite correct in this assumption. Consider two additional statistical conclusions, based upon studies in New York City and Washington, D.C.

A New York police study of how the city's prosecutors and judges handle robbery cases has found that 15.7 percent of a sampling of suspects arrested on a charge of purse-snatching ultimately were sentenced to jail.

The study, released in 1972 by the Police Department's Criminal Justice Bureau, also found that less than one-quarter of a sampling of suspects charged with committing robberies in hallways, entrances and elevators served time in a city or state institution.

The police robbery study involved an examination of the disposition of one out of five of the arrests made for purse-snatching or residential robbery in the city in April, May and June of 1971. A total of 207 out of 1,035 such cases were analyzed.

The study found that by December 20, 1971, a total of 71 percent of a sampling of those arrested for robbing someone in building entrances or hallways during April, May and June of 1971 had been disposed of. Among the dispositions were the following: 24 percent, some kind of jail sentence; 22 percent dismissed; 7 percent probation; 6 percent awaiting sentence; 3 percent discharged on their own recognizance; and 4 percent either withdrawn or given a conditional discharge.

David Burnham, writing in the *New York Times* of April 20, 1972, notes that "the Criminal Justice Bureau is known to have made similar studies on the disposition of other kinds of cases, including those involving persons charged with possession and sale of narcotics and with the illegal possession of hand guns." He reports that according to the study on hand gun cases, a sampling of 136 felony charges and 20 misdemeanor charges resulted in no defendants being convicted of a felony but in 48 percent being convicted on a reduced charge or the original misdemeanor charge.

The report declared, "The study revealed 8.3 percent of all defendants were imprisoned and 11.6 percent were fined." The longest sentence was one year, and the highest fine was $300. Under the law, while the defendants could have received a total of 972 years in prison, actual sentences totaled 5 years, 4 months and 11 days. This amounted, the study said, to "six-tenths of one percent of the total penalty the law permitted."

In Washington, D.C., almost one of every five persons arrested in May 1972 was on probation or some other form of conditional release one month later. A report compiled by the major violators unit, a branch of the police department whose major function is to find out what happens to prisoners released to halfway houses, on probation or on self-recognizance, stated that the District Police made 2,040 arrests in May 1972 compared to 1,568 arrests in May 1971. Of the total arrested in May 1972, 375 were rearrests. Of the total for May 1971, 193 were rearrests.

Thus, while total arrests department-wide increased 30 percent in May of 1972 over May of 1971, rearrests of persons on release status increased 94.3 percent.

The report said that of the 2,040 arrests in May, 1972, 935 were for major crimes, including homicide, rape, and other sex offenses, robbery, burglary, auto theft and narcotics violations. Of these 935, there were 172 arrests of persons who were free on conditional release. In May 1971, 12 percent of all those arrested were conditional release cases. For May 1972, 18 percent of all arrests were in that category.

Senator James L. Buckley of New York declares that "contrary to the old adage, crime in America does indeed pay—and, for those who are prepared to undergo certain manageable risks, it can pay rather handsomely." Professor Gordon Tullock made some extrapolations on the rationality of crime as a profession and calculated, on the basis of 1965 figures, that if you commit a crime, your chances of being arrested are only one in seven, and if you are convicted, only one in 60 that you will be sent to prison.

We find, when considering the various causes for the increase in crime and violence in the American society, a variety of contributing factors. On the one hand, the family is breaking down, permissiveness has become the prevailing morality and transience has eliminated the sense of roots and neighborhood. To this must be added the influence of radical political rhetoric, violence on television and in the movies and the increasingly accepted concept that men are not responsible for their deeds but that such deeds are the fault of poverty, the environment or other societal factors. Then, on the other hand, we witness the breakdown of our legal system and the fact that criminals are able to get away with their crimes without punishment. All of this adds up to the crisis we face—unsafe streets and a growing threat to the very fabric of our civilization.

In his volume *Contemporary Sociological Theories,* Professor Pitirim Sorokin provides a list of eight findings based upon a lengthy and detailed survey of the available data concerning the causes of crime.

He notes, "Several studies . . . have shown that an extraordinary increase of crime in the periods of social upheaval is due to other than purely economic conditions. Secondly, not everywhere nor always do the poor show a greater proportion of crime. Third, many poorer countries have had less crime than the richer countries."

Professor Sorokin continues: "Fourth, the improvement in the economic conditions of the population of the Western countries in the second half of the 19th century, and at the beginning of the 20th, has not been followed by a decrease in crime. Fifth, among those who commit crimes against property there is always a considerable number of well-to-do people and, on the other hand, many of the poorest people do not commit such crimes."

He concludes, "Sixth, it is an ascertained fact that, in the causation of crime and criminals, a great many noneconomic factors play an important role. Seventh, practically all correlations between economic conditions and crime are far from being perfect, or even notably high. Eighth, there is only a relatively low coefficient or correlation found between crime and business conditions . . . . "

Once we understand the things which are *not* the causes of the increase in crime we have faced, and begin to understand the things which *are* contributing factors, we will see the irrelevance of most of the suggestions and programs which have come from the political arena.

It has been easy and convenient to believe that our society was taking important steps to cut the rising crime rate by appropriating money for more police, by urging vast comprehensive crime plans and by increasing welfare payments and other programs which were meant to redistribute wealth and, in effect, produce less resentment and anxiety on the part of those at the bottom of the economic ladder.

Each of these individual programs has merits and demerits. These merits and demerits, however, must be considered separate from the question of crime, its causes and possible solution. Crime has no simple cause and, as a result, can have no simple solution, despite the fact that simple solutions are the only kind our political process seems capable of implementing.

As we have seen, the very fabric of American society is what has produced the situation we face today. Just as all Americans, white and black, are part of that society, and just as all Americans, of both races, observe violence on television, see communities fall away and families break up, so all Americans are affected by it. Black Americans, however, are not only affected by all these factors which they share with the larger society, but are subjected to a number of additional forces which work upon them in somewhat different ways.

The Negro crime rate is as high as it is because of the unfortunate combination of these forces. Just as white society does not fully understand why it has become the way it is today, so black society is equally unaware of the real causes of the social breakdown it has witnessed. These causes are complex, but unless they are understood the problem will deteriorate further, to the detriment of all, white and black together.

Chapter 4

Politicization, Urbanization and Black Crime

All of the forces in society which tend to disrupt established social patterns and place all traditional values in a state of upheaval and impermanence work upon Americans of both races.

Americans of both races watch the violence on television and in the movies. Americans of both races have been torn from their roots and live in a transient and ever-changing society. The divorce rate and accompanying breakdown of family life affect both races, as does the lowering respect for law and the growing belief on the part of criminals and potential criminals that men, in today's American society, do not have to pay for their crimes.

Every force which leads the larger American society away from its traditional values and ways of living affects black and white Americans together, but not necessarily in the same way. The fact is that black Americans are even more dramatically influenced by the changing values and social structure they must live with and to which they must accommodate.

If families in general are breaking down, black families were weaker at the start. If men and women in general are leaving their homes in the ever-increasing trend toward urbanization, this movement is even more swift for Negroes, whose predominantly rural life patterns in the South have been most subjected to the winds of change. If the larger society is faced with a philosophy of moral relativism which is tearing it from its concepts of what is right and what is wrong, black Americans, who have lived for so long on the margin of American society, were less wedded to the philosophical precepts of the older America, and find it easier to abandon them.

It may be said that every negative force in America is even more negative with regard to its impact upon black Americans. In addition, black Americans must cope with all the forces affecting the larger society, as well as with a separate group of forces which are unique within the black community itself.

A study issued by the US Census Bureau in 1971 indicates, for example, the extent of Negro transience and migration in recent years. The study shows that migration was a major factor in the rapid growth of Negro populations in big cities outside of the South. New York, Chicago and Los Angeles all showed net migration gains of 100,000 or more Negroes in the decade from 1959 to 1970. New York's migration gain was by far the largest—a net of 435,840. Eleven other cities had migration gains of 25,000 or more.

It is in the large cities outside the South that the proportion of Negroes in the population has increased fastest. Table 1 gives several examples

Table 1
Negro Population in Ten Selected Cities (%)

City	1950	1960	1970
New York	9.5	14.0	21.2
Chicago	13.6	22.9	32.7
Detroit	16.2	28.9	43.7
Philadelphia	18.2	26.4	33.6
Washington	35.0	53.9	71.1
Los Angeles	8.7	13.5	17.9
Baltimore	23.7	34.7	46.4
Cleveland	16.2	28.6	38.3
St. Louis	18.0	28.6	40.9
Newark	17.1	34.1	54.2

The trend in Negro migration is also shown by regional statistics. In the South, the black population has grown only 5.8 percent in the last decade. It has also declined in the East South Central States. But the number of Negroes has increased 43.4 percent in the Northeastern States, 32.7 percent in the North Central States and 56.1 percent in the West.

In the nation as a whole, the Negro population has gone up

19.6 percent since 1960, while whites increased 11.9 percent. Although 102 counties in the South remained predominantly black in 1970, all but four of those counties have a smaller percentage of Negroes than they did in 1960.

The effect of transience and uprootedness upon Negro crime and violence is a subject that has not been studied with sufficient thoroughness and interest. One study which has appeared, however, tends to place this question in a much needed proper perspective. It is a volume entitled *Violence in the City,* published in 1969 by the Texas Christian University Press and written by Dr. Blair Justice.

Most analyses of the recurrent eruption of urban crime and violence have tended to follow either one of two simplistic formulas, which are:

1. The violence is engendered primarily by economic deprivation and social discrimination, and can be ended by removing these causes.

2. The violence results from a failure of law enforcement due in large part to obstacles created by recent rulings of the courts; the remedy lies in sterner laws and in stricter enforcement by police and judiciary alike.

In either case, the analyses appear to work toward pre-established conclusions derived from ideological prejudice or conviction rather than direct observation.

In his study, Professor Justice shows that the problem is far too complex to fit either interpretation, and far too difficult to admit of either solution. In addition to being clinical professor of social psychology at the University of Texas and a research associate at Rice University, Dr. Justice is director of human relations for the mayor of Houston. It was in that city that a great part of his investigation was undertaken, but his findings have a far wider applicability and deserve the attention of all who seek to understand the real ingredients of the "urban crisis."

It is not poverty, but unfulfilled expectations, according to Dr. Justice, that spread the seeds of discontent and unrest among urban Negroes. One of the most influential agencies in arousing these expressions, he states, is television, from which a great many Negroes derive their misconceptions about what kind of life most white persons lead.

Most urban Negroes have a very limited contact with whites, or none at all. This was brought out in a random sample survey taken in Houston in the summer of 1966. Out of 533 Negroes questioned, 46 percent admitted they had no contact whatever with whites; 29 percent had jobs which brought them into contact with some white persons for four or more hours a day; 17

percent said they had less than four hours daily contact; 4.5 percent gave no answer. According to H. Edward Ransford, the sense of social "isolation" felt by a black man increases the likelihood of his participation in some form of violence. In other words, those Negroes who had least contact with whites were, generally speaking, those readiest to employ violence.

In comparing the attitudes of Negroes in Houston with those in the riot areas of Watts, Los Angeles, Dr. Justice noted that "many Negroes coming from East Texas found conditions better than those they left, but they did not bring with them excessively high expectations toward Houston. From interviews in Watts, I found that Negroes moving to California, on the other hand, looked toward it as promising much more than it could deliver . . . . The same can be said about Harlem and Chicago."

But Dr. Justice also found that a single episode could bring about sharp reversals of attitudes toward violence. There was, for example, an exchange of gunfire between police and students during a disturbance at the predominantly Negro Texas Southern University. Before this incident the police had been looked upon with a high degree of acceptance, apparently because of the patience and restraint they had shown in dealing with other incidents on campus. Yet, as Dr. Justice observes: "One residual effect of violence is that a strong shift to a highly vocal Black Power personality may occur in the Negro community, particularly in situations where white authority is considered as having wronged other black people—even those with whom members of the community formerly disagreed."

Before the disturbance at Texas Southern University, in random sample interviews among 2,271 members of the black community, there were 19 percent who said they had never even heard of "Black Power," 46 percent who said that they were against it, and only 35 percent who spoke favorably of Stokely Carmichael and his program. After the violence at TSU, the black community was not only more aware of "Black Power," but was more in sympathy with its leaders.

The statistics assembled in this study show that those Negroes who have moved frequently from place to place are more likely to be involved in acts of violence than those who were born and have grown up in a given community. Today, three-fourths of all American Negroes are living in urban areas. This is a higher proportion than for white Americans and includes almost all Negroes outside the South. In 1910, fully 90 percent of all Negroes lived in the South; in 1967 only 54 percent lived there.

The sense of identity, of "belonging," depends in part at least on being able to call some place home. Studies by E. H. Powell have shown that a background of rootlessness, broken homes and fractured relationships with others constitutes the "decisive variable" in criminal behavior. An analysis of the files of 108 Negro prisoners under the Texas Department of Corrections disclosed that more than 90 percent recalled four or more migrations in childhood. More than 90 percent had been born in small towns or in the country, but 85 percent of this group had committed their crimes of violence in cities that they now considered their home. Mobility and complexity were especially evident in the backgrounds of those who had been convicted of murder, assault and rape.

In his work, Professor Justice examines many other aspects of violent unrest. He deals at length with student violence and advises us to "quit pushing the black student into the pressurized environments of large white universities where he becomes the object of 'charity' of white students and faculty members seeking a catharsis for guilt on the race question." He wants us to "recognize that Negro colleges and universities have an expertise for helping ill-prepared high school students to catch up and gain some sense of competency" and urges us to give these colleges "the substantial support they need to do a better job."

Elsewhere he discusses the relationships between black slum residents and the police. The city of Houston managed to siphon off some of the hostility and rage existing between these two groups by bringing them together in face-to-face confrontations under the guidance of psychologists. The techniques of psychodrama and role-reversal were employed to enable members of each group to understand what it felt like to be in the other's shoes. "The problems of the blue-collar minority were understood, probably for the first time, by members of the black community, as were the problems of the Negroes by the police."

In the United States in 1956 more than 20,500 police officers were assaulted, 6,838 were injured and 53 were killed. It has been reported that in the late 1960s one officer out of every eight was assaulted. Clearly, this is a state of affairs which must be corrected. Dr. Justice declares that Americans must recognize "the fact that historically the Negro male has had to play a passive role in American society and he sees the police officer as the symbol of white authority . . . . Let's accept that there is much unvented rage from the passivity and that a high degree of hostility is likely to be felt. The challenge is to find constructive avenues for release of the rage, avenues that do not lead to violence."

Professor Justice recalls that during a riot in Houston when a supermarket and a service station were set afire he received a telephone call from the mayor, who asked him to call a certain number, saying it belonged to a concerned citizen who had "an urgent message" to deliver. Justice dialed the number; it was that of a friend and this was his message: "Let them do their burning. It will be a catharsis. They need this." The professor broke off the conversation and the connection. "The reason I relate this story," he tells his reader, "is that I cannot ever accept the notion that violence brings good."

It is impossible to understand the rise in black crime and violence without understanding the impact upon the black family of the move from the rural South to the large cities of the North and their accompanying slums to which most arriving black families are consigned.

While black families in the South lived in rural communities where they had, in most instances, lived for generations, they suddenly found themselves in impersonal, mass urban societies where they knew no one. In their rural homes the influence of the church was significant, while in the urban inner city the influence of all of the forces of the street—gamblers, prostitutes, drug peddlers, gangs—replaced the church, the family and the community as sources of value and of "belonging."

The impact of the move from South to North, and from rural to urban area has been expressed by many black writers. One of the best descriptions comes from Claude Brown, in his book *Manchild in the Promised Land.*

At nine, Brown was a member of the Harlem Buccaneers, a notorious gang, and of the Forty Thieves, an elite stealing division of the Buccaneers. At 11 he was sent to Wiltwyck School for "emotionally disturbed and deprived boys" where he stayed for two years. At 14 he was sent to Warwick Reform School for the first of three times. He was graduated from Howard University in June 1965, and the next fall entered law school. His is one of the success stories to come from the streets of Harlem. Claude Brown battled the odds, and he won. Too many lose.

Discussing the characters in his book, which is the story of his own youth, he writes, "I want to talk about the first Northern urban generation of Negroes. I want to talk about the experiences of a misplaced generation, of a misplaced people in an extremely complex, confused society. This is a story of their searching, their dreams, their sorrows, their small and futile rebellions, and their endless battle to establish their own place in America's greatest metropolis—and in America itself."

The characters in his book, declares Brown, are the sons and daughters of former Southern sharecroppers: "These were the poorest people of the South, who poured into New York City during the decade following the Great Depression. These migrants were told that unlimited opportunities for prosperity existed in New York and that there was no 'color problem' there. They were told that Negroes lived in houses with bathrooms, electricity, running water, and indoor toilets. To them, this was the 'promised land' that Mammy had been singing about in the cotton fields for so many years."

The move from the rural South to New York, and to other large cities of the North, was "goodbye to the cotton fields, goodbye to 'Massa Charlie,' goodbye to the chain gang, and most of all, goodbye to those sunup-to-sundown working hours. One no longer had to wait to get to heaven to lay his burden down; burdens could be laid down in New York."

The blacks from the rural South came to the urban cities of the North by the tens of thousands. "They felt," writes Brown, "as the Pilgrims must have felt when they were coming to America. But these descendants of Ham must have been twice as happy as the Pilgrims, because they had been catching twice the hell. Even while planning the trip, they sang spirituals such as 'Jesus Take My Hand' and 'I'm on My Way' and chanted, 'Halleluja, I'm on my way to the promised land!' "

Speaking of those who had encouraged them to go North, Brown notes, "It seems that Cousin Willie, in his lying haste, had neglected to tell the folks down home about one of the most important aspects of the promised land: it was a slum ghetto. There was a tremendous difference in the way life was lived up North. There were too many people full of hate and bitterness crowded into a dirty, stinky, un-cared-for closet-size section of a great city . . . . The children of these disillusioned colored pioneers inherited the total lot of their parents— the disappointments, the anger. To add to their misery, they had little hope of deliverance. For where does one run when he's already in the promised land?"

The city has had a dramatic, and often negative, impact upon those who turned to it for a better life. Census data released in 1971 showed that a fourth of all nonwhite families are headed by women, and that the curve is still rising. In a memo to President Nixon in 1970, Daniel P. Moynihan wrote that "the problem does not get bet-ter, it gets worse. In 1969 the proportion of husband-wife families of Negro and other races declined once again, this time to 68.7 percent. The illegitimacy ratio rose once again, this time to 29.4 percent of all live births. (The white ratio rose more sharply, but was still only 4.9 percent.)"

Moynihan declared, "Increasingly the problem of Negro poverty is the problem of the female-headed family. In 1968, 56 percent of Ne-gro families with income under $3,000 were female-headed. In 1968, for the first time, the number of poor Negro children in female-headed families (2,241,000) was greater than the number in male-headed families (1,947,000). The incidence of antisocial behavior among young black males continues to be extraordinarily high."

In Washington, D.C., a city which is predominantly black, the sta-tistics tell this story in some depth. In a report issued in March 1972 and compiled by the Department of Human Resources of the District of Columbia, it is shown that the percentage of children born out of wedlock had increased from 19.8 percent in 1960 to 37 percent in 1969.

Roberto Fuentes, chief of the human resources' research and statistics division, said that 1970 figures, not included in his report, show the percentage exceeding 40 percent. "If this rate of increase continues," the report said, "half of all births will be out of wedlock by 1973."

The percentage of illegitimate babies increased for both black and white District residents. Fuentes said that in 1970, 44.7 percent of all births to black District residents were out of wedlock, up from 40.9 percent in 1969 and 29.8 percent in 1964. For whites, the figures increased from 10.1 percent in 1964 to 13 percent in 1969, to 13.3 percent in 1970.

A large portion of the increase in illegitimate births can be traced to an increase in births to teenage mothers. In 1969, out-of-wedlock births to teenage girls involved 18.5 percent of all births, up from 7.5 percent in 1960. In 1969, more than 70 percent of all births to teenagers in the city were out of wedlock. The study projects that in 1973, almost 30 percent of all live births will be births to unwed teenagers.

The District of Columbia figures are far higher than those for the nation as a whole and also higher than those in the Washington suburbs. Dr. Carl Shultz, director of the office of population control in the Department of Health, Education and Welfare, said that the national illegitimacy rate in 1972 was approximately 10 percent. In the predominantly white Washington suburb of Fairfax County, Virginia, the figure in 1970 was 4.9 percent. In predominantly white Montgomery County, Maryland, in 1970 it was 5 percent, and in Prince Georges County, Maryland, also predominantly white, it was 7.8 percent.

The breakdown of the black family and the rising rate of illegitimacy, together with the rapid urbanization of black Americans and the deteriorating quality of life in the nation's core cities, added to the changing morality of the total American society, are all essential ingredients of the causes of the rising black crime rate.

Yet, the problem is far more complex. At the same time that statistics show family breakdown and inner city deterioration, other statistics show quite clearly that black Americans are much better educated than ever before, and are holding better jobs and earning higher salaries.

In 1971, Andrew F. Brimmer, the only black member of the Board of Governors of the Federal Reserve Board, told a convention of the National Association for the Advancement of Colored People that in the 1960s Negroes left low-paying jobs on farms and in households at a rate almost three times as fast as whites. The number of nonwhites in high-paying professional technical positions jumped by 131 percent, compared with a gain of 49 percent among whites—and the black share of such jobs rose from 4.4 to 6.9 percent.

The 1960s saw a great breakthrough for blacks. A third (32 percent) of all families of Negro and other races earned $8,000 or more in 1968 compared in constant dollars with 15 percent in 1960. Outside of the South, young husband-wife Negro families have 99 percent of the income of whites. For families headed by a male age 25 to 34, the proportion was 87 percent.

Black occupations improved dramatically. The number of professional and technical employees doubled in the period from 1960 to 1968. This was two and one half times the increase for whites. In 1969, Negro and other races provided 10 percent of the other-than-college teachers. This is roughly equal to their proportion of the population, 11 percent.

In 1968, forty-five percent of Negroes 18 and 19 years old were in school, almost the equal of the white proportion of 51 percent. Negro college enrollment rose 85 percent between 1964 and 1968, by which time there were 434,000 Negro college students. The total full-time university population of Great Britain, by comparison, is 200,000.

Thus, on the one hand, we see a deteriorating family life and a deteriorating city while, on the other, we see dramatic improvement in Negro education, employment, and earnings. From a purely statistical approach, we might properly blame the increase in crime and violence on one factor as on the other. It may be, however, that, quite to the contrary, the cause—or at least part of the cause—is to be found elsewhere.

In his 1970 memo to President Nixon, Daniel Moynihan noted that "with no real evidence I would nonetheless suggest that a great deal of the crime, the fire-setting, the rampant school violence and other such phenomena in the black community have become quasi-politicized. Hatred—revenge—against whites is now an acceptable excuse for doing what might have been done anyway. This is bad news for any society, especially when it takes forms which the Black Panthers seem to have adopted."

One major cause of increasing black crime appears to be the growing politicization of the black community and the feeling on the part of militant spokesmen, who are given prominent coverage by the media, that crime and violence are justifiable if they can be explained or rationalized in political terms. While the average black murderer, rapist or burglar may not himself think in political terms, the fact remains that he is part of an atmosphere in which crime and violence have been pronounced as acceptable forms of social behavior.

The claims made for themselves by those who argue that their crimes have been "political," and that they are, accordingly, being incarcerated and "persecuted" not because of their actions but because of their political opinions, are clear and precise. One well-known advocate of this view is Eldridge Cleaver, the Black Panther leader, who set forth his position in the much-publicized volume *Soul on Ice,* published in 1968.

Cleaver, arrested and convicted on charges of rape, declares that "I became a rapist. To refine my technique and modus operandi I started out by practicing on black girls in the ghetto—in the black ghetto where dark and vicious deeds appear not as aberrations or deviations from the norm, but as part of the sufficiency of the Evil of a day—and when I considered myself smooth enough, I crossed the tracks and sought out white prey. I did this consciously, deliberately, willfully, methodically—though looking back I see that I was in a frantic, wild and completely abandoned frame of mind. . . . I know that if I had not been apprehended I would have slit some white throats."

Although he admits that he was in a "frantic, wild, and completely abandoned frame of mind" and that if he had not been apprehended he "would have slit some white throats," he proceeds to set forth the proposition that his acts of violence and passion were, in fact, "political."

He writes, "Rape was an insurrectionary act. It delighted me that I was defying and trampling upon the white man's law, upon his system of values, and that I was defiling his women—and this point, I believe, was the most satisfying to me because I was very resentful over the historical fact of how the white man has used the black woman. I felt I was getting revenge."

Cleaver declares that "we are a very sick country" and "perhaps I am sicker than most." He condemns judges, policemen and prison administrators for not understanding that Negro convicts, be they murderers, rapists or thieves, are all really "political prisoners." He writes, " . . . rather than see themselves as criminals and perpetrators of misdeeds, they look upon themselves as prisoners of war, the victims of a vicious, dog-eat-dog social system that is so heinous as to cancel out their malefactions: in the jungle there is no right or wrong."

Thus a man, simply because he is black, and because those who are black have, at different times and in different ways in American society, suffered discrimination, now receives justification for the commission of the most heinous crimes. Rape, murder and other acts of brutality are "political" because by committing such acts the black prisoner shows his hostility to "white society."

Cleaver, of course, overlooks the fact that most crimes of violence committed by blacks are against other blacks, not against the white society which is oppressing them. "Rather than owing and paying a debt to society," Cleaver states, "Negro prisoners feel that they are being abused, that their imprisonment is simply another form of the oppression which they have known all their lives. Negro inmates feel that they are being robbed, that it is 'society' that owes them, that should be paying them a debt."

Behind the flamboyant rhetoric, what Cleaver is saying, quite simply, is that every black American in prison, for whatever reason, is a "political" prisoner, even if he has no political opinions, or if he has political opinions diametrically opposed to those held by Cleaver himself. By this definition, "political" crime is synonymous with racial identity, and has little to do with intent or action of the accused individual.

Another well-known advocate of the concept of "political crime" is George Jackson, who was killed during the San Rafael, California, shoot-out which implicated radical leader Angela Davis in the charge of murder. Jackson had been convicted of a series of crimes and, according to his own admission, did not develop a political philosophy until after his incarceration in prison. It was not, as a result, even possible for him to argue that he had committed such crimes as a consequence of a motivating political worldview.

In his book *Soledad Brother,* a collection of letters sent from prison, he sets forth his philosophy. A great portion of his hostility is reserved for those who call for positive change through nonviolent activity. He considers such individuals to be completely out of touch with history, and not to realize, as his own historical studies in prison had apparently taught him, that violence is the best and, probably, the only means through which affirmative social change may be brought about.

He writes, "The concept of nonviolence is a false ideal. It presupposes the existence of compassion and a sense of justice on the part of one's adversary. When this adversary has everything to lose and nothing to gain by exercising justice and compassion, his reaction can only be negative."

Establishing this alleged "adversary" situation between all black Americans, on the one hand, and the remainder of American society on the other, Jackson declares, "Our response . . . must necessarily be negative when we consider that blacks in the U.S. have been subjected to the most thorough brainwashing of any people in history. Isolated as we were, or are, from our land, our roots, and our institutions, no group of men have been so thoroughly terrorized, dehumanized, and divested of those things that from birth make men strong."

What does Jackson think of his nonblack fellow citizens? He does not hesitate to vent his hatred and his view of the innate superiority of everything black. He writes: "People the world over are not the same but those that we meet here in the U.S. are generally of a single type. By and large they are all fools, intellectual nonpersons, emotional half-wits. Status symbols, supervisory positions, and petty power motivate their every act. Personal, individual, financial success at any price is their social ethic, the only real standard upon which their conduct is built."

Black Americans, Jackson writes, are heir to a far different approach to life: "Black culture is a monumental subject that covers countless years. The first man and consequently the first culture was black." Writing to his younger brother Jon, later to be killed during the San Rafael incident, on December 28, 1969, he says this of Western religion: "Forget that Westernized backward stuff about god. I curse god, the whole idea of a benevolent supreme being is the product of a tortured, demented mind. It is a labored, mindless attempt to explain away ignorance, a tool to keep people of low mentality and no means of production in line."

Comparing the challenge facing black Americans with the challenge which he imagined to be facing Chinese, Cubans and Vietnamese, Jackson advanced the view that what is needed to solve racial problems in America is a program of armed insurrection: "People's war, class struggle, war of liberation means armed struggle . . . . How can we deal with these men who have so much at stake, so much to defend? Honesty forces us to the conclusion that the only men who will successfully deal with the Hoovers, Helmses and Abramses will be armed men."

While he seemed intent upon making racial distinctions, seeing all virtue in all that is nonwhite, whether black or yellow or red or some indeterminate color, and evil in all that is white, still his limited reading within the prison walls taught him that distinctions based upon race did not tell the whole story. There was something, he learned, beyond race, and that was economic class. This he learned from Karl Marx, and if he had a difficult time keeping his hatred of whites and white society separate from his adoption of the essentially white and European Marxist philosophy, this seemed not to bother him very much.

"Our principal enemy," he wrote, "must be isolated and identified as capitalism. The slaver was and is the factory owner, the businessman of capitalist Amerika, the man responsible for employment, wages, prices, control of the nation's institutions and culture. It was the capitalist infrastructure of Europe and the United States which was responsible for the rape of Africa and Asia. Capitalism murdered those 30 million in the Congo."

Those black Americans who refused to share his view of the enemy became, for him, simply a part of the enemy. One for whom Jackson had special wrath was comedian Bill Cosby. Using the rhetoric of Mao Tse-tung, he said this of Cosby: "Bill Cosby . . . this running dog in the company of a fascist with a cause, a flunky's flunky, was transmitting the credo of the slave to our youth, the mod version of the old house nigger. We can never learn to trust as long as we have them.

They are as much a part of the repression, even more than the real live rat-informer-pig. Aren't they telling our kids it is romantic to be a running dog?"

It is clear that Jackson's view was that any black man who did not seek to destroy American society through the use of force, and who did not believe that communism would provide a better life for people, particularly minorities, was not in any sense an honorable man with whom he might disagree. That man had, of course, to be a "running dog" of the enemy. He had to be an "Uncle Tom," a "house nigger," or whatever other epithet came conveniently to mind.

George Jackson's warped view of reality led him to conclusions which logically followed from such a misapprehension about the society surrounding him. Thus, if black Americans really lived in slavery, the only way out was to destroy the slave-master. Jackson's philosophy is inherently logical, but is based on a premise that is hopelessly false, a premise in which he had been carefully indoctrinated while in prison by those professional totalitarians who assumed for themselves the task of "revolutionizing" inmates in prisons across the country.

As a result, Jackson's analysis of the police, his reference to them as "pigs" who must be eliminated, follows from the rest of his worldview. In a letter written on April 17, 1970, he expresses this view: "The pig is protecting the right of a few private individuals to own public property. The pig is merely the gun, the tool, a mentally inanimate utensil. It is necessary to destroy the gun, but destroying the gun and sparing the hand that holds it will forever relegate us to a defensive action, hold our revolution in doldrums, ultimately defeat us . . . . Spare the hand that holds the gun and it will simply fashion another. The Viet soldier has attacked and destroyed the pigs and their guns, but this alone has not solved his problems. If the Cong could get to the factories and the people who own and organize them, the war would end in a few months. All wars would end. The pigs who have descended upon the Vietnamese colony are the same who have come down on us."

For Jackson, the struggle of the Viet Cong and what he conceived of as the struggle of another "colonial" people, black Americans, is the same. Black Americans, however, have one opportunity lacked by the Viet Cong. They exist within America, rather than outside of it, and the damage they are able to inflict could be fatal. He notes, "We . . . are on the inside. We are the only ones (besides the very small white minority left) who can get at the monster's heart without subjecting the world to nuclear fire. We have a momentous historical role to act out if we will. The whole world for all time in the future will love us and remember us as the righteous people who made it possible for the world to live on."

Almost precisely the same view was expressed by Eldridge Cleaver.

He noted that "black Americans . . . are a Black Trojan Horse within white America and they number in excess of 23,000,000 strong. That is a lot of strength . . . . The police are the armed guardians of the social order. The blacks are the chief domestic victims of the American social order. A conflict of interest exists, therefore, between the blacks and the police. It is not solely a matter of trigger-happy cops, of brutal cops who love to crack black heads. Mostly it's a job to them. It pays good. And there are numerous fringe benefits. The real problem is a trigger-happy social order."

Unfortunately, the difference between the old-fashioned criminal and the "revolutionary" criminal has confused many into believing that men such as George Jackson and Eldridge Cleaver are indeed "political prisoners." This, however, is not the case.

Discussing this difference, Professor Murray Rothbard notes that "the old-fashioned criminal has always tended to be a 'right-winger,' for he has generally acknowledged that his actions were morally wrong, that he had broken the moral law. Hence, while personally trying to keep out of prison as much as possible, the old-fashioned criminal does not challenge the correctness or propriety of the prison system per se. Hence, when sent to prison, he tries not to be a trouble-maker, tries to win privileges and early parole by good behavior, etc.

"But," he continues, "in the last few decades, liberals and leftists have turned their mischievous attentions to the prison system, and to the concept of crime and punishment. They have promulgated the absurd theory, for example, that 'society' (i.e., everyone *except* the criminal, including his victim) is responsible for crime, and not the criminal himself. Criminals have of course become adept at using their increasing literacy to wrap themselves in left-wing justifications for their misdeeds. In the thirties and onward, it was sentimental liberalism that they clasped to their bosoms, whining that *they* were not responsible, but only the fact that not enough playgrounds had been provided for their childhood, or because their mother and father hated each other. In recent years, this liberal cop-out has been succeeded by revolutionary leftism. Now the murderer, the rapist, the mugger, can preen himself as a member of the vanguard of 'revolution'; every time he knifes an old lady he can proudly proclaim it a 'revolutionary act' against the Establishment."

George Jackson, who has come to exemplify the current approach to the radical critique of "political crime," was not in prison for his political views. He was initially jailed for a number of crimes, including armed robbery, and most lately was accused of murder. He was shot in an attempted escape in which a number of guards were brutally murdered. It may serve the purpose of today's radicals to make a martyr of Jackson, but he was not a "political prisoner" by any objective standard, and his death resulted, it seems clear, not from his political activities or views but from his acts of violence.

Almost precisely the same arguments were used by the radical left concerning the riot at Attica Prison in New York as in the case of George Jackson. The aftermath of the riot at Attica has seen a complex analysis of prison conditions and almost a reflex condemnation by the political left of Governor Nelson Rockefeller's decision to order the forced liberation of the prison and hostages held by rebelling inmates. The criticism of Governor Rockefeller has not been based upon the fact that reports had it that a number of hostages had had their throats cut by rioting inmates, that this information was false, and that therefore the Governor's action was not called for by the facts. The criticism which has been most vocal, and most disturbing, is that which stated that *even if* the prisoners had in fact slit the throats of the hostages, still the Governor should not have acted.

We are told by such critics as radical attorney William Kunstler that the Governor was guilty of murder, that prisoners riot because of oppressive prison conditions, and that our society itself is to blame for such disturbances, not those individuals who actually perpetrate them. Since it is society which is to blame, the Kunstler argument would seemingly have us alter society itself rather than take any particular action to free the hostages or bring order to the prison. This is only a consistent application of the idea that rapists and murderers are not guilty of their crimes but have become criminals because of a racist or harsh environment. Thus, Kunstler and others advance the view that Eldridge Cleaver is a "political criminal" even though he was sentenced for rape, and George Jackson is a "political criminal" even though he was sentenced for armed robbery. Previously we considered murder, rape and armed robbery to be something other than "political crimes." But the radical analysis of today would disagree.

Commenting upon this view, Professor Daniel Glaser of the University of Southern California noted that "the concept of 'political crime' as giving a special status to certain prisoners is alien to American legal philosophy . . . . American prisoners are sentenced for violation of criminal codes which make no references to political motivation, and are all sent to the same jails and prisons. Traditionally, most offenders approve laws against the kinds of acts—such as burglary, theft or robbery—for which they are convicted, although many of them claim they are innocent or were victims of extenuating circumstances."

Professor Glaser points out, "This viewpoint has changed . . . almost everyone who is degraded by others strives to interpret his experience so as to view himself favorably. It is normal to excuse oneself by blaming others or by complaining about conditions." The fact is that nearly 100 million Americans saw representatives of the prisoners at Attica on television saying in clear and precise terms that unless every one of their demands were granted they would proceed to execute hostages. The prisoners may have been bluffing. Still, Governor Rockefeller was compelled to act upon the possibility that they were not.

The simple fact of Attica was that a group of hardened criminals, stimulated by New Left rhetoric and ideas, held 38 hostages to the bitter end, beat them, killed at least one of them—the first hostage to be killed—and intended to murder them all unless their incredible, nonnegotiable demands were met by the state of New York. If the Governor erred, it may have been in his hesitancy to act, not the action itself.

Washington Post columnist Nicholas Von Hoffman, often a supporter of New Left causes, wrote, "Rule Number 1 in one of these joints is that you never bargain with inmates holding hostages. Never, not ever. The reason is that the jail guards—unless they're on the walls or in some other inaccessible place—must work unarmed. That's because they're always mixing with the prisoners and can be disarmed and made hostage too easily. Their one protection is making absolutely, unshakably clear to the inmate population that grabbing a guard will do no good."

Discussing the situation at Attica, San Quentin, Soledad and other prisons, Fred T. Wilkinson, director of the Missouri State Department of Corrections and formerly deputy director of the U.S. Bureau of Prisons, stated, "We are reaping a harvest of the cult of permissiveness. Disciplines and controls in communities have been destroyed. And this has now reached our prisons, where so many militants and violence-oriented people from outside have been confined within the last year or two. They have carried with them hostility against any kind of law enforcement and order. You must have reasonable discipline—the kind of discipline we impose upon ourselves in a community. A prison is a community."

With regard to the question of outside influence, Mr. Wilkinson states, "Trouble is being generated in many cases from outside sources. Aggressive militants in prison still have contacts outside. Many people engaged in law practice today are practicing barratry [the incitement of lawsuits]. They are willing to create incidents. Some 85 percent of the people in prisons want nothing to do with this, but they fall under control of the militants through intimidation and violence."

Commenting upon the statement by many political radicals, such as George Jackson and Angela Davis, that they are not only "political criminals" but are also, in fact, "prisoners of war," Professor Rothbard makes this observation:

One begins at least to sympathize with the exasperated Conservative Party leader in Queens, who, after the umpteenth justification by Black Panthers and others of themselves as "political prisoners" or "prisoners of war" finally said: "OK, if these people are prisoners of war, let them be locked up until the 'war' is over." For another curious aspect of this whole line of argument is this: why do criminals expect, and often get, preferential treatment when they proclaim that they are "revolutionaries" dedicated to overthrowing society and the existing system? If you knife a candy-store owner and then trumpet this as an "act of the revolution," why shouldn't you expect to be treated even *worse* than otherwise by authorities whose very task it is to protect existing society? Why expect "acts of violent overthrow" to be treated especially gently by the very people who are being "overthrown"? On the contrary, they should expect even harsher treatment as a result, for what kind of boobs are they who take threats of violence against themselves as passports for that violence? And yet, such boobs have obviously abounded in recent years.

The fact is that during the latter part of the 1960s and the early years of the 1970s American society has witnessed repeated calls for violence by leaders of New Left and other radical organizations. Black Americans have been particularly victimized, both by black radicals and white extremists who sought to use them for ends of their own. The language used by the two groups has been very similar.

Weatherman leader Mark Rudd, for example, speaking at the City University of New York, advocated closing schools and government bureaus "in whatever manner is necessary." There is "nothing too strong," he added, noting that it was "good to be violent against the pigs"—which, in this case, he identified as bureaucrats, members of the Establishment, policemen and "even the workingmen who are drafted and fighting in Vietnam."

Similarly, the Black Panthers pursue precisely the same approach. In every issue of *The Black Panther* newspaper, its articles, drawings, photographs and caricatures concentrate on "killing the pig," and the Panthers' Minister of Education, George Mason Murray, extolled in these words the virtues of black "revolutionary culture":

"Our painters must show piles of dead businessmen, bankers, lawyers, senators, congressmen, burning up inside their stores, being blown up in cafes, restaurants, night clubs. Our music, rhythm and blues, jazz, spiritual music, must burst the eardrums of the whites who dare to listen to it . . . .Those are the battle cries of mad, crazy black men and the screams are coming from the honkey's throat as he and his wife are strangled to death, and robbed, looted, and then set afire . . . ."

For a number of years black and white radicals have together made every effort to radicalize the black community, to alienate it from American society, and to advance the idea that violence is the only means through which a better society may be brought about.

There have been significant successes in this effort, and much of the street crime, prison unrest, and politically motivated sabotage are,

101

at least in part, a result of the concentrated efforts to politicize and radicalize the black community. This, more and more, is being made clear, even to the casual observer of today's American society.

Early in January 1972, the city of New Orleans, Louisiana, was the scene of a sniper attack which left seven people dead and 21 wounded in 32 hours of arson and near-guerrilla warfare. Finally killed on a hotel rooftop by police sharpshooters was Mark James Robert Essex, the young man who had been responsible.

Essex had grown up protected by a religious family in Emporia, Kansas. His father had worked up to a foreman in a slaughterhouse and his mother taught in a local Head Start program. Young Jimmy himself was remembered as a sensitive lad who had tithed his part-time earnings to the Baptist Church. It was only after he joined the Navy in 1969 that the racial animosities of the outside world intruded.

Mark Essex was described as a happy-go-lucky youth and a "darned good sailor" until two or three months before his discharge from the Navy two years previously for bad behavior. At the Imperial Beach Naval Station in California where he served for seven months as a technician in the dental clinic, he was described as a hard worker who, until he became 21 in 1970, was on friendly terms with both blacks and whites.

Essex was court-martialed on January 15, 1971, for being home in Emporia for a month without official leave. Reverend W. A. Chambers of St. James Baptist Church said that Essex had built up a tremendous hate for whites while he was in the Navy. "I baptized him in the religion when he was quite young. But when he came back, he was denouncing all this as a white man's religion."

Reverend Chambers said that both he and Mrs. Essex tried to counsel him. "But he wouldn't listen. He just hated white folks." Mrs. Essex said that the last letter she received from her son included a section torn out of the book *Black Rage*, written by black psychiatrist William H. Grier and Price M. Cobbs. She said that the torn section was "a part on becoming a man." Essex wrote a note on it that said, "Africa—this is it, Mom. It's bigger than you and I and even God."

After Essex died, investigators visited his shabby rented shack in the black New Orleans slums along Dryades Street. They found a cheap waterbed, some clothing—and four walls scribbled with anti-white graffiti. "The quest for freedom is death," said one slogan. "Then by death I shall escape to freedom."

Mark Essex was, much like the people he cold-bloodedly murdered, a victim of the politicization to which the black community has increasingly been subjected. He grew up seemingly without prejudice or racial hatred. When he died, however, he was very much a part of the radical, racist, violence-prone black radicalism to which he had been attracted. The real cause of the sniper attack which shocked New

Orleans and the nation was as much the black extremism which has been growing in recent years as anything to be found in the background of Mark Essex, the individual man.

The Essex attack came at a time when policemen throughout the country were being increasingly victimized by black radicals. In 1971, a group calling itself the "Black Liberation Army" claimed credit for having killed two New York officers and wounded two others in two ambushes a few days apart. Since then, similar slayers have been linked to the Black Liberation Army in Atlanta and in Houston. In all, 32 policemen were killed by snipers from ambush in a two-year period. In addition, 328 policemen were killed in the line of duty in the period from 1971 to 1973.

The link between black radicalism and politicization is clear, and the number of crimes of violence which have been stimulated by the radical hatred spread by the Black Panthers and numerous other groups is difficult to assess. In discussing the causes of black crime, however, a serious mistake is made in not carefully considering the impact of the radical organizations and their rhetoric of violence and of racial warfare.

Any discussion of crime and violence in the black community must, in addition, consider the impact of narcotics addiction. The connection between narcotics addiction and crime is well-known. What is often less easily understood is exactly why drugs have had the impact and influence they have.

The individual stories of narcotics addicts are pathetic. John A. Hamilton, a member of the editorial board of the *New York Times,* related the story of 12-year-old Ralphie de Jesus. He reached his twelfth birthday on February 22, 1970, and stated that "my birthday is the same as George Washington's." But he was officially 11 when he was admitted to Odyssey House in New York for treatment as a drug addict.

Short at four feet, one inch, and quite frail, at 60 pounds, he looked even younger. He was still pale after a recent bout with hepatitis, which may have caused permanent liver damage. He had contracted the disease from a dirty needle used in shooting heroin with friends on top of roofs in the Hunts Point section of the Bronx.

"I started using dope because my friends were using it, and I didn't want to be left out," he said. He explained that he had been using it for about six months, "skin popping," or shooting it into his shoulder two or three times a week. Packs of heroin cost $2 each "I'd steal to get the money," he confessed, snatching purses and picking pockets, and "once I stole clothes from a store."

How did he become an addict? "You mean who hit me first? My friend Johnny."

According to drug experts, there are at least 25,000 children in New

York who are similarly addicted to drugs, and untold numbers in other cities across the country—the majority of them black. The Medical Examiner's Office in New York reports that there were 35 deaths in the first six weeks of 1970, an alarming figure because drug deaths rise sharply in the warmer months.

Another case, reported in the *Journal of the American Medical Association*, describes an infant, born limp, who died with severe respiratory distress at the age of nine hours. The infant weighed five pounds. She had a sloping forehead, poorly differentiated, low-set ears, a broad nose with prominent bridge, and bilateral epicanthic folds. A slight fatty hump was noted at the nape of the neck. Both hands had simian creases. The left hand had four fingers; a rudimentary sixth finger was attached to the right hand. The right foot showed a slight deformity. A roentgenogram taken after death showed 11 pairs of thin ribs, absence of part of the sacrum, and dislocation of both hips.

The infant described was born with equally severe internal problems. An autopsy showed that she had an enlarged right heart, two holes in the walls dividing the chambers of the heart, and a long catalogue of abnormalities involving the kidneys, lungs, liver, pancreas, digestive tract and genitalia. What had caused her horrible deformation?

The Mount Sinai School of Medicine doctors who reported the case found that the infant's cells contained an abnormal chromosome that was made up of two joined chromosomes. This extra chromosomal material had garbled the genetic message. Something must have happened during the parents' lifetime to change the chromosomes in their germ cells, either the father's sperm or the mother's ova. That something may well have been identified by the Mount Sinai doctors. The mother, the doctors found, had taken three doses of LSD nine months before her infant was conceived. The father had taken two doses a few years earlier.

"While coincidence cannot be excluded," say the doctors, "the possibility of chromosome damage to germ cells by LSD, with production of abnormal offspring, must be emphasized."

Another case highlights the continuing plight of young people, in many instances black young people, caught up in narcotics before they are even able to understand the dangers that might confront them.

Antoinette Dishman was an attractive 17-year-old black girl, a freshman at Barnard College, who sniffed heroin and perhaps cocaine at a middle-of-the-night party and never woke up again. She was not an addict, not hooked, only entering into the spirit of feeling free and cool and liberated. Her teachers and fellow students spoke of her bright promise. Columnist Max Lerner noted, "We almost forget this —that it is not the worst but often the best of our young people who are thus cut down."

Among the estimated 100,000 heroin addicts in New York City alone, there are an average of 900 deaths a year, a quarter of them teenagers. Many teenagers, particularly in the black inner city, have become pushers, while many become criminals to get money for the drug. Still others, not addicts themselves, are caught up in the traffic. There are numerous stories of boys 11 and 12 years of age being arrested for selling heroin.

Why do young people turn to drugs? If all the answers were known, the solution to the problem would be clear and straight-forward. We live in a confusing age, and the young, facing life in the midst of a society which neither they nor their parents nor their teachers fully understand, seek an escape from a reality which often seems hopeless to them.

Dr. Sidney Cohen, chief of Psychosomatic Medicine at Wadsworth Hospital Veterans Administration Center in Los Angeles, makes the following point in his important volume *The Drug Dilemma*:

"If drug taking becomes habitual, it usually represents either a gratification which the young person should have been able to derive from daily living or an evasion of life experience due to inability or unwillingness to meet life's day-to-day rebuffs. Those most attracted to drugs are those who are bored, cannot enjoy, or cannot tolerate stress and frustration. The drug fits their emotional discontent and removes the necessity to plan, to struggle, to endure. In other words, the drug abuser was usually made long before the drug appeared. Drug dependence serves to compound the individual's problem with dependence."

Dr. Cohen notes that "it is a feeling of existential meaninglessness which attracts some people to the drug state. The acquisition of a sense of meaningfulness is the antidote. The current problem can be seen as a disease of affluence and nondirection. For many, this generation has not found ways and means of constructively using the time formerly expended on work to evade hunger. Freedom from want has produced a vacuum of time which must be filled with meaningful activities, not time-consuming activities."

Just as affluent young people suffer from a sense of meaninglessness, so young people in the black inner city suffer from a lack of a strong family life, of schools and teachers which are truly concerned about their education, and of an overhanging rhetoric of despair which is fueled by the vocal and militant black power organizations which repeatedly tell them that it is not possible for a Negro to succeed in American society.

The root of the despair of many young people, of both races, seems to be a vacuum of values in the midst of a society which appears to have abandoned so many of the traditional virtues and has not replaced them with anything more than the cynicism and relativism of a self-proclaimed "sophisticated" age. There are many who see in the protest and alienation of the young an essentially religious pursuit. English poet Stephen Spender, for example, observed, "It might be misleading to say that the true aims of the student movement are religious rather than political. Nevertheless, one finds oneself constantly forced back onto religious examples to describe them. For it is in religion rather than politics that the revolution precedes the goal, and that the aim of the revolutionaries is . . . to retain the original vision."

Spender points out that "the grievances and demands of the students, the issues and confrontations—reasonable or unreasonable as they may in themselves be, excusable or deplorable—express their total rejection of the depersonalizing forces of modern society. The feeling of the young is that the claims, the powers, the 'production' of this world are opposed to the spirit, flesh, imagination, instincts and spontaneous self-realization that are life."

Although all of us, young, middle-aged and old, live in the mid-20th century, only the young, those who have come of age in the innocent fifties and since, are truly of this narcotic-crisis period. Those who lived through the Depression or through World War II have been frozen by the dramatic and intense experience of those days.

The Southern writer Walter Hines Page wrote this with regard to the generation that lived through the Civil War in the South: "It [the Civil War] gave every one of them the intensest experience of his life, and ever afterwards he referred every other experience to this. Thus, it stopped the thought of most of them as an earthquake stops a clock. The fierce blow of battle paralyzed the mind. Their speech was the vocabulary of war . . . they were dead men, most of them, moving among the living as ghosts; and yet, as ghosts in a play, they held the stage."

Thus the young, and particularly the young in the black inner city, are the only ones who are, in a sense, frozen with the peculiar dramatic and intense experience of these days. Many of them do not relate the upheavals of today with the past, for they know no past, except through the books most of them do not read, to their great misfortune. They live in the present and wonder what kind of future they may hope for in so transient and unstable a world. If there is a generation gap it is of this nature. In few places does the generation gap exist in starker contrast than in the black inner city, with rural parents and grandparents trying and failing to keep the influences of the urban city streets away from their children. One of the most sinister of such influences, of course, is narcotics.

Many of the problems facing black young people are similar in nature to those involving more affluent whites. A young man growing up in Europe one or two hundred years ago would have faced a life situation in which the major decisions in his life were preordained. More than likely, he would have been born in the same house in which his father had been born, almost surely in the same town. He would pursue the same means of earning a living as did his father. If his father was a tailor or a butcher, the son would also live his life in this manner. His marriage would have been arranged. His own range of decision-making was very slight. Life was circumscribed by religious faith and communal custom. The individual was part of the community, of the group. His responsibility was more that of playing out his role than grasping life as a horseman at the reins and riding in whatever direction he willed.

Today, man's situation—for those of both races—is far different. Today, young Americans have choices to make—with regard to career, location, marriage partners, and other basic elements of lifestyle. Certainly there are restrictions. The draft until recently, claimed two years out of the lives of many young men. Some start life in humbler surroundings than others, thereby limiting upward mobility. Yet, on the whole, the young man or woman coming of age in America at this time has perhaps a greater freedom to choose his pattern of living than has any individual at any other time in history.

Freedom to choose, however, becomes a very difficult task when no one provides any knowledge or information about the basis upon which such choices may beneficially be made. At one time the family, the school and the church spent a good deal of time pointing young people in particular directions which they considered to be valid and time-tested. Today the family, and particularly the black family in the inner city, is in a state of disarray; the school pursues what it calls a "value-free" curriculum, and the church doubts its own message, being swept away in the modern tide of relativism and political action.

What many young people are searching for is a perspective about life which is no longer presented by the institutions which once seemed to perform this task. Young people are asking the "ultimate questions" to which theologian Paul Tillich referred—questions about life and death and purpose. Where they will find answers to such questions, in what they view as a materialistic and dehumanized age, is difficult to say.

Author and critic James Burnham has compared many of today's alienated young people with those who at the time of the Industrial

Revolution felt that the new machines would make their own lives meaningless and obsolete. He writes that many young people resemble "contemporary Luddites trying to smash the new machinery of production in this initial phase of the technological revolution, just as the original Luddites tried to smash the steam engines and spinning jennies of the initial phase of the Industrial Revolution." He points out further that the original Luddite movement coincided with the high point of an earlier romanticism.

Young people of both races, in a variety of ways, are rebelling against the impersonal, technocratic modern world. Some are, in a confused and confusing way, searching for many of the traditional values which the society as a whole has abandoned. Others have simply declared that traditional values are irrelevant. As we enter the technological revolution, and move further and further into the mass society, we must be as concerned with the quality of life which young people will face in the future as we are with the quality of the material things with which they will be able to tinker.

While urbanization and the advent of new technology have had a dramatic impact upon our total society, most particularly upon young people within that society, they have had a more immediate and more damaging effect upon the black community than upon others.

The new agricultural technology has forced unskilled blacks in rural areas off the farms. It has driven them to mass metropolitan areas at the very time when new industrial technology had eliminated the need for unskilled factory work. Millions of black Americans have migrated from rural to urban areas at the very moment when millions of unskilled jobs, both agricultural and industrial, were being eliminated. Thus, they found themselves in large cities, subjected to all of the negative forces of inner city slums, and without available employment. They increasingly became wards of the state through the welfare system, and their children grew up in the streets, often with little idea that a better life might be had.

Many young people, as a result, turn to drugs as a means of escape from shallow and meaningless lives, or simply for purposes of experimentation and "kicks." Many also turn to drugs because they believe that narcotics represent something new, modern and different. It is unfortunate that they are not aware that drug usage, experimentation and addiction are as old as man himself. The stories of ruined lives also are recorded far beyond our modern period.

Drugs that affect behavior have been known since antiquity. Even people in the Stone Age may have been familiar with opium, hashish and cocaine. Primitive people used these drugs to induce states of intoxication during religious rites or, in the case of hashish, to prepare warriors for battle. As far back as 2700 B.C., marihuana was known to the Chinese Emperor Shen Neng and recommended for gout, con-

108

stipation and "absent mindedness," among other uses. And in 500 B.C., the Scythians were reported by the Greek author Herodotus to be using the drug.

In July 1842 a young British immigrant, William Blair, described his experiences with opium in *The Knickerbocker,* a New York magazine. He wrote: "I knew that for every hour of comparative ease and comfort its treacherous alliance might confer upon me *now,* I must endure days of bodily suffering; but I did not, could not, conceive the mental hell into whose fierce corroding fires I was about to plunge."

By the end of the 19th century over 100,000 Americans—and possibly as many as a million—were in some degree addicted to opium or its derivatives. A widely published estimate put the number of addicts in the general population at one in 400—about 190,000 people.

Opium has been used since earliest times as an agent of indulgence. Opium and its derivatives have the power to allay anxiety, gloom and despair, as well as to provide escape from boredom, loneliness and even from reality itself. There is an apparent reference to opium in Homer's *Odyssey,* written in the ninth century B.C. Rouse's translation tells of "a drug potent against pain and quarrels and charged with the forgetfulness of all trouble; whoever drank this mingled in the bowl, not one tear would he let fall the whole day long, not if mother and father should die, not if they should slay a brother or a dear son before his face and he should see it with his own eyes."

For many years the danger of opium addiction was not recognized. The problems of addiction were compounded in the 1800s by the discovery of two opium alkaloids, morphine (1805) and codeine (1832). Ignorant of their dangers, doctors administered morphine and codeine to cure the opium habit—with the result that opium addicts were merely transferred from one addicting drug to another.

Perhaps the most important factor influencing the spread of narcotic addiction was the invention, in 1843, of the hypodermic needle. Brought to this country in 1856, it was used widely during the Civil War to administer morphine, not only to battle-wounded, but also to those suffering from dysentery. Vast numbers of soldiers were returned to civilian life addicted to morphine. A term prevalent at the time, "soldier's illness," actually meant narcotic addiction.

The final link in the opiate chain was forged in 1898 when a morphine derivative, heroin, was synthesized. Also initially considered nonaddictive, heroin was available in many easily obtained pharmaceutical preparations and became a prime drug for treatment of morphine addiction. Heroin-created addicts by the thousands firmly established the hypodermic needle as the instrument of drug abuse.

It was not until the 1890s that public attitudes toward narcotic use and users began to change from its previous tendency to compare narcotics with alcohol. One reason was that many physicians now fully recognized the destructive nature of narcotic dependence and gave widespread publicity to their findings. Public awareness also came from addicts who wrote accounts of their experiences, and from newspapers which published sensational stories of addiction among young people. Added to these factors was the growing realization that great numbers of people had become addicted. By 1901, when both lay and professional groups were expressing alarm over the narcotics problem, a special committee of the American Pharmaceutical Association surveyed pharmacies to learn the extent of the public's demand for addiction-producing drugs. In its report, the group termed the problem "appalling."

Many young people today, particularly in the black inner city, who regard drugs as the answer to their problems, have discovered, at great cost, the dangers they face. Dr. Cohen notes that "even in the Hashbury District of San Francisco, one of the many posters in a poster-loving community says, 'Speed kills.' And it can. 'Speed-freaks' on 200 to 1,000 times the average dosage of speed lose interest in food or body care. Abscesses develop at injection sites. They heal poorly because of impaired health. In fact, all the dangers of 'skin-popping' and 'mainlining' are present when speed, heroin or any other substance is injected carelessly . . . . Other infections can be introduced: tetanus, syphilis, malaria, or viral hepatitis. There is some evidence that enormous doses of Methadrine can, over time, injure brain cells."

The most persuasive testimony with regard to the dangers involved in the consumption of drugs comes from young people themselves, those who have learned of these dangers from their own experiences. One young man wrote this letter concerning his own life: "Two years ago when I was 18, I took over a dozen trips. I tripped in San Francisco, Colorado and Philadelphia. I was tripping on acid on a bus in the mountains, at a concert, while driving a truck, and in my own bedroom. During my trips I experienced some beautiful visions and sensations, and some moments which I wished I hadn't begun at all. During my last trip I had a desire to cut off my leg and actually did feel as if I were taking my own life. Luckily I had enough self-control to get up and flush the remaining LSD (about $50 worth) down the toilet."

This young man's advice to others: "Acid, as well as being a synthetic chemical, is dangerous. Its effect on the mind, in my case, was disastrous. Even under the guidance of an experienced friend, the results are never predictable. I have heard that the effects of an acid trip wear off completely after three years. I have one year, and for me it will be a tortuous one. You want to take acid? Eat good food, exercise, read a book. Carry your life and treasure it. Don't carry around an artificial chemical that will harm you. I hope that my words will be taken seriously."

It is clear that many young people begin using drugs simply because their friends do—and because on the streets in the inner city it is easily available. Not doing it may cause them to be ostracized and looked down upon. Others try drugs for the excitement of doing what is now illegal, or for the hallucinatory effects of expanding their consciousness. The reasons for using drugs are many, but the results are unfortunately the same, and they are never good.

How to cope with this situation is a question to which few answers have, thus far, been given. Discussing the problem, the black columnist for the *Washington Post,* William Raspberry, writes, "We talk about eliminating the really significant traffickers and taking the profit out of drug dealing, when the truth is, there's only one significant figure in the scene and only one person who can take the profit out of the traffic—the idiot who buys the stuff."

Raspberry continues: "I know it's not nice to call him an idiot, and I do understand that frustration, alienation and pain of various sorts can make you do foolish things. But somehow it has never sounded very convincing to me—even when I've said it—that 'conditions' make people turn to dope."

Criticizing those who see all fault in society and little or no fault with the individual addict, Raspberry points out that "there must be some flaw—and not just in society but in the individual drug abusers. And yet, the clear trend is to treat the individual abuser as though he is 100 percent victim. It just won't wash. I am fully aware of the peculiarly degrading effects of black urban poverty. But I'm also aware that nobody chases anybody else down and jabs a needle into his arm. You've got to search for the stuff, and it isn't always easy to find. It would be awfully interesting to know just what it is that makes some of us go looking."

To fully understand the growth of crime and violence among Negroes in the black inner city it is essential to put all the pieces together in some semblance of order—the breakdown of the family, the migrations of millions of people from the rural South to the urban North, the influence of the street leading to narcotics addiction, the general permissiveness of the society at large, the growing belief that it is possible to commit crimes and escape punishment, the radical rhetoric of black militants calling for a violent overthrow of society— all these are important contributing factors.

The trends in the period since World War II give every indication of continuing into the future. In his volume *Crisis in Black and White,* Charles B. Silberman points out that "even if the Negro migration were to stop completely (and it's bound to slow down), the Negro population of the large cities would continue to grow at a rapid rate, and Negroes would account for a steadily increasing proportion of the cities' population. For the Negro population is considerably younger than the white population in these cities; in addition, the Negro birth rate is considerably higher than the white. (In New Haven and Buffalo, for example, Negroes represent one person in eight out of the total population, but account for one birth in four.) Thus, Professor C. Horace Hamilton of the University of North Carolina has predicted that the Negro population outside the South will have doubled again by 1980, and that by the year 2,000 nearly three Negroes in four will be living in the North and West."

Professor Philip M. Hauser, Chairman of the Sociology Department at the University of Chicago, declares, "The problems which confront the Negro today, although perhaps differing in degree, are essentially the same kinds of problems which confronted our migrant groups in the past," and they will be solved in essentially the same way.

Professor Hauser concedes that Negro migrants do not need "Americanization" as did their European predecessors, but he argues that they do need "acculturation." This need for acculturation, in his view, forms the heart of the Negro problem in the large city. For Negroes have "been drawn from a primitive folk culture into a metropolitan way of life" in little more than a single generation—"as severe a problem of acculturation," Hauser argues, "as any group in history has ever faced." To solve the "Negro problem," he concludes, "the older residents must teach the newcomers what is expected of them in the city," thereby equipping them "to enter into the opportunities of the dominant culture."

"A Negro in the Mississippi Delta," Dr. Hauser suggests by way of illustration, "tosses his empty whisky bottle or beer can in a cotton patch, and what difference does it make? But on the asphalt pavements of a city it can make a difference, esthetically and with respect to safety. If physical violence is accepted in the south as a means of resolving conflict, nobody cares much; but in the urban community, such acts become felonies, with much more serious consequences."

There is, of course, a serious generation gap within the black community. "Don't let this Harlem git you," a motherly Harlem matron advises the young hero of Ralph Ellison's *The Invisible Man,* just recently arrived from the South. "I'm in New York, but New York ain't in me, understand what I mean? Don't get corrupted." Still, notes Charles Silberman, "many do . . . . The fact that city-born youngsters read no better than recent arrivals from the South is all the more striking in view of the fact that the former have somewhat higher IQs—in the sixth grade, an average of 90, compared to 85.8 for the in-migrants. Thus, the native-born children perform at a lower level relative to capacity than the newcomers. Residence in the

Northern city seems to dull rather than to stimulate achievement."

While the problem of crime in our urban areas may largely concern Negroes, and primarily black young people, we should not be misled into thinking that the problems we face are entirely unique. In an important study of crime in Great Britain, Professor Howard Jones, head of the Department of Sociology at the University of Keele, discusses crime among young people in some depth.

He points out in his book, *Crime in a Changing Society,* that those found guilty of indictable offenses among boys and girls between the ages of 14 and 21 on the basis of numbers of offenders per 100,000 amounted to 2,090 in 1938. By 1960, however, this figure had increased to 5,136. By 1965 it was 6,529.

Professor Jones notes that "it is not only in rate per 100,000 that teenage delinquency has been increasing. There has also been an increase in the proportion of our crimes committed by older adolescents as compared with other people . . . the share of this group in the crime problem increased by over one-third, while that of the age group 30 and over declined by one-fifth . . . . Crime is, it seems, increasing faster among our young people than among the older age groups . . . . The other major tendency has been for the amount of violent crime to increase more rapidly than such offenses as simple stealing or false pretenses. The statistics suggest that this new-found destructiveness is also mainly a teenage trend."

Similar conclusions were reached in F. H. McClintock's study of crimes of violence, showing that the proportion of youths aged 14 to 17 committing these offenses increased by 216 percent and of those aged 17 to 21 by 153 percent between 1950 and 1960. Well under half of the teenagers found guilty in the Leicester Juvenile Court in 1953 stood before the magistrates alone. Of 200 older teenage boys in Borstal studied more recently by Gibbens, 143 committed their offenses in company.

Professor Jones provides this analysis: "Could anything more clearly indicate that this is an age group with a problem than these collective acts of defiance? But their group character is remarkable in another way. Adolescence is a time when one expects the gregarious 'swarming' of the middle years of childhood to be superseded by a growth in individuality. Yet here we see a gang motive extending among delinquents into the later teens."

Years before, declares Professor Jones, "Fritz Redl, a tremendously insightful student of young people, argued that this was a regressive tendency; a sign of emotional immaturity, a fear of growing up and going forward in life, arising from emotional insecurity. Many observers have noted how insecure and emotionally deprived the members of delinquent gangs seem to be. T. R. Fyvel spoke of the frequency with which they come from emotionally unsatisfactory homes; and Dr. Peter Scott, a London psychiatrist, after investigating the backgrounds of 151 boys for the juvenile court, wrote that the real gangs he found among them did not 'conform with the picture of healthy development, adventurousness, pride of leadership, or loyal lieutenancy, that is often painted. Gang members who come before the courts usually have a gross antisocial character defect and come from homes in which the emotional atmosphere has been obviously disturbed and detrimental!' "

In the most thorough study carried out of the juvenile gangs of a great city, Chicago, Thrasher showed how frequently young members of immigrant families seemed to form gangs. Rejected equally by the modern American society they sought to enter, and by the traditional backward-looking European family which deplored their willingness to change, they had only each other in whom to find comfort.

The crime wave we have witnessed in the black inner city of our major metropolitan areas combines all of the causes that have been discussed as well as a number of other, more general, difficulties, with which we are yet to deal.

Too many observers have attempted to simplify this complex problem in order to make it amenable to the simple solutions which the political process can offer. Those who have done so have, in a number of ways, made the problem increasingly more dangerous, and have made any real solutions even more difficult to contemplate.

Chapter 5

Black Crime and the Community—Black and White

Many in the black community have found themselves in the position of apologizing for rather than condemning crime and violence in the black inner city. They have argued that calls for "law and order" are merely veiled attacks upon Negroes, and that black crime is simply the result of a bad environment and the racism which is endemic to American society.

Bayard Rustin, for example, declared in 1968 that the cry of "crime in the streets" had turned into a slogan for keeping the Negro in his place. According to him, "The term 'crime in the streets' is rapidly becoming a slogan for keeping the 'nigger' in the street in his place. But it will not work."

Carrying this philosophy to an extreme, a large portion of the black "leadership" in Washington, D.C., actually found itself in the position in July 1968 of calling the shooting of a policeman "justifiable homicide." This case, in many respects, is an unfortunate but typical example of how many spokesmen for the black community have failed to come to grips with the problem of crime in the streets.

In an almost unprecedented statement, the Black United Front, an organization of so-called "civil rights" leaders, including extremists such as Stokely Carmichael and alleged "moderates" such as Reverend Walter Fauntroy, then vice-chairman of the District of Columbia City Council, called the slaying of a District policeman "justifiable homicide." The resolution, which was unanimously adopted by 450 members meeting at the Douglas Memorial Church, said, in part: "The methods of self-defense used by the family charged with the alleged slaying of the honky cop is justifiable homicide in the same sense that police are allowed to kill black people and call it justifiable homicide."

Private Stephen Williams, 32, was killed and his partner, Private Frederick L. Matteson, 38, was critically wounded in a struggle with a robbery suspect, the latter's son and the suspect's wife. Both officers were shot with their own revolvers in the 1300 block of Columbia Road after attempting to arrest Johnnie White, 39. White, his son Dwayne, 19, and his wife, Ethel, were all charged with homicide.

Several hours after the issuance of the Black United Front's statement, Mayor Walter Washington, himself a Negro, asserted that "the Black United Front resolution with respect to the slaying of Officer Stephen A. Williams . . . is inflammatory, irresponsible and unfortunate . . . . If this community is to thrive and prosper, it must do so within the framework of the law. As citizens we must continue to work together—black and white, policeman and civilian—so that law and order with justice, will be the code for all."

Director of Public Safety Patrick V. Murphy called the resolution "very dangerous" and "not well founded." He said that the resolution could not "help but be inflammatory" and he noted that he did not think it spoke for "any significant number of citizens." Murphy said that Police Department evidence suggested nothing like justifiable homicide and that anybody with different evidence had a responsibility to come forward. He said: "I think it's tragic that such a statement should be made concerning a policeman who has given his life protecting other citizens."

The D.C. Federation of Civic Associations, a predominantly black organization, voted to oppose the Black United Front's resolution. It sent a condolence card and $50 to the family of Private Williams and an additional $50 and a card to Private Matteson.

But the real news was not that many responsible citizens and organizations had condemned this inflammatory statement, but that many refused to do so.

Reverend Channing Phillips, the Democratic National Committeeman from Washington and board member of the Black United Front, was asked whether he approved of the front's statement. "Well, I was there and the vote was unanimous," Mr. Phillips said. "Both the officer and the citizen deserves protection from this system that provides for the deaths of both." Reverend Walter E. Fauntroy, then vice chairman of the D.C. City Council and also a board member of the Black United Front, was not present at the time the resolution was adopted. Subsequently, however, he refused to repudiate it.

The city's new Democratic Central Committee adopted a resolution condemning what it called assaults on citizens by police. At the same time, the Committee deleted from the proposed language of the resolution a statement of sympathy for the family of the murdered police private, Stephen Williams. The section cut from the resolution said: "We strongly condemn assaults against police officers who are properly carrying out their vital responsibilities to protect the public."

The public outcry was significant. Representative William G. Scherle of Iowa called upon Reverend Fauntroy either to resign his position as vice chairman of the D.C. City Council or to resign from the Black United Front. He stated: "The Reverend Fauntroy . . . has balanced on the tightrope between violence and law and order long enough. It is time for him to choose between his membership in the D.C. City Council and his membership in the Black United Front. By his silence, the Reverend Fauntroy has in effect endorsed the inflammatory, irresponsible and outrageous statement issued by the Front . . . . Reverend Fauntroy cannot be both an officer in the City Government and an officer in an organization pledged to disorder and violence."

The criticism was by no means partisan. Maryland's Democratic Senator Daniel Brewster stated, "It is unbelievable that the membership of the Black United Front includes such a community leader as Walter E. Fauntroy . . . . He and others of his stature should realize that there is no place in this community for organizations that exhibit the malicious irresponsibility of the Black United Front. . . . Mr. Fauntroy can best serve the city in this case by denouncing the Black United Front and resigning from it. If he is unable to do that, he should resign from public office."

When they refuse to condemn black crime and violence, Negro leaders are, in large measure, following the lead of white liberals who have for many years been advancing a philosophy holding that society, and not the individual criminal, is responsible for crime. With regard to the Negro, such white spokesmen argue that racism and discrimination have driven him to crime and if an end is sought to crime, the way to proceed is by correcting white society.

This approach has been carried to its extreme in Sweden, where it has been decided by expert debate, and accepted by public opinion, that crime is a sickness. "This," writes Roland Huntford in his volume *The New Totalitarians,* "is connected with another debate, that on free will against determinism which, in Sweden, took the form of personal responsibility against environment. This has been settled in favor of environment, and the general conclusion is that all crime is not only a form of mental disease, but the product of unfavorable circumstances . . . . Lawbreakers in Sweden are, therefore, not punished for an evil act, but treated for a disease. Their care is considered to belong to the domain of social welfare, rather than criminal law."

Huntford notes that "crime is defined not in terms of moral depravity or ethical wrong but purely and simply as asociality. It is not the act but its asociality that is the crime. It is not a long step to the belief that asociality by itself is a crime, and therefore a kind of mental illness."

In our own country we have heard many alleged "experts" argue against the traditional view that criminals should pay for their crimes and that those who perpetrate crimes are, in fact, guilty of them. After the slaying of Robert Kennedy, University of Houston psychologist Richard Evans characterized the Kennedys as "victims in search of assassins." Evans' concept—that victims often invite and help to shape crimes—is now established as a new discipline known as "victimology."

At a recent conference, the International Criminological Society included a special session on the behavioral patterns of victims. For the first time in the United States, courses in victimology are being offered—at the University of California, Northeastern University and Boston University Law School.

Fortunately, those who advance the view that society and not criminals are responsible for crime have been challenged. Daniel P. Moynihan told his fellow liberals in Americans for Democratic Action that the time had come for them to stop "sticking up for and explaining away everything, howsoever outrageous, which Negroes individually and collectively might do." He told ADA leaders that liberal Democrats must:

1. Recognize that "their essential interest is in the stability of the social order" and promote that goal through "much more effective alliances with political conservatives who share that concern."

2. Abandon "the notion that the nation, especially the cities of the nation, can be run from agencies in Washington," and instead place more emphasis on local programs.

The theme that the responsibility for most crime lies not with the criminals but with society, and more specifically that poverty is the main cause of crime, persists, both among white liberals and many in the black community who find it convenient to echo this point of view. This view, for example, was set forth in the volume *Crime in America,* by former Attorney General Ramsay Clark. In his book, Clark declared that the solutions to the problem of crime are primarily economic solutions. We must, he wrote, "contain our acquisitive instinct" and relegate "selfishness" to the past.

That this overworked thesis denying criminals responsibility for their own actions is, increasingly, being held in disrepute, is an indication that society may be inching closer and closer to facing the problems that really do exist.

In his review of Ramsay Clark's book, Professor Sidney Hook declared that "the old and overly simple thesis that most crime is caused by economic deprivation is difficult to prove. First of all, it is based on statistical correlations that cannot by themselves establish causal connections. Second, as economic conditions have improved, crime rates have increased instead of decreasing. Third, at any economic level, the behavior of most individuals is not criminal. There must, therefore, be other factors at work."

Professor Hook notes that "those who . . . keep insisting that we devote all attention to the 'real' or 'true' or 'underlying' causes perform a double disservice. They not only oversimplify complex and subtle questions of causation, but also impede and undermine imperfect but nonetheless worthwhile efforts to reduce the amount of actual harm being done."

Ramsay Clark, declares Dr. Hook, "displays a heartwarming and commendable interest in the human rights of criminals—but alas, little concern for the human rights of their victims. The fundamental weakness of his analysis is his failure to realize that there are conflicts of human rights, and that the requirements of wise decision-making impose an order of priority. . . . In a period when the number of violent crimes is rising rapidly, when in almost every large city citizens fear to leave their homes at night, it is psychologically unrealistic as well as morally unjustifiable to expect the potential victims of criminal behavior to give priority to the human rights of criminals if these conflict with their own rights."

Despite the fact that the mass media give disproportionate coverage to those black "spokesmen" who apologize for lawlessness and crime, it is within the black community itself that the disproportionate numbers of the victims of such crime are to be found.

Table 2 gives some indication of rate of victimization which is suffered by members of the black community.

The results of this survey show that blacks are victimized disproportionately by all index crimes except larceny of $50 and over. The President's Commission also considered the extent to which violent crime involved interracial attacks. For evidence on the way in which the race and sex of the victims and offenders might affect the probability of criminal assault, the Commission, with the cooperation of the Chicago Police Department, studied 13,713 cases of assaultive crimes against the person, other than homicide.

It was found that Negro males and females were most likely to be victimized in crimes against the person. A Negro man in Chicago

119

Table 2. Victimization by Race*
(Rates per 100,000 Population)

Offenses	White	Nonwhite
Forcible rape	22	82
Robbery	58	204
Aggravated assault	186	347
Burglary	822	1,306
Larceny ($50 and over)	608	367
Motor vehicle theft	164	286
Total	1,860	ˊ 2,592.
Number of Respondents	27,484	4,902

*The President's Commission on Law Enforcement and Administration of Justice, 1967.

runs the risk of being a victim nearly six times as often as a white man, and a Negro woman nearly eight times as often as a white woman.

Table 3 shows that Negroes are most likely to assault Negroes, whites most likely to assault whites. Thus, while Negro males account for two-thirds of all assaults, the offender who victimizes a white person is most likely also to be white.

Table 3. Victim-Offender Relationships by Race and Sex
In Assaultive Cases Against the Person
(Except Homicide)*
(Rate per 100,000 population)

| | White Offenders | | Negro Offenders | | All Types |
Offenses Attributable to	Male	Female	Male	Female	of Offenders
White males	201	9	129	4	342
White females	108	14	46	6	175
Negro males	58	3	1,636	256	1,953.
Negro females	21	3	1,202	157	1,382.
Total					
Population	130	10	350	45	535

*Source: Special tabulation from Chicago Police Department, Data systems Division, for period September, 1965, to March, 1966.

The President's Commission on Crime in the District of Columbia discovered similar racial relationships in its 1966 survey of a number of serious crimes. Only 12 of 172 murders were interracial. Eighty-eight percent of rapes involved persons of the same race. Among 121 aggravated assaults for which identification of race was available, only 9 percent were interracial. Auto theft offenders in the District are three-fourths Negroes, their victims two thirds Negroes. Robbery, the only crime of violence in which whites were victimized more often than Negroes, is also the only one that is predominantly interracial:

in 56 percent of the robberies committed by Negroes in the District of Columbia, the victims are white.

Despite the fact that Negroes are the primary victims of crime in the nation's cities, the impression has somehow been given that the black community is tolerant of crime and violence, apologizes for it and perceives "racism" in all efforts to combat it. Nothing could be further from the truth.

Yet this impression has been developed primarily because it has been carefully cultivated, particularly in the media. Consider some of the charges that have been made and documented by those who have been concerned about the false view of the black community presented to the American public, both black and white, particularly by television.

On June 1, 1968, *TV Guide* writer Neil Hickey published a revealing report of the failure of Detroit's local television stations and network affiliates to cover life in the black community. He interviewed a variety of black citizens: the managing editor of a black publication, religious leaders, sociologists and urban officials, and over and over again his black informants charged television with being racist and declared that normal black existence was never covered. They noted that "the television cameras only show up when a black man steals or rapes or kills—or to film rioting, looting and violence . . . television creates its own black 'leaders' to feed the newsmen the line they want."

In her important book, *The News Twisters,* Edith Efron publishes her findings of television bias during the 1968 presidential campaign. With regard to the treatment of Negroes, she writes:

> What was shatteringly missing from black coverage was the essence of "normalcy" in the United States: a vision of black achievement. Not once during this period did we hear opinions from black scholars, doctors, engineers, poets, businessmen, magazine editors—from the black middle class with its many dignified, sophisticated, intellectual and able people. Not once did we hear the opinions of law-abiding, honorable, and noncriminal black workers . . . . Because the "normal" range of black existence was excised from the screen, what was missing above all was a vision of black diversity—of individuals with different personalities, different minds, different moral qualities, different levels of knowledge, different levels of aspiration and achievement. The view of blacks as real human beings who range, like whites, from illiterate, mindless thugs to men of tremendous intellectual, spiritual and social distinction, is totally absent from network news coverage. By creating a black stereotype and a criminal stereotype at that, the networks were reinforcing the essence of race prejudice—a negative, indeed degraded, view of blacks.

In October 1969, Max Ways, a member of *Fortune*'s Board of Editors, wrote:

> From the end of the post-Civil War Reconstruction period to the mid-

fifties, American journalism was virtually silent on the subject of how black Americans lived. Lynchings were reported and deplored, as were race riots and the more sensational crimes committed by blacks against whites. But crimes by blacks against blacks were regularly ignored as a matter of explicit news policy on most newspapers. This was symptomatic of an implicit journalistic assumption that blacks were not a significant part of the American white society's disengagement from the Negro and his problems.

While the media have spent much time and effort portraying black militants, the fact is that the Negro community has little respect or regard for such "leaders" appointed for them by the white press. In a poll whose results were published on April 6, 1970, Lou Harris revealed the magnitude of the difference between the majority of blacks and the most extreme militants. When asked to assess the effectiveness of four different types of black leadership, a majority of blacks made the distinction that although militants may build up black pride, they are not the most effective leaders. At the top of the list are "elected black officials" cited by 71 percent as "very effective." They are followed by "civil rights leaders, such as the NAACP," viewed as "very effective" by 67 percent. Behind them are black ministers and religious leaders, given a "very effective" rating by 56 percent. At the bottom of the list are "leaders of the black militant groups," who are given a "very effective" rating by only 29 percent. The poll also showed that 84 percent of all blacks are opposed to violence.

In her book Edith Efron concluded, "The black on network television . . . is as intense a selective distortion as is the fascist-honky 'white American'—against whom he is used as a terrifying threat. They are two malevolent caricatures—both artificially divorced from the full context of the American race problem . . . network news coverage has given white Americans no insights into black dignity or achievement, and few insights into the magnitude of black pain."

The fact is that the real black community is yet to be discovered by the majority of whites. Vincent Baker, parliamentarian for the New York Branch of the NAACP, declared that "for the great majority of Negroes in our big cities, law and order is not a code phrase for white racism. It is a crying necessity, for we live under unbelievable terror by day and night. We hold no brief for crime or criminals. We are their chief victims. Help from our fellow Americans would be welcome."

It is high time that we discover that real black community.

Speaking at the University of Iowa on the subject "New Frontiers in Race Relations," Carl Rowan, former head of the US Information Agency and a syndicated newspaper columnist, termed black power "most unfortunate" and blamed the nation's press for giving "irresponsibles" large play as Negro leaders.

Black State Senator Charles Chew of Chicago, discussing the violence in that city in 1968, called for stepped-up police action against looters whom he described as "thieves in hiding" who represent less than 1 percent of the Negro community.

"The people who did the looting and are now in hiding are thieves all around and would use any measure in their secret desire, which is to steal. The police department should be aware that decent citizens, I mean Negroes in Chicago who have tried to contribute something to the growth of the city, would support police action in a 'get-tough' policy. This is what is needed. The thugs and looters don't make up 1 percent of the Negro people."

Chew said that he was astounded when he saw looters carrying out goods from destroyed buildings and then saw the "restraint" exercised by police. He declared, "I would like to see the law enforced at all costs, and I don't care whose toes are stepped on. The only people who lose through this destruction are the Negro people."

Speaking in St. Louis, Gloster B. Current, director of branches and field administration for the NAACP, declared that the Negro middle class is under "devastating attack" by Negro militants. He lashed out at "black power" extremists and said that they scorn the progress made toward integration as "tokenism" and stir hatred and violence against those of their own race who disagree with their views.

"Today," declared Current, "the Negro middle class, who pulled themselves up by their own boot straps, are made to feel guilty at having done so." He spoke with what the *St. Louis Globe Democrat* called "obvious bitterness" of the Negro "leaders," such as H. Rap Brown and Stokely Carmichael, as having been "created" by newspaper and television publicity. "They got the exposure that made them 'leaders.' They became the pundits, the statement makers . . . . Young Negroes are being taught to hate not only whites but Negroes who do not agree with them."

Rather than being radical, the majority of black Americans are, in fact, quite conservative. This point was made in a lecture at Howard University by the dean of its law school, former United States Ambassador to Luxembourg Patricia Roberts Harris.

Mrs. Harris noted that Negro Americans are "politically and economically conservative, with all that term conveys." She explained that Negroes want to conserve the good in American society and do not seek radical solutions, "as the failure of every far right and far left institution to recruit significant numbers of Negroes attests."

Calling for observance of law, Mrs. Harris declared, "We must never minimize the fact that freedom of speech, petition and the press as guaranteed by the Federal Constitution, not guns and bombs, have been the weapons with which the Negro minority, with its friends in the majority, have assailed the walls of segregation."

"Our fortunes as Negroes," she stressed, "cannot be separated from the fortunes of the United States. Therefore, self-interest requires that we, as Americans, use all our resources to interpret the position of this Nation."

After rioting occurred in the South Bronx area of New York City in July 1969, Martin Arnold, a reporter for the *New York Times,* interviewed residents concerning their opinion of the police and of the disorder which had occurred in their community.

"The police are too lenient with some of these people," William Massas, a labor union employee, said. "They should be treated like criminals."

Arnold noted that "from his window in a dirty brown six-story building on Brook Avenue, between East 138th and 137th Streets, he had watched a group of rioting teenagers and young men smash the windows in a hardware store across the street and strip down the shelves before moving next door to twist the iron grating from the jewelry store, which was looted clean.

" 'There are people always begging for money, the addicts and the young ones who won't work,' Mr. Massas said."

Such attitudes are widespread and are echoed by countless leaders who find it almost impossible to receive proper coverage from the nation's media.

One example of a man who must be considered a black leader by any objective standard is Dr. Joseph Harrison Jackson, president of the six-million-member National Baptist Convention, U.S.A. He is also pastor of the Olivet Baptist Church in Chicago and, as opposed to the self-proclaimed militant "leaders," he has, in fact, been elected a leader by those in whose name he speaks.

Asked to discuss the concept of "black power," Dr. Jackson noted that "if 'black power' means the Negro cultivating his abilities and expending his energy to develop strength, standing and creative ability within his social order, then it means the same thing as that which the National Baptist Convention has been preaching for some time. But if the term indicates a separatist movement of Negro against white, then it is unfortunate and doomed to failure because it becomes a form of segregation of the minority against the majority and as such cannot work."

Asked about his attitude toward violence and demonstrations which have, in many instances, developed into violence, Dr. Jackson stated, "The Negro is not by nature violent. But the age of nonviolent doctrine has witnessed more violence on the part of the Negro than any other time in history. I believe the Negro has been used by persons with interests contrary to the best interests of the United States. The destruction of a city is not in the mind of the Negro, especially the destruction of the neighborhood in which he lives like we saw in Los Angeles. Someone else has to put this idea in his mind."

Asked about the charge that he and those who represent views similar to his own are, in fact, "Uncle Toms," Dr. Jackson declared:

> I don't work for white people, so I have nothing to gain from them by my views on the racial problem. My church in Chicago has called me for life. I have no political ambitions, so I don't need the favors of the white man in this area. Yet the men who call me Uncle Tom, these men do receive money from white people. About 80 percent of CORE's [Congress of Racial Equality] income comes from white people, for example. I hold the views I do, I take this position because I believe in myself, my race, my country and I have faith in God. I do not believe there is any other system in the world whereby a man can use his powers to become as strong and great as under the Stars and Stripes. It is my responsibility as an American to uphold this system and to oppose those, white or Negro, who attempt to destroy it.

Many Negroes who have been urged by militants to repudiate their white friends and their attempt to be a part of the larger American society have been intimidated, and have failed to respond. Others, however, have responded forcefully.

Claudia McNeil, who played Mama Younger in Lorraine Hansberry's "A Raisin in the Sun," both in the play and in the film, responded this way concerning black anti-Semitism in particular, and hostility to whites in general:

"Yes, this race thing, nowadays, Negroes and Jews . . . I'm prejudiced . . . I was raised by Jews. And this is ridiculous, this business now. I don't like a bad black man any better than a bad white man. People are people. You don't reverse segregation. I'm 50 now. I came through the Depression. I don't like some young whippersnapper telling me how to live [with great scorn] particularly when he can't even wear a whole suit."

Miss McNeil declared, "I'm for the man who's been fighting for over 35 years in a dignified way—men like Roy Wilkins, Whitney Young. Everybody is giving me a leader. Well, the Pope is my leader. I'm a Catholic. If you can't fight it with dignity, you can't achieve dignity. You can't fight it with rocks and bottles. If you have no dignity, you walk alone."

Similarly, former light heavyweight champion Archie Moore has criticized those who advocate violence as a means for achieving a better life. In an article in the *San Diego Union,* which was reprinted across the nation in 1967, he wrote, "The devil is at work in America, and it is up to us to drive him out. Snipers and looters, white or black, deserve no mercy. Those who would profit from their brother's misfortunes deserve no mercy, and those who would set fellow Americans upon each other deserve no mercy."

Discussing those who have tried to intimidate him by labeling his attitude that of an "Uncle Tom," Moore responds forcefully: "I'll fight the man who calls me an 'Uncle Tom.' I have broken bread with heads of state, chatted with presidents and traveled around the world. I was born in a ghetto, but I refused to stay there. I am a Negro, and proud to be one. I am also an American, and I'm proud of that."

With regard to young men and women growing up in today's inner city, Moore notes, "The young people of today think they have a hard lot. They should have been around in the 1930s when I was coming up in St. Louis. We had no way to go, but a lot of us made it. I became light heavyweight champion of the world. A neighbor kid down the block, Clark Terry, became one of the most famous jazz musicians in the world. There were doctors, lawyers and chiefs who came out of that ghetto. One of the top policemen in St. Louis came from our neighborhood."

The reason for such success stories, wrote Moore, was that "we made it because we had a goal, and we were willing to work for it. Don't talk to me of your 'guaranteed annual income.' Any fool knows this is insanity. Do we bring those who worked to get ahead down to the level of those who never gave a damn? The world owes NOBODY —black or white—a living. God helps the man who helps himself."

Archie Moore grew up facing all of the racial injustices to which black Americans have been heir. He cautions his readers not to get the idea that he did not hate the injustices of the world: "I am a staunch advocate of the Negro revolution for the good of mankind. I've seen almost unbelievable progress made in the last handful of years. Do we want to become wild beasts bent only on revenge, looting and killing and laying America bare? . . . If you listen to the professional rabble-rousers, adhere to this idea of giving up everything you've gained in order to revenge yourself for the wrongs that were done to you in the past—then you'd better watch your neighbor, because he'll be looting your house next. Law and order is the only edge we have. No man is an island."

Another prominent former athlete who has spoken out against black violence and extremism is one-time Brooklyn Dodger baseball star Joe Black. "Dropout," he tells black youths, "is another word for quitter. Quitting is a cinch. You walk away. For the time being you're the boss. Free as a bird. And because you're young, people excuse a lot of things. But when you get older, people stop feeling sorry, and that gets you sore, but what are you good for? A quitter is trained for nothing but being angry."

Speaking to black adults, he declares, "This reawakening of racial pride is a fine thing. African styles in clothing, jewelry, and hairdos are important. But what's more important is what we do to solve community problems. The future is the young; it's in the schools. A new hairdo solves no problems, but wearing the new hairdo to PTA meetings is something else. That's feeling racial identity and trying to make the ghetto schools a better place. But if you had to pick one to skip, skip the hairdo. Make the PTA."

During an Honors Day program at Virginia Union University, a predominantly black school in Richmond, Virginia, Black spoke about the responsibilities as well as the rewards of black power: "Our efforts have to be more positive than shouting, 'Sock it to him, Soul Brother,' or 'We are victims of a racist society,' or 'Honky!' I'm in favor of black history because it makes whites realize that American blacks have done more than make cotton king. But I'm opposed to all-black dorms, and violence. If the black student wants to use a loaded gun to make a point, what can we expect of uneducated blacks? By now some of you must be saying I'm a Tom, a window-dressing Negro. But I learned two things early. A minority cannot defeat a majority in physical combat and you've got to let some things roll off your back. Because my name is Joe Black, whites called me 'Old Black Joe.' After a few years of scuffling, I still hadn't silenced all of them and throwing all those punches had made me a weary young man. Call me 'Old Black Joe' today and you agitate nobody except yourself."

Recalling his own experiences as one of the first Negroes in the major leagues, Roy Campanella cautioned against those who preached racial hatred in the black community. He stated: "Being one of the first blacks to play in the major leagues with this, as they say, revolution taking place today, these teenagers refer back to Ebbets Field. And I tell them the press, the white press, really helped me, and the fans across all the years. I never had a single racial slur happen to me from the fans, nothing out of the way, and maybe they've been listening to people talking about hate and I want to tell them it isn't all hate, hate don't do good and I have no hate—no hate, but friends."

Similarly, Dr. Kenneth B. Clark, the distinguished Negro psychologist, has denounced the philosophy preached by black militants as a "shoddy moral product disguised in the gaudy package of racial militance" but grounded in a genuine Negro fear of the removal of racial barriers.

In an analysis of black militants, Dr. Clark called on thoughtful Negroes to refuse to be "cowed into silence by unrealistic Negro racists." He warned that they could become accessories in leading the nation back to the racial separatism and white advantage of the post-Reconstruction years. Dr. Clark laid principal emphasis on the need for Negro intellectuals to "choose sides," to reject the idea that the enemy may be understood in terms of color, and to take aim at "human irrationality, ignorance, superstition, rigidity and arbitrary cruelty."

He declared that "in many ways the problems of race relations in America today are similar to those of the post-Reconstruction period of the late 19th century, which continued and intensified through

World War I. This period culminated in the institutionalization of rigid forms of racism. This retrogression in racial democracy in America was imposed by white segregationists with the apathy, indifference or quiet acceptance of white liberals and moderates as necessary accessories."

There seems to be, stated Dr. Clark, a "stark and frightening" parallel between that time and the present. Whereas moderate whites in the post-Reconstruction era were bullied by white extremists, the thoughtful Negro today may be cowed by Negro racists into becoming "an active partner in fastening the yolk of impossible racial separatism more tightly around the neck of America."

A poignant example of a black educator who sought harmony rather than racial tension and separatism came in March 1972, when, in order to make his voice heard, Paul L. Cabell, Jr., frustrated and discouraged, put a shotgun to his head and pulled the trigger.

"I die to emphasize to you and all minority people who ever dream to be free that it can only come through working together," the teacher wrote his students before the fatal shot. "It seems that there is no other way for me to get your attention."

Mr. Cabell was assistant principal at the racially troubled Beecher High School in Flint, Michigan. He was charged with the responsibility for discipline at the school, which had an enrollment of about 1,000 —65 percent white and 35 percent black.

The 26-year-old administrator left two notes before he committed suicide. One, which remained private, was to Carlitta, his wife of three years. The other, made public by Mrs. Cabell, was addressed simply: "For Beecher."

Proud of his blackness, convinced of his need to be just, weary of his inability to reach hotheads of both sides, and distressed by the apathy of those in the middle, Mr. Cabell wrote:

> I am a leader but I cannot march alone. To all those black students who worked hard at bringing sense to the errant and foolish brothers and sisters at Beecher, thanks for your efforts—I appreciated them.
> To the white student body, I commend you for keeping your cool as long as you did. Tolerance and patience be yours forever.
> To the vast majority of blacks who did not take a stand but let the words of a few hotheads and several others turn your mind away from what it is all about—I say it is for you I die.

Shelly Grammer, a white cheerleader who was beaten by black students twice in a week of scattered violence at Beecher, conferred with Mr. Cabell and another black teacher 12 hours before his death.

"All I could see was a very frustrated man who couldn't find the answer," she said. "He was in a trap. He was called a 'nigger' by some whites and a 'Tom' by some blacks."

Mr. Cabell, in the note, told of the intolerable line he said he had been forced to walk. He wrote:

128

The cultures of the races have been manipulated by a few for capital gain. These cultures, as the races, have been programmed to be so diametrically opposed that seeking a common plane from which to establish "relations" often leads one to totter precariously on the line between the two cultures. And for what?

For whom do I isolate myself in the middle, never right, always wrong? Lonely, for no one, but no one immediately present can comprehend the continuous agony that those situations present.

It may be argued that to discipline those black students who are overcome with the myopic singleness of blackness and choose to show this narrow view of proving their "blackness" in groups of two, three and more to one white person, is right and must be done to preserve the system—to that, I say, do you punish a child who is learning to walk when he falls? These young blacks are hostile to all sense of reason, for reason is based on white-instigated values. On the other hand, I cannot stand by helplessly and turn my head while innocent white youths are abused and misused as sport for these young black egotists.

In many respects, it may be said that Paul L. Cabell, Jr., was a casualty in the battle for a free and equal American society. Unfortunately, voices such as his have all too often been unheard and unheeded, in both the black and white communities.

Throughout the late 1960s and early 1970s, while black militants occupied the center of the national stage, there were numerous black voices speaking out against them. Somehow, they did not make themselves heard amidst the bias of the press and the desire of many white liberals to, in effect, create Negroes in their own image.

One who spoke out forcefully, and continues to do so, is General Daniel James, known as "Chappie."

When he was an Air Force Colonel in Vietnam in 1967 he declared, "Stokely Carmichael is a big-mouth who is making a profession out of being a Negro, and he's got no damn business speaking for me. This Black Power garbage is for the birds."

Chappie James was then the biggest fighter pilot in the Air Force, and had already become something of a legend in the air war in Vietnam. He flew an F-4 Phantom fighter and was vice wing commander of the 8th Tactical Fighter Wing based in Thailand. The commander was James' closest friend, Colonel Robin Olds, the Air Force's top ace.

In Danang on a short visit, Colonel James discussed the racial turmoil which was plaguing the United States: "These riots are the worst thing that could happen to the Negroes' cause. This could set the civil rights movement back 100 years. A lot of the fence-sitters are jumping off on the wrong side now. We're fighting to get laws passed to protect civil rights. You've got to obey laws. You can't have a double standard."

James was especially critical of Stokely Carmichael. "I resent Stokely's setting himself up as spokesman for Negroes," he said. "This SOB is leading too many kids astray. And when he advises Negro servicemen to come back and fight at home—that's sheer stupidity."

In the event that anyone questioned his own credentials in the civil rights movement, James added, "Hell, I was in the original sit-in back in 1943." He and nearly 100 other Negro Army Air cadets refused to accept segregation at Selfridge Air Force Base in Michigan. They were all arrested and threatened with court-martial, but they held their ground and the charges were later dropped.

"What I really don't buy is that back-to-Africa stuff," James concluded. "I'm not an African immigrant. I'm an American with several generations behind me in this country. If something is wrong with my country right now, then I'm willing to hold her hand for a while until she pulls out of it and is all right."

Washington Post black columnist William Raspberry tells of a phone call he received from a woman who identified herself as "an ordinary Negro." "Why is it," she wanted to know, "that people never pay any attention to what we ordinary Negroes think? Let Stokely Carmichael or somebody come into town to raise hell, and you can't see him for the reporters. People get the impression he's speaking for us. He's not, but we don't have any way to make our voices heard."

Similarly, Nelson C. Roots, president of the D.C. Federation of Civic Associations, a kind of black Chamber of Commerce, declared, "We've been working hard for years, and we have won a lot of respect in this city. Yet our statements are ignored, while the press gives full play to anything a radical Negro has to say."

Here is William Raspberry's explanation for this unfortunate state of affairs:

> The extremists on both ends are considered news because of the sheer shock value of their utterances and actions. By this system of news judgment the man who gets up in the morning, kisses his wife, goes to work, comes home and gets a good night's sleep isn't news. But the man who does something out of the ordinary is.
>
> The priest who upholds the views of the church isn't news; he is doing just what he is expected to do. Let the same priest denounce the church, and he finds himself in the news. The opinions of the silent middle— which is the overwhelming bulk of the population—simply aren't news in the conventional sense. The eccentric view or action is.

This problem becomes even more serious with regard to Negroes. "The problem," writes Raspberry, "is that no one believes the eccentrics or the wayward priest to be representative members of their groups. But when a handful of Negroes express radical views, there is the tendency to believe that these views are held by most Negroes. Complicating the problem is the increasing reluctance of nonradical Negroes to say what they think; they are too afraid of being put down by the militants as Uncle Toms."

Part of this fear to speak out was seen in a meeting held in May 1963, by then Attorney General Robert Kennedy with prominent Negroes such as James Baldwin, Lena Horne, Lorraine Hansberry and Harry Belafonte. Robert Kennedy had hoped to build bridges toward a rational and responsible leadership but he found this impossible to do.

"They didn't know anything," Kennedy later told Arthur M. Schlesinger, Jr., "They don't know what the laws are—they don't know what the facts are—they don't know what we've been doing or what we're trying to do. You couldn't talk to them .... It was all emotion, hysteria. They stood up and orated. They cursed. Some of them wept and walked out of the room."

Others remained silent while Robert Kennedy was attacked and vilified, then went to him privately to express their appreciation for his efforts. When he asked why they hadn't spoken up to defend him before the others, their reply was: "If I were to defend you, they would conclude I had gone over to the other side."

This, unfortunately, is the mentality of fear that has caused many Negroes to remain silent in the face of crime and violence, of disorder and chaos. To a large extent, those who know better and refuse to say so must share the blame for what follows with those who have actively agitated and perpetrated the disorder we have witnessed.

The idea that Negroes are, in fact, quite conservative is not a new idea, and not one that anyone with an understanding of black history in the United States would challenge. The calls for "black identity" and for returning to Africa are by no means unique to the mid 20th century. Such calls have been heard, and have been rejected, before.

In his important volume *The Negro in the Making of America,* Benjamin Quarles, Professor of History at Morgan State College, writes that the northern Negro reacted to his lot in America in this manner:

> At the outset, he made one important decision: he would remain in America. From the time of the Revolutionary War the Negro had been advised to return to Africa. Those giving such advice were variously motivated. To some whites the back-to-Africa movement was a good way to get rid of the troublesome free Negro. To humanitarians the movement was a way to send to Africa Christianized population and to discharge a moral obligation to return the Negro to his ancestral homeland. Moreover, reasoned the humanitarians, masters would more readily free their slaves if there were a place to send them outside the United States.

The sentiment to deport the Negro culminated in 1817 in the formation of the American Colonization Society. Composed of men prominent in public life, this organization sought the aid of Congress in acquiring a place to which to send the Negroes. In 1822, the colony of Liberia, on the west coast of Africa, came into existence under the auspices of the American Colonization Society, with an assist from the United States.

Dr. Quarles points out that "the Negro did not share this enthusiasm for colonization. By 1852 fewer than 8,000 Negroes went to Liberia, and 2,800 of these were free Negroes, the others being some 3,600 slaves emancipated on condition they go to Liberia and some 1,000 Africans who had been liberated from slave ships. In 1855 not a single

Negro from Indiana sailed for Liberia, despite increased state aid to such emigrants. Even in the South, the response was cool: in Tennessee only 55 Negroes had gone to Liberia by 1841, and in Virginia the colonization efforts resulted in repeated failure."

The failure of the Liberian colonization resulted in part from its high cost, but the key reason was the attitude of the Negro himself. Dr. Quarles notes that "despite the Colonization Society's support by influential groups, the majority of free Negroes disliked the proposal from its inception. They believed that deportation was a device to get rid of the free Negro in order to make slavery secure—that colonization was the twin sister of slavery. Moreover, the Negro, although not forgetful of his plight, regarded America as home."

"A few may go," said Negro leader Robert Purvis, "but the colored people as a mass will not leave the land of their birth."

One of the most significant expressions of social action among Negroes in the 19th century was the Colored Convention Movement. Held annually for seven years, the convention assembled sporadically after 1837—at Buffalo in 1843, Troy in 1847, Cleveland in 1848 and Rochester in 1853. At the Rochester meeting 140 delegates from eight states answered the call for "the amelioration of the condition of the colored people."

Presiding over this Rochester convention was the scholarly clergyman, J. W. C. Pennington, and chairman of the committee on declaration of sentiments was the noted orator, Frederick Douglass. The statement drawn up was quite clear as to what the Negro wanted. It declared:

"We ask that in our native land we shall not be treated as strangers, and worse than strangers."

The delegates voiced an official disapproval of colonization and supported the proposal to establish a manual labor school which would teach the skilled trades. In addition to the committee on a manual labor college, the convention established three other committees: one on safeguarding the civil liberties of the Negro, a second on business relations—a job-finding agency—and a third on publications, designed to collect data on Negroes and to refute slurs upon them.

Some Negroes refused even to participate in the meeting on the grounds that organizations made up exclusively of Negroes tacitly accepted segregation, perhaps the worst kind of self-segregation. William C. Nell of Boston declared that Negroes should abandon separate action and become "part and parcel of the general community."

In 1862, Congress voted to set aside $100,000 to aid in colonizing Negroes of the District of Columbia and later voted an additional $500,000 for the colonization of the slaves of disloyal masters. With this $600,000, of which President Abraham Lincoln was the sole trustee, Lincoln took up the task of getting the Negro to agree to be colonized and of finding some place for him to go. To place his views before the Negro people, Lincoln arranged to have an interview on August 14, 1862, with a five-man Negro delegation. The interview was widely published, as Lincoln had intended, and was widely read by Negroes.

Dr. Quarles notes that "their response, however, was something less than he had hoped for. A number of colored leaders wrote open letters condemning his proposal, and Negroes in various cities held protest meetings."

The general sentiment of these gatherings was expressed in an "appeal" sent to Lincoln by the Negroes of Philadelphia: "Many of us have our own house and other property, mounting, in the aggregate, to millions of dollars. Shall we sacrifice this, leave our homes, forsake our birthplace, and flee to a strange land, to appease the anger and prejudice of the traitors now in arms against this Government?"

The essential conservatism and patriotism of the overwhelming majority of American Negroes rejected the appeals of radicalism in the 20th century just as it had rejected the idea of African colonization in the 19th century.

In the days of the Depression in the early 1930s, the Communist Party made every effort to recruit Negroes to their cause. How significant was their failure is reflected in a presidential condidate poll published by *Opportunity* magazine in May 1932 which showed that out of 3,973 Negroes polled, only 51 planned to support the Communist nominee.

Benjamin Quarles writes that "Negroes simply did not seem to be attuned to the Communist message, for reasons that are not hard to fathom. Typically American, the Negro was individualistic, not likely to submerge his personality in conformity to a party line from which there could be no deviation. Most Negroes took their cues from their clergymen or their secular leaders, both of whom had a middle-class outlook on the economics of property and each of whom had special reasons for disliking the Communists. Moreover, the Negro, again like other Americans of his day, was not class-conscious—the very vocabulary of the Communists struck him as foreign. Basically, too, the Negro was a man of conservative mold. Because he protested against 'Jim Crow' he was thought to be a revolutionary, but at best he was a 'forced radical,' and, even then, only on the issue of race. And, finally, Negroes were cool toward communism because they were skeptical of utopias and somewhat suspicious of the intent of their promoters."

Richard Wright was one of the bright young Negroes whom the Communists sought to recruit, who joined the Party for a time, and left, disillusioned with the manner in which it was seeking to use him for ends of its own. He wrote of his experiences in a volume of reminiscenses by a group of former Communists, *The God That Failed.* When the Communists first approached him, he wrote, "I felt that Communists could not possibly have a sincere interest in Negroes. I was cynical and I would rather have heard a white man say that he hated Negroes, which I could have readily believed, then to have heard him say that he respected Negroes, which would have made me doubt him."

He recalls one of the early meetings he attended: "I sat in a corner and listened while they discussed their magazine, *Left Front.* Were they treating me courteously because I was a Negro? I must let cold reason guide me with these people, I told myself. I was asked to contribute something to the magazine, and I said vaguely that I would consider it. After the meeting I met an Irish girl who worked for an advertising agency, a girl who did social work, a school teacher and the wife of a prominent university professor. I had once worked as a servant for people like these and I was skeptical. I tried to fathom their motives, but I could detect no condescension in them."

Richard Wright soon learned that the Communist Party was a hospitable place only for those who were willing to say precisely the things they were told to say, and who were unwilling to deviate from authority. He describes a meeting in which he expressed his own opinions, which differed from official Communist policy:

"I found myself arguing alone against the majority opinion, and then I made still another amazing discovery. I saw that even those who agreed with me would not support me. At that meeting I learned that when a man was informed of the wish of the Party, he submitted, even though he knew with all the strength of his brains that the wish was not a wise one, was one that would ultimately hurt the Party's interests."

His own American values in such concepts as free speech were so ingrained that Richard Wright made a very poor Communist. He noted that "it was not courage that made me oppose the party. I simply did not know any better. It was inconceivable to me, though bred in the lap of Southern hate, that a man could not have his say. I had spent a third of my life traveling from the place of my birth to the North just to talk freely, to escape the pressure of fear. And now I was facing fear again."

Describing a meeting of the National Writers Congress in New York, in which he was representing the John Reed Club of Chicago, Wright recalls the manner in which he was treated by his white Communist comrades:

"I waited while one white Communist called another white Communist to one side and discussed what could be done to get me, a black Chicago Communist, housed. During the trip I had not thought of myself as a Negro; I had been mulling over the problems of the young left-wing writers I knew. Now, as I stood watching one white comrade talk frantically to another about the color of my skin, I felt disgusted ... I cursed under my breath. Several people standing nearby observed the white Communist trying to find a black Communist a place to sleep. I burned with shame. A few minutes later the white Communist returned, frantic-eyed, sweating. 'Did you find anything?' I asked. 'No, not yet,' he said, panting. 'Just a moment. I'm going to call somebody I know. Say, give me a nickel for the phone.' 'Forget it,' I said. My legs felt like water. 'I'll find a place. But I'd like to put my suitcase somewhere until after the meeting tonight.' "

Communism, Wright learned, feared the man who thought for himself, who would not permit himself to become simply a means for the ends of others. He summed up his attitude this way:

"In trying to grasp why Communists hated intellectuals, my mind was led back again to the accounts I had read of the Russian Revolution. There had existed in Old Russia millions of poor, ignorant people who were exploited by a few educated, arrogant noblemen, and it became natural for the Russian Communists to associate betrayal with intellectualism. But there existed in the Western world an element that baffled and frightened the Communist Party: the prevalence of self-achieved literacy. Even a Negro, entrapped by ignorance and exploitation—as I had been—could, if he had the will and the love for it, learn to read and understand the world in which he lived. And it was these people that the Communists could not understand."

Richard Wright's story is, of course, similar to the story of many white idealists who entered the Communist Party, viewing it as the vehicle through which a better world might be achieved, only to learn that its goal was the total subjugation of the individual human spirit, not its fulfillment and development.

The fact that Communists and other radicals, until the decade of the 1960s, made little headway in the black community indicates that the innate conservatism of American Negroes was a pervasive and deeply felt system of values, as was religion, as indicated by the traditional primacy given to the black church. Only when the value structure of the larger American society seemed to weaken could a similar weakening be found within the black community. For every Stokely Carmichael there were innumerable Abbie Hoffmans, Jerry Rubins and Rennie Davises. Nevertheless, the view became widespread that radicalism was becoming a dominant phenomenon in the black community. This view, clearly at variance with the facts, was the one which the mass media brought to millions of Americans—of both races. It made the role of Negroes seeking to resist the calls to violence and disorder by the small minority of vocal militants that much more difficult. Unfortunately, it scared many away completely.

The goal of the majority of Negroes, rather than being a revolution or the destruction of American society, has traditionally been one of gaining entry to that society. This view was explicitly expressed by the most important black spokesman of the Civil War era, Frederick Douglass. In his article, "The Present and Future of the Colored Race in America," which appeared in *Douglass' Monthly* in 1863, he wrote:

> I shall advocate for the Negro, his most full and complete adoption into the great national family of America. I shall demand for him the most perfect civil and political equality, and that he shall enjoy all the rights, privileges and immunities enjoyed by any other members of the body politic . . . this is the only solid, and final solution of the problem before us. It is demanded not less by the terrible exigencies of the nation, than by the Negro himself for the Negro and the nation, are to rise and fall, be killed or cured, saved or lost together. Save the Negro and you save the nation, and to save both you must have but one great law of Liberty, Equality, Fraternity for all Americans without respect to color.

Douglass asked himself the same question many are asking today: "Can the white and colored people of this country be blended into a common nationality, and enjoy together, in the same country, under the same flag, as neighborly citizens of a common country? . . . Equality . . . can this thing be done? Can white and colored people of America be blended into a common nationality under a system of equal laws?"

Frederick Douglass' answer, in 1863, was the same answer which the overwhelming majority of black Americans have given from the days of slavery to the current period. "I answer most unhesitatingly," declared Douglass, "I believe they can."

Many of the programs being inaugurated by black separatists today are not as new and unique as they often claim. They are, in fact, suggestive of those initiated in the 1920s by Marcus Garvey. Garvey created the Universal Negro Improvement Association, the African Communities League and "The Black Star Line," a steamship company. In addition, he spearheaded efforts to develop black businesses. Throughout his life he was vitally concerned about the "unity and liberation" of black people throughout the world. To him, the racist exploitation of Africa was as intolerable as that in America. Because of his inability to manage his affairs, however, he was imprisoned for mail fraud in 1925 and deported to his native Jamaica upon his release.

Garvey, a visionary, an idealist and a black nationalist, failed to obtain massive support for his "back to Africa" movement. He set forth his philosophy in his "Appeal to the Conscience of the Black Race to See Itself." He noted that "progress of and among any people will advance them in the respect and appreciation of the rest of their fellows. It is such a progress that the Negro must attach to himself if he is to rise above the prejudice of the world. The reliance of our race upon the progress and achievements of others for a consideration in sympathy, justice and rights is like a dependence upon a broken stick, resting upon which will eventually consign you to the ground."

He declared, "The Universal Negro Improvement Association teaches our race self-help and self-reliance, not only in one essential, but in all those things that contribute to human happiness and well-being. The disposition of the many to depend upon the other races for a kindly and sympathetic consideration of their needs, without making the effort to do for themselves, has been the race's standing disgrace by which we have been judged and through which we have created the strongest prejudice against ourselves."

After proclaiming his interest in self-help and self-improvement, Garvey set forth the thesis that the Negro was not at home in America, but should return to Africa. He wrote, "The Negro needs a nation and a country of his own, where he can best show evidence of his own ability in the art of human progress. Scattered as an unmixed and unrecognized part of alien nations and civilizations is but to demonstrate his imbecility, and point him out as an unworthy derelict, fit neither for the society of Greek, Jew, nor Gentile."

He believed that "no Negro, let him be American, European, West Indian or African, shall be truly respected until the race as a whole has emancipated itself, through self-achievement and progress, from universal prejudice. The Negro will have to build his own government, industry, art, science, literature and culture before the world will stop to consider him."

Just as many self-proclaimed black leaders do today, Marcus Garvey urged his followers to turn away from the "alien" American society and return to their African roots. He received a number of supporters, and gathered a good deal of money. Part of the reason, of course, was that he spoke of black pride and achievement. This found a real response in the black community, as it does today. What did not find a significant response was the idea of leaving America and returning to Africa. No more Negro Americans felt that this was the answer to their difficulties than they did in the 1850s when colonization schemes were being proposed. Both then and in the 1920s, the overwhelming majority made a firm commitment to being Americans. Similarly, the overwhelming majority share that commitment today.

Nevertheless, individual Negroes have frequently traveled to Africa in search of what they believe to be a "lost identity." What they find, however, is often quite different from what they had expected.

"It's ridiculous," one American Negro in Africa told Harold Isaacs, "but I never before realized how much of my life had nothing to do with the race problem at all. I mean just the way you do everything you do, what you mean when you say something, and how you understand what the other fellow means."

Almost every American Negro he met in Africa in 1960, Isaacs reports, had "discovered that he was much more alien in Africa. Whether he liked it or not, he found that he was an American, and that in Africa he became an American in exile."

Charles Silberman, in the book *Crisis in Black and White,* concludes that "it is in the United States and only in the United States that American Negroes will be able to resolve their problem of identification. For American Negroes have been formed by the United States, not by Africa; Africa gave them their color, but America gave them their personality and their culture.

"The central fact in Negro history," writes Silberman, "is slavery, and Negroes must come to grips with it, must learn to accept it—to accept it not as a source of shame (the shame is the white man's) but as an experience that explains a large part of their present predicament. Only if they understand *why* they are what they are, can Negroes change *what* they are. Identity is not something that can be found; it must be created."

Thus, Solly Sanders, the hero of John Oliver Killen's novel *And Then We Heard the Thunder,* is transformed by reading a copy of Richard Wright's *Twelve Million Black Voices,* which his race-conscious sweetheart had sent him. This pride in self dissolves Solly's hatred of the white: "One day he was reading the book, and it suddenly came to him, and he said to himself, if I'm proud of me, I don't need to hate Mr. Charlie's people. I don't want to. I don't need to. If I love me, I can also love the whole damn human race. Black, brown, yellow, white."

Those, both black and white, who have portrayed the Negro as an advocate of crime and violence, as an opponent of traditional American values of individualism, hard work and respect for law, have presented a highly distorted and unrealistic view. The world is not the way it is painted in the rhetoric of black militants or in the journalistic renditions of white intellectuals.

Black Americans do not, contrary to widespread belief, constitute a poor, uneducated "underclass" of the American society. The real fact of recent American history is the dramatic increase in black education, black income, and black living standards. Consider some of the facts, rather than fancies, in this area.

By 1969, 99.5 percent of all nonwhites 14 to 24 years old in America were literate. By 1970, 56 percent of all blacks 25 to 29 had completed high school, up from 38 percent in 1960. Black student enrollment in all American medical schools in 1971 was a record 26 percent higher than in 1970. Black family median income rose almost 50 percent between 1960 and 1970. By 1970, 24 percent of all black families had an income of over $10,000—almost two and one half times as many as ten years before.

Blacks in professional, technical and clerical jobs doubled between 1960 and 1970. "About two-thirds of the net increase in Negro employment from 1962 to 1967 was in professional, technical, managerial, clerical and sales positions," according to John S. Morgan and Richard L. Van Dyke, authors of the book, *White-Collar Blacks, A Breakthrough.* "Black employment in those years," say the authors, "fell by 600,000 in the less attractive categories—domestic service, industrial labor and some farm work." During the five year upgrading, salaried managerial jobs held by blacks went up 49 percent.

Since 1940, blacks as a national group have raised the median years of schooling for 25- to 29-year-olds (the ones just launching their work careers and families) from 7.0 years of school in 1940 to 12.2 years in 1970. The addition of 5.2 years of education for the average young black was more than twice the national gain for all Americans. It raised the average education level for young blacks to within a fraction of a year of that enjoyed by the population as a whole.

The facts regarding the nature of Washington, D.C., a city which is predominantly black, illustrate clearly that black Americans have been steadily advancing in almost all respects.

Writing in the *Washington Daily News* of May 29, 1972, Judy Luce Mann notes that "the District has, during the past decade, developed into a predominantly black, middle-income city rather than a poor, black city as has been widely assumed," according to an analysis of 1970 census figures conducted by the Washington Center for Metropolitan Studies.

"The recent growth in the black middle and upper-income population can be a hopeful sign for the District's economic future," the report said.

Using the census figures listing 537,712 blacks out of a population of 756,510 and adjusting for inflation, the center found:

• The number of black families in the District with incomes in excess of $12,000 a year has tripled during the past decade, while the number of families with incomes under $4,000 has remained constant.

• The number of black families with incomes over $8,000 a year has doubled from an estimated 31,000 in 1960 to 66,000 in 1970.

• In addition to 122,000 black families in D.C. there are more than 72,000 "unrelated individuals—persons unrelated to anyone else in a household, and those living in group quarters or other institutions." These people tend to have lower incomes than black families, the study said, with a median income of $3,881 in 1969 compared to $8,497 for families.

• The number of black families with incomes of over $15,000 a year has tripled, from an estimated 7,000 in 1959 to 21,000 in 1969. (Census income data is derived from the full year preceding the taking of the census.)

• More than half of the black families in the District enjoy incomes of $8,000 a year.

The study found that black families in the suburbs are even "more prosperous overall" than those within Washington itself. "Of all suburban black families, nearly 62 percent have incomes over $8,000; the figure is 53 percent in the District. About 13 percent have incomes below $4,000, compared with 17 percent in the District," the study found.

The study was prepared as part of the Washington Center for Metropolitan Studies' "Agenda for the 70s" project, which is supported by the Ford, Cafritz and Meyer foundations. The monetary adjustment factor for 1959 and 1969 figures used in the study is the Consumer Price Index for the area, derived by the Bureau of Labor Statistics.

Black Americans have steadily improved their educational and economic status and, as new opportunities have been made available, have taken advantage of them. It is ironic, but not atypical, that crime has increased within the black community at the very time when opportunities have been expanding, when income has been rising, and when educational levels have been advancing. The same is true with regard to the white society, where crime and affluence are both steadily increasing.

While crime is increasing in the black community, it is blacks themselves who are its primary victims. Although the media have portrayed a picture of black apology for and sympathy with narcotics addiction, violent crime and civil disorder, the truth about black attitudes is far different.

At the height of the racial tension which plagued the nation in the mid-sixties, shortly after riots in Watts and in Harlem, polls were taken within the black community of both areas. The poll conducted in Watts by John F. Kraft, Inc., an independent public opinion research organization, showed that the majority of Negroes sympathized with police problems and wanted more instead of fewer policemen in their neighborhood.

The Kraft Company interviewed 527 individuals in the Watts area one month after the riots in August 1965. The Harlem survey involved interviews with 1,200 persons and was released by the American Broadcasting Company in September 1966.

The people of Harlem believed that the worst problems facing their community, in this order, were the following: Dope addiction, 21 percent; crime and juvenile delinquency, 11 percent; the need for better schools, 11 percent; the breakdown of family life, 10 percent.

When Harlem residents were asked about the biggest problems on their block, rather than in the black community generally, the answers were: Crime in the streets, 28 percent; dope addiction, 20 percent; the need for better police protection, 15 percent; and murders and drunks in the hallways of buildings, 3 percent each.

"Problems of police brutality are conspicuous by their absence," the report said. "It appears that police malpractice in Harlem is an issue only insofar as the police are inadequate in doing their jobs. Police brutality, as such, was not a volunteered problem of concern for the people of Harlem."

In Watts, when residents were asked directly about police brutality, 46.8 percent of those interviewed believed that some police brutality existed, 15.1 percent said "none at all," and 38.1 percent were not sure.

However, the report said, "a number of people did not feel that the blame for the brutality was altogether the policeman's part." When asked what might be done to prevent violence, nearly one-third of all respondents said there should be "better" police protection and "more" police protection.

During the disturbances in Washington, D.C., in 1968 there were countless examples of members of the black community working as "counter-rioters" in an effort to stop the violence and looting which had broken out.

City Councilman Stanley J. Anderson, for example, roamed the streets in Anacostia when trouble broke out on Good Hope Road. Anderson, youth leader Rufus Mayfield, and Clinton Mitchell of the Council of Human Relations staff helped avert an ugly incident when a crowd gathered around a Negro man lying on the sidewalk. The man had fallen, but the word that he had been shot by police had drawn the crowd. The three explained what had happened and also told policemen why the group gathered, "so they wouldn't jump out with their guns," Anderson said.

At the Central Cardozo Youth Center, a group of 35 teenagers being chased by National Guardsmen poured through the center's doors and a curious crowd materialized. Center Director Darryl Dargan thought the troops were about to throw tear gas and intervened. He got the youths and the Guard talking. The crowd dispersed, the youths apologized to the troops for not obeying the order to halt, and stayed behind to sweep up the glass from the center door, which had been broken in the melee.

In Anacostia, Director John Kinard of the Smithsonian Institution's Anacostia Neighborhood Museum was startled to see a white man walking down the street apparently oblivious to angry stares from Negro teenagers. About 60 yards from the museum a crowd fell on the man and pummeled him to the ground. Kinard and other adults chased the youths away and carried the bleeding man into the museum, from where police took him home.

Most of the "counter-rioters," according to a report in the *Washington Post* of April 9, 1968, "reported considerable help from private citizens."

To help calm the disturbed Washington area James Brown, the popular black soul singer, voluntarily appeared on network television to urge a return to nonviolence. Speaking of his own rise from very humble beginnings, James Brown emphasized that the most effective black power is brain power. He counseled youngsters to stay in school, and urged families to stay off the streets, to return to their homes.

In his television talk Brown told his audience, "I just left Africa. I always wanted to go to Africa because I wanted to know where my soul came from. I wanted to know where it really started. They say I have so much in common—my music, I even have the drums, the syncopation, the movement, the sound. So I went to Africa and I found people working for $200 a year, $40 a month. Then I thought of something else. But, do you know, with all the minor things that have happened out there, America is the greatest country in the world. Everybody has had their problems. My home is Augusta, Georgia, and you know I had my problems. I know what they are. But the main thing is that you've got determination, enough believing confidence in yourself to go all the way."

Speaking to those militants who view those who oppose violence and disorder as "Uncle Toms," Brown declared, "You know, I'm not what we call around the country a man who would do anything anybody says . . . take sides. I am not what a black man describes as a 'Tom.' I am not a 'Tom.' I am a man. Nobody can buy me. I do what I want, I say what I want, because this is America. A man can get ahead here. Through you, I got ahead. I've been able to say what I want to say and say it to whom I want to say it. I say to you . . . get off the streets, go home. Take your families home . . . . This is our country . . . . We are not going to tear the country up because we love the country. You aren't going to burn your house down. You aren't going to cut up the streets, throw your shoes in the trashcan—this is your home, your life."

From the beginning of the American experiment in a free and democratic society, there have been those, both white and black, who told the American Negro that this was not his country, that his future was someplace else, that he need not obey the laws and customs of the alien, white culture. There were always a few who listened, and who agreed. The overwhelming majority of black Americans, at all points in our history, and at this point in our history, have rejected that analysis. America, they continue to believe, is as much their country as anyone else's. Its laws are their laws, and their commitment to fulfilling their responsibilities as well as pursuing their legitimate rights is as great as is the commitment of other Americans.

It is unfortunate that the small minority of black militants, aided and abetted by their allies in the white community, have been permitted, in recent years, to become the "voice" of black America. They are *not* the voice of black America, as anyone who has taken a closer look can readily see.

Chapter 6

What Some Negroes Have
Been Doing About Crime

Although their efforts have been given little publicity, and the majority of Americans of both races remain unaware of them, the fact is that many black Americans have been busy organizing, in a variety of ways, to fight crime, violence, narcotics addiction and other forces of social disruption within the nation's inner cities. It is their own successful efforts in recent years that provide an indication of the real hope that exists for the future.

In an editorial entitled "Private Citizens Must Help Reduce High Rate of Crime," the *Philadelphia Tribune,* a biweekly newspaper serving that city's black community, declared, "Wringing our hands and lamenting the growing prevalence of crime in our neighborhoods is not the answer to reducing the crime rate in our city. The private citizen must do something more than that."

In its issue of October 21, 1972, the *Tribune* calls for "the formation of local citizens' alliances, comprised of civic, business, labor and other groups organized on the block and neighborhood level."

This suggestion, the paper points out, "is workable. It is being tried by the Boy Scout movement in Philadelphia and elsewhere throughout the nation, and thousands of boys hitherto outside the Scout movement are being reached by the growth of block action."

The active participation of citizens in the fight to control crime was also called for in a paper prepared by the 1972 Democratic National Convention. "There should be more programs in which police and citizens join together to combat crime," said the panel headed by Senator Harold F. Hughes of Iowa and Representative Claude D. Pepper of Florida.

In October 1972 a meeting took place at the Masonic Temple in Baltimore, bringing together more than 200 of that city's black citizens. "I saw my boy take a last breath in the streets of Baltimore," said Hattie Taylor, "and I don't want any other mother to ever have to suffer like I did."

Toward the end of her brief presentation to the group she began to cry, and her sobs were amplified over the loudspeakers. The occasion was described by several black politicians and clergymen who were present as "the beginning of a war on the murder rate in Baltimore city."

Representative Parren J. Mitchell, the black former college professor who represents Maryland's Seventh Congressional District, was the organizer of the meeting. He said that the rally was the first of several "consciousness-raising efforts" to be staged. The idea, according to Representative Mitchell, is to start a grass-roots movement that will gradually reduce Baltimore's rising rate of homicides, 85 percent of which, he points out, are in the black community.

"Ninety percent of all city homicide victims are black," said Delegate John J. Douglass of Maryland's Second Assembly District, "and most of the murderers are also black. Did you know that for black males, homicide is the second most common way to die? We're wiping out our future leaders."

In Mrs. Taylor's personal tragedy, according to police reports, her 17-year-old son Randolph was walking with a friend in South Baltimore on May 25, 1972, when they were approached by two other youths. Police said that one of the approaching youths asked, "Where's the narcotics?" The Taylor youth said that he knew nothing of narcotics, and was hit in the face with a .45 caliber semiautomatic pistol. The gunman then shot him in the face and fled.

At the Masonic Temple meeting were approximately two dozen families whose members had experienced similar tragedies. Mr. Douglass, addressing the group, declared, "There are those among us of our own race who are taking advantage of our circumstances. There is something illogical about black crime. Usually you have the oppressed striking out against their oppressors. But with black crime the oppressed are striking against the oppressed."

Other speakers, clergymen and students, stressed the need for "pride" and "self-love" in the black community as the most effective way to lower black crime. "Above all we need pride, dignity and self-

144

respect," said one clergyman. "Then we can start working on concrete things like housing and education."

According to Earl Lawrence, president of the Student Government Association at Morgan State College, it is a "positive philosophy of self-love that makes killing impossible. Most killings are examples of a lack of such love, resulting in fatal crimes by one black person against another black person."

Between January 1972 and October 1972 more than 250 people were killed in Baltimore, which is more than the total number of American soldiers killed in Vietnam during the same period.

Five years before the Baltimore meeting, a Harlem clergyman organized an armed militia and advised local residents to buy guns to protect themselves against what he called "criminalization."

"A rising tide of crime has swept over Harlem streets in the past six months," stated Reverend Oberia D. Dempsey in October 1967. "Crime is at its worst. The citizens fear to venture out after dark. Church members are afraid to go to their meetings at night. The law seems to be in the hands of the muggers and robbers. There's panic among the people."

Mr. Dempsey organized a police militia that he called "Operation Interruption." The group had approximately 2,600 members, 200 of whom were active and armed. Volunteers were recruited from among retired policemen, guards and others who have been trained and hold pistol permits. Mr. Dempsey himself has a permit, and stated that he always carried a .32 caliber pistol, even in church.

The *New York Times* reported that "the volunteers are supposed to be ready to stop muggings and robberies in the streets of Harlem whenever they encounter them. They are regularly assigned . . . to escort parishioners to church and women to market, and also serve as police informants, working with the city police and with the Federal Bureau of Investigation and Federal Narcotics Bureau agents."

A rally was held on October 18, 1967, at St. Charles Roman Catholic Church in Harlem which more than 700 Harlem residents attended. They demanded more police protection and James F. Brodie, program director of the Drew Hamilton Community Center, which is sponsored by the Catholic Youth Movement, was chairman at the meeting. He said that he would not go so far as Mr. Dempsey in recommending that citizens arm themselves, but noted:

"The muggings and rapes and robberies around here have reached the point that the people must do something. I would suggest forming an auxiliary civilian police. Civilians could ride in the prowl cars, for instance, freeing uniformed police to patrol on foot, where they're needed."

In the 12 years preceding 1961, Reverend Oberia Dempsey was chief assistant to Representative Adam Clayton Powell, Jr., at Mr.

Powell's Abyssinian Baptist Church. Dempsey has also served as "Mayor of Harlem," a nonofficial but prestigious elective position, and has worked with many Harlem civic groups and has been active in the rehabilitation of narcotics addicts. He contends that increasing addiction is a prime reason for the increase in Harlem crime and points out, "We're losing some of our vital services in Harlem as a direct result of the impact of crime. We've had 12 drugstores close and only three open in the past four months. Stores by the dozen are closing. Business is going out, which means that people are going to suffer. You can't blame the merchants, because who wants to gamble his life just to make a few dollars?"

Captain William J. O'Rourke, commanding officer of the 25th Precinct, has worked closely with Mr. Dempsey, and concedes that there are not enough patrolmen to control crime in Harlem without the active support of the community. "It's a case of the good guys against the bad guys," he says, "and without the good guys of the community working with us, we can't make Harlem safe."

In Chicago's West Side ghetto the Afro-American Group Attack Team, a band of ten street-wise black vigilantes, took upon themselves the difficult mission of ridding their neighborhood of its number one problem: narcotics.

Newsweek magazine of September 27, 1971, reports the following incident:

> The youthful drug pusher was slouching in his usual spot outside the OK Lounge, a seedy, graffiti-stained bar in Chicago's West Side ghetto. Suddenly a dark-blue auto slid to a stop at the curb and its driver—a 32-year-old black named Hosea Lindsey—ordered the pusher over to the car. "The next time you help someone in this neighborhood take dope," Lindsey told him softly, "I'm gonna beat your ass. And if you run, I'll chase you with a gun." The pusher glanced from Lindsey to his three scowling passengers and then he began backing away from the car. "OK, I won't do that any more," he stammered. "I won't do that anymore." Then he walked quickly off as the four in the car exchanged satisfied looks.

One member of the Afro-American Group Attack Team, 23-year-old Edward Meade, stated, "We know we can't stop the use of drugs, but we think we can get the junkies and dealers out of our community. Sure they'll move to another one, but maybe that community will organize and chase them out. Pretty soon they won't have anywhere to go but the river."

Operating out of a shabby building lent to them by the University of Illinois Medical Center, equipped with two cars and a mimeograph machine, the team first passed the word that junkies were now marked men. They inundated the neighborhood with 1,500 leaflets that read: "If you are caught selling or using dope in this community, you will be in serious trouble." Then the team organized daily street patrols,

146

monitoring the pushers' favorite corners and threatening both dealers and buyers.

Not only has the Afro-American Group Attack Team turned in many heroin users, but the concept quickly spread to Chicago's Italian and Spanish-American communities, which organized similar groups. The police did not react favorably. Edward Meade charged, "the cops here take money from the pushers. Every so often they bust a chump, but they just do it to keep their statistics up."

In Washington, a "Crime Stoppers" group was started by Margie R. Wilber, and won its founder a national award from ACTION, the citizens service corps, for outstanding voluntary community service.

"We the Crime Stoppers of D.C. pledge to obey all laws, respect police officers and all other citizens," is the way in which all Crime Stoppers meetings begin. Law and order, a respect for it and adherence to it, is the message and purpose of this group in which boys in their formative years, eight to 12 years old, are taught to "stop crime by not committing crime," as their motto reads.

Mrs. Wilber, who says that she started Crime Stoppers because of her concern for "the vast numbers of our people in prisons, and the torture they suffer," declared that "black people need to be taught at an early age to avoid prison records."

Founded in 1966, Crime Stoppers had approximately 300 members in January 1973. The oldest of the 1,500 boys who have joined since its inception was about 18 years old in 1973, and at that time none of them, to the knowledge of their former teachers and principals, had been in trouble with the law.

An editor for the Department of State, Mrs. Wilber states that they were not exceptional boys, "just average, ordinary children." Many of them were underprivileged, and some had parents on public assistance.

Principal William Curtis of Payne Elementary School said that the boys "do get into mischief, as all boys will," but that their Crime Stopper membership is often a sufficient deterrent. He said that he sees the group as "a positive outlet for their talents, and it teaches responsibility."

Arriving an hour before school begins, boys at Lovejoy, Maury, Payne, Tyler and Mott elementary schools meet once a week. Other Crime Stoppers meet evenings and Saturdays at Wheeler Road, Potomac Gardens and Greenleaf community centers. On the premise that knowing the law is a prerequisite to obeying it, they memorize definitions of "misdemeanor," "felony" and other legal terms. They are awarded badges and titles such as attorney or judge for their performance. On occasion, a U.S. marshal or an FBI agent speaks to the groups. Every meeting is opened with the pledge, followed by each boy's testimony of why he is a Crime Stopper. Reasons such as,

"I don't take dope" and "I respect my elders," are given. The meeting ends with their song.

Mrs. Wilber uses lunch hours and leave time from her job at the Department of State's Publishing and Reproduction Services Division to meet with the boys. She says that she was prompted to start the organization by a 1967 newspaper article concerning the rising rate of crime. It said that more than 50 percent of all criminals in the District of Columbia committed their first offenses as juveniles.

She says that she sees Crime Stoppers as "a vital organization" and would like it to become nationwide. "Minority groups have enough problems being assimilated without adding criminal records."

Another woman who has made an important contribution in improving the black inner city is Mrs. Mary Iemma, a resident of the Upper Park Avenue area of East Harlem in New York. The area is one ridden with crime.

"In 1965, it looked a hopeless case—an area of despair," recalls Mrs. Iemma, a resident of the area and president of the Upper Park Avenue Community Association. "There were no facilities for youth, no communication between the elderly; the buildings were decaying from lack of services."

The Upper Park Avenue Community Association (UPACA) began when several women, determined to improve their neighborhood, sponsored a barbecue party. The noisy music attracted neighbors and 75 to 100 women got together and decided to take action. They organized their children into play groups and went to the city and applied for loan money to rehabilitate apartments.

The city told them that they needed a co-sponsor, such as a long-standing church or paternal organization or union, as well as an architect and a lawyer. They found a lawyer and an architect and the New York Federation of Reform Synagogues became the co-sponsor.

"Then," states Mrs. Iemma, "we went back to the city for a loan and before we knew it, we had 62 buildings under management contract, and 13 of them we owned outright. No one actually knew what we were doing. No one believed we women were actually doing anything!"

As of November 1972 UPACA had built 405 new units and is continuing with construction plans until 2,500 apartments, housing 12,000 people, are built and renovated. UPACA also learned of a training program offered by Cornell University and it was not long before Cornell was in East Harlem teaching residents of UPACA's housing how to clean floors, buy furniture, put clothes in drawers and run appliances.

"We had the Fire Department teach them how to get out if there was a fire. The Health Department told them how to wrap garbage and dispose of it," recalled Mrs. Iemma. "This turned out to be a most successful part of our program. And people became real friends. In April 1968, people moved into our first building, and unless a piece of paper blows in from someplace, there is no garbage in the halls."

Mrs. Betty Fitzgerald, who supervises economics for the New York City Housing Authority, states that "UPACA really initiated the first preoccupancy training program for tenants. Their tenant-training classes are not voluntary: the tenants must go before they can get an apartment—so there is no pussyfooting about it, like with the housing authority, which is afraid to make such classes compulsory. When you make it voluntary, the people who need it won't come."

In an interview with *Christian Science Monitor* reporter Jo Ann Levine, Mrs. Iemma was asked if she had any advice for those who look at an area that seems hopeless and wish to help. She answered: "Don't come into an area and try to do something that you would not want done in your neighborhood. We are the same people. We want our children to go to college, to have good jobs, to get into the professions and into politics, too. And you must realize you can't start things on a large scale. You must pick leaders. It is not important that they have an education—you can always get a secretary to write a proposal."

Challenging the idea that all social problems can be solved by the appropriation of additional funds, Mrs. Iemma noted that "it's not always more money. We've never had money . . . but you've got to have a feeling for people. You've got to really care."

One black American who has shown an overwhelming ability to "care" is former light-heavyweight boxing champion Archie Moore— who has started an organization called ABC—"Any Boy Can"—in an effort to keep young people away from crime and narcotics and to lead them toward productive and meaningful lives.

When asked, "Any boy can what?" Archie Moore replies: "Any boy can improve himself if he wants to." The program is designed to help them do it.

ABC started in 1962 in Vallejo, California, and is an after-school project for the boys and "Instructor Moore," as the boys call Archie, with this goal: "We have only one objective in ABC . . . and that is to teach the young boys to *want* something better, to give them the desire to grow into good and decent human beings, to show them that they, too, can be police chiefs, school principals, teachers, doctors, lawyers or anything else. We teach just what we call it, 'Any Boy Can.' "

It began for Archie Moore when, as he says: "I started thinking. I got weary with thinking about boys and how to help . . . then it came to me that we could help if we could show them they don't have to act 'big' in bad ways, they can be 'big' in good ways."

ABC is not backed by the federal government but by money from the city, civic agencies, private industry and from Archie himself.

In the ABC program the boys learn self-respect, self-assurance, sports, including football, softball and boxing—for defense only; they also learn the Ten Commandments by heart and the rules an ABC boy is expected to live by. These include, "A boy shall not steal. A boy shall not drink. A boy shall not lie, steal or show disrespect."

Discussing his approach to young people, Archie Moore says, "We start out by getting their interest . . . maybe we do this with a free feed, or a party, or just taking them to talk with them, not at them, and then we emphasize that they must teach as they learn. It isn't enough that the boys, who are from eight to 15 years old, learn our code and rules . . . . They must feel they are teaching them too."

Discussing the results of the ABC program on the floor of the House of Representatives, Representative John Ashbrook of Ohio declared, "The most important thing about ABC is that it works. It takes boys who are either juvenile delinquents or headed in that direction, and the underprivileged boys, and helps them find a life of responsibility and respect—and shows that they have a future, if they want it."

Representative Ashbrook noted, "Congratulations from the recreation district in which the Vallejo project operates were emphatic. In a resolution of commendation and congratulations, recreation members stated that the ABC program had developed 'a basic program, providing opportunities for physical, mental and moral improvement to youngsters' with results which are 'obvious, immediate and conclusively successful in the judgment of this community.'"

Archie Moore set forth his philosophy and the sentiments he tries to instill in "his boys" in an article written for the *San Diego Union*, and later reprinted across the country. He wrote:

> There are members of the black community who call for a separate nation within America. Well, I do not intend to give up one square inch of America. I'm not going to be told I must live in a restricted area. Isn't that what we've all been fighting to overcome? And then there is the element that calls for a return to Africa.
>
> For my part, Africa is a great place to visit, but I wouldn't want to live there. If the Irishmen want to go back to the Emerald Isle, let them. If the Slavs want to return to the Iron Curtain area, OK by me. But I'm not giving up my country. I fought all my life to give my children what I'm able to give them today: a chance for development as citizens in the greatest country in the world.
>
> I do not for a moment think that any truly responsible Negro wants anarchy. I don't think you'll find intelligent—no, let's rephrase that—mature Negroes running wild in the streets or sniping at total strangers. God made the white man as well as the black. True, we haven't acted as brothers in the past, but we are brothers. If we're to be so many Cains and Abels, that's our choice. We can't blame God for it.

Archie continued, "As a matter of plain fact, I have been doing something for the past several years. I have been running a program which I call the ABC—Any Boy Can. By teaching our youth, black, white, yellow and red, what dignity is, what self-respect is, what honor is, I have been able to obliterate juvenile delinquency in several areas."

Discussing militant and radical spokesmen who encourage violence and disorder, Archie declares, "If some bigot can misguide, then I can guide. I've spent too much of my life building what I've got to put it to the torch just to satisfy some ancient hatred of a man who beat my grandfather. Those men are long dead. Do we have to choke what could be a beautiful garden with weeds of hate? I say no!"

Another black leader who "cares" is Charles E. Lloyd, a young Los Angeles attorney who heads an organization called the Youth Inspirational Foundation of America. This organization is dedicated to the inspiration and motivation of the disadvantaged young blacks in the inner city toward success and achievement.

Charles Lloyd was graduated from a segregated high school in Mississippi and was told by his father at the age of 16 that he would never be more than a dishwasher. He attributes his own achievements to a strong motivation and a positive outlook which he says are the chief ingredients of success. He states, "The disadvantaged suffer more from a lack of motivation than any other factor. A man, properly motivated, can do the impossible because he doesn't know it can't be done."

While conditions exist in this country which must be changed, states Lloyd, "Americans still enjoy freedoms which are denied and opportunities which are not available in other countries. Never have so many had so much. America is not a perfect country, just the best of those available."

In 1952, after graduating from high school in Mississippi, Charles Lloyd arrived in Los Angeles with 12 cents and one pair of pants. At the age of 20 he took the Los Angeles Police Examination, and was accepted at the Police Academy at age 21. He received his bachelor's degree from State College at Los Angeles, and attended the University of Southern California Law School during the day while working full time as a juvenile officer in South Central Los Angeles for the Police Department at night. He received his law degree in 1961.

In 1962, Lloyd was appointed a Deputy City Attorney for the Los Angeles City Attorney's office and served as Chief Prosecutor of the Criminal Division. In this position, he had a direct command of 25 Deputy Prosecutors, and won 140 out of 145 jury trials. In addition, he taught law at Van Norman University and in April 1964 entered private practice.

Of black Americans, Lloyd says that they are the most recent victims of slavery and have long suffered the worst forms of oppression, discrimination and segregation. He feels that because of this fact, many capable blacks lack motivation and do not take advantage of opportunities which are available. He tells them to "stop wallowing in your own misery, and blaming other people. You can achieve and conditions do not absolve you of your responsibility to do the best you can. Your effort means you will be the recipients of a better life."

Lloyd is opposed to violence in any form. "Violence must be put down with vigor," he contends. "The overwhelming majority of black Americans are for law and order and always have been. There is a silent black majority composed of hard-working people, but this segment of the black community has been ignored while radical elements have received a lot of attention."

The list of black Americans who "care," and have been working in their own way to fight crime and narcotics, is virtually endless. Another is Henry Womble, referred to by the *Washington Post* as "The Don Quixote of Division Avenue and Grant Street, NE."

For ten years, notes the *Post,* Womble has been hanging around that corner, "looking conspicuously out of place among the young drug addicts who spend a good part of the day and night jiving and hustling. For ten years, Womble has been luring a few of them away from Division and Grant into schools, job training programs and recreation programs."

Henry Womble has been espousing a social theory that he feels has fallen on deaf ears in the city government. The theory is that all of the heavily funded and widely publicized youth rehabilitation programs in Washington are geared to helping trouble-prone youths who are already in schools, recreation yards and juvenile courts, or even jail. "But what about the problem boy who has never seen the inside of a recreation program, who is not in school and has been smart enough to avoid being taken to court?" asks Womble.

"I have 20 boys who haven't been in school for years, and who have never seen a recreation program. Their recreation is hanging around the corner, or in the pool halls, hustling," says Womble.

Henry Womble has a private outreach program to deal with what he calls the "anonymous trouble kids." It is an unpretentious program, operating out of several private homes; it does not have an official name. It is alternatively known simply as "the street program" or—because Womble's nickname is Shorty—is sometimes called "Shorty's program." This private effort has 15 volunteer workers and, during the summer months, upward of 200 youths. Most of them are school drop-outs without jobs.

"We just go out there and get them," says Womble, referring to Division Avenue and Grant Street and other popular corners where aimless youths hang out with nothing to do. "There's nothing out there but dope addicts. This is a haven for them, and they stand out there from ten o'clock in the morning to midnight."

In his neighborhood, says Womble, "you get fellas 18 and 19 years old driving Cadillacs but they don't have any jobs. You see Cadillacs some nights parked from one end of the street to the other."

152

Womble, who owns a small grocery, says that his interest has always been in youth guidance. He previously worked for the D.C. Recreation Department and it was in this position that he became concerned about tough young kids who turned their backs on city-sponsored programs.

Money is raised for his volunteer program by youths at bake sales, dances and other paid admission events. During the summer the program sponsors out-of-town sightseeing excursions, and focuses its attention on athletics. A baseball team called the "Hustlers" raised $2,000 in 1971 and bought a second-hand school bus for trips. "If we can get one or two out of ten, we have helped," says Womble.

An organization founded in 1970 to help rehabilitate drug addicts is RAP (Regional Addiction Prevention), Inc. The organization, located in the black inner city of Washington, D.C., not only helps drug addicts rid themselves of their habit, but seeks to build a positive value system around them by the RAP lifestyle.

Led by Ron Clark, an ex-addict from California's Synanon program, RAP is dedicated to community service and has strong ideas on just what "prevention" means. "The best way to educate the community is to meet some of their survival needs first," says Clark.

As a result of this philosophy Clark, co-director Constance Clark and the 104 men and women living at RAP, give out free vegetables and clothes every week and offer free information on legal aid and where to get medical attention. They help to clean up neighborhood streets and run workshops for young people in everything from tutoring to photography to how to deal with the realities of everyday life, called "survival teaching."

"You just can't talk to people about the evils of drugs,"states Clark, explaining the RAP philosophy. "You have to first get out there with brooms and shovels and help them clean up dirty streets and trash-filled alleys. Then they know you care and will listen to you."

RAP advocates a totally drug-free existence. "We don't want to see people rely on another drug, like methadone—or even rely on RAP. Self-reliance is what we're after. Then you can survive as a complete person anywhere," Clark says.

In New York City, 20 teams of young people, armed with antidrug comic books, music, plays and posters they have prepared, began in the Fall of 1972 to visit the city's schools to discuss the dangers of narcotics addiction. The teenage "consultants" were trained for leadership in a drug-abuse prevention program known as ACTION (not related to the federal ACTION programs). They talked to students in elementary, junior high and high schools.

Discussing the program with *Christian Science Monitor* reporter Mary Kelley were four young participants in the program.

Marian Rogers, from Brandeis High School, stated, "I think ACTION is a really great program. It works both ways. It responds to kids. They respond to it. There are so many pressures on youth today—that's why they turn to drugs. But find the drug user's real potential. Everyone has a potential. We don't say to them, 'It's wrong to use drugs,' because they rarely listen to that. We do say, 'Don't throw away your talent—perhaps you can write, paint or take photographs.' We were able to turn one boy off drugs when he found he could write commercials. He's going to be on our TelePrompTer show."

"Rather than preach to the kids," observed young Ron Jenkins, "I say open up a new road to them. Maybe sports or public speaking or other things. If they like music, I bring my guitar along."

To put the antidrug message over, the young people have written music, produced sculptures, plays, posters and comic books in their own style. Four coordinators, familiar with their areas, were set up in east, central and west Harlem, and in a middle-income area in Nassau. "In learning the basic facts about the drug problem, they interviewed everyone they thought had honest information—from seven-year-olds to janitors," said Charles Schwep, film-maker and educational consultant to the group. "Youth listens to youth—and out of it came some specific designs" (including the comic books and posters).

The depth of feeling within the black community is so strongly against crime, violence and narcotics that it is difficult to believe that the nation as a whole has been so successfully victimized by the false view presented by the media. In a variety of ways, concerned black Americans have been trying to make their voices heard.

When he was promoted to the rank of general, Colonel Daniel (Chappie) James, Jr., was asked by the *Washington Post*'s black correspondent, Jesse W. Lewis, Jr., whether both being on the promotion list for general and being a Negro had special significance for him. This was the reply:

> Yes, but only in the sense of showing black kids that it can be done. Today black kids hear so much bitterness from the militants, who are so steeped in their own bitterness that they're trying to cure the disease by killing the patient. I'm not saying all the barriers are down. They are not. I'm not a starry-eyed idealist. But separatism is not the answer. There are opportunities today . . . in the Air Force, everywhere in America.

Discussing the militant calls for self-segregation on the part of black Americans, James noted, "I'm all for teaching black history so kids will know about the Negro contribution to our country. But I'm dead set against separatism. And I am dead set against disloyalty, black or white, and racism, black or white. You will find prejudice of some kind everywhere in the world. I think our country is closer to true freedom than any other country in the world. Our system—if justly applied—will lead to eventual true freedom for all its people."

The best way to bring out affirmative change, states James, "is first to ensure that the nation survives, to cast the vote, to participate in the political life, to contribute to its welfare and to fight for it whenever asked . . . . My getting promoted is not just getting a star but it means being able to make a larger contribution to the Air Force and to make a stronger America."

Another black American who has faith that our system of freedom and free enterprise will work to make a better life for all of our citizens is W. Leonard Evans, Jr., publisher of *Tuesday* magazine. Mr. Evans' predominantly black-oriented magazine has soared into national prominence, and has a circulation in the millions.

It is Evans' belief that to make tangible social and economic gains, black Americans must increasingly own their own business enterprises. He believes that black universities and colleges, now basically oriented toward the liberal arts, must establish business programs, and expresses the view that political or social separatism by blacks is "foolhardy," "defeatist," and "unnecessary."

Tuesday magazine, like another Chicago-based journal, *Ebony*, is geared to the increasingly mobile and affluent Negro middle class. It is issued as a Sunday supplement each month by newspapers throughout the country, and spotlights black history, black family life and cultural trends, as well as the type of "general interest" story that was carried in magazines such as *Life, Look* and the *Saturday Evening Post*. The magazine's staff is integrated.

"When I was with a Chicago advertising agency in the late 1950s I saw quite clearly that the spectrum of magazines for the American Negro was just totally insufficient," Evans says. "I was concerned about the image that my children—black children living in a white-led society—would form of themselves. I decided that I just had to do something about this gap.

"Most major black publications—like the *Chicago Defender*—were first founded as protest sheets. We want to affirm the positive, the enduring, the constructive in Negro life. The mass-circulation daily press focuses on the negatives—sit-ins, wrongdoers, militants, and political activists. But what about black social and family life? How do white Americans—or even Negroes who read only the white press— know what goes on in black homes, churches, businesses? We want to show the richness of black life."

Mr. Evans, who was graduated from the University of Illinois School of Commerce in 1935, and subsequently undertook legal training at Kent College of Law, argues that the black community must be built up through "black economic power."

"If you look at black America as a whole," he says, "We're a wealthy people. In fact, in dollar statistics, the tenth richest nation in the world, with a wealth of about $32 billion. Yet blacks control less than 1 percent of American industry."

Contrasting the false premises of most government programs designed to help in the inner city with free enterprise, Evans notes that "unfortunately, capitalism just isn't functioning in the ghetto today. What's functioning there is a sort of 'welfare socialism.' Federal and state relief continues to be all too necessary. Workers must settle for inferior local jobs or travel great distances to the suburbs where industry is relocating. And all the while, black money keeps flowing out of black areas. We've got to start up our own businesses—creating products and services that whites as well as blacks can use. That way money will flow back to the inner city, and we'll all be enriched."

Can the black man build a successful enterprise in the face of lavishly financed and stiff competition from white-led firms?

"My experience shows that it can be done," states Evans. "I had an idea, and I had the preparation and experience to make it work. My creditors evaluated me on the basis of integrity and purpose, not just on the fact that I'm a Negro; I conducted myself in a manner that won their confidence and trust, and that paid off in capitalization and backing and eventually success for *Tuesday.*

"Yes, the system does indeed work," he states. "If I could do it, so can other Negroes."

Another successful black businessman is S. B. Fuller of Chicago. Born in Louisiana, where he started door-to-door selling, Fuller's family moved to Memphis when he was 15 years old with only a sixth-grade education. When he was 17, his mother died, leaving seven children. According to Fuller:

"The relief people came and offered us some relief, but we did not accept it, because it was something of a shame for people to receive relief in those days. We were embarrassed just because the relief woman came to talk to us. We did not want the neighbors to know we couldn't make it. So we youngsters made it for ourselves."

At 23 he hitchhiked to Chicago. That was 1935. When he left Memphis he had $25 in his pocket, and when he got to Chicago he still had that same $25. He bought some soap and started selling door to door. From that meager beginning the Fuller Products Company has grown to a widely diversified producer and seller of goods. It requires the services of several hundred home office employees to back up thousands of salespeople—black and white—still using the door-to-door techniques of S. B. Fuller. When Fuller started in business he sold his products—mainly soap—only to blacks. Twenty-eight years later he was operating a multimillion dollar gross income business with both black and white employees and salesmen, and with consumers from both races.

Through the years the Fuller Products Company has bought out a number of white companies that were having financial troubles, and thus it has expanded to one of the major firms in Chicago. When Mr.

Fuller was asked what he thought was the answer to the race problem in this country, he replied:

> Well, the problem is one the Negro has to work out himself. Negroes are not discriminated against because of the color of their skin. They are discriminated against because they have not anything to offer that people want to buy. The minute that they can develop themselves so they excel in whatever they do—then they are going to find they don't have any real problems.
>
> An example is baseball. There was discrimination in the big leagues. But when the owners of the big leagues found that Negroes could play just as well as whites, discrimination in the big leagues ended as far as Negro players are concerned.

While blacks have many legitimate complaints, states Mr. Fuller, he believes that the answer to most of them lies within themselves: "They will find that you cannot sue a man and make him want to live next door to you. You have to sell him the idea that you are just as good as he is, by performance. You must perform well in your job. You must train your youngsters. You must keep your community as clean as the white man's community. You must keep up the home as well as he does."

Negroes still do not perform at their peak, declares Fuller, but they are making rapid progress. He notes, "The Negroes have been free for 100 years, but during that time the white man has not told Negroes the truth. He always taught the Negroes that they were at a disadvantage. He never told Negroes that they should do business for themselves, that they should clean up their own community, and that they should accept community responsibility. They have never told him this in plain English. Nor has the white man told Negroes what the white people say about the Negro when the Negro is not present. This is what they should start doing—telling Negroes in their presence what they say about them in their absence."

With regard to militant spokesmen, Fuller declared, "They speak for certain small groups of people. If they were speaking for the Negro people, you would find more Negroes demonstrating. Those who are demonstrating and 'sitting in' are a very small minority of the Negroes."

S. B. Fuller is also concerned about black radicals who denounce as "Uncle Tomism" every opinion which disagrees with their own militant analysis of American society. "I think that this is very dangerous," states Fuller. "It is an attempt to muzzle free speech. I think that every man should have a right to his own opinion . . . . There are more moderates than we hear of, but some are afraid to give their opinions. They are being muzzled; they are somewhat fearful of speaking out."

"The crimes that you find in Harlem," Fuller points out, "are caused by the people of Harlem. I came from a very poor family, and in those days we didn't have the crime you have today. When I was a boy they kept us busy doing something. Today it's hard to find a boy in Harlem to sell newspapers. Negroes want integration—but not as the white man thinks they want it. Negroes want to know that they have the opportunity to go wherever they want to go and live wherever they want to live .... They have the same ambition in life that white people have, but they don't know how to go about satisfying that ambition .... Negro people do not understand that they must own their own businesses. They must give jobs—not just ask for jobs. They have as much right to employ the white man as the white man has to employ them. They must remember that every one of us is born with a spark of divinity, but it's up to the individual to fan that spark."

The voices of S. B. Fuller, of Archie Moore, of Chappie James—these are not isolated voices. In fact, they represent the majority of black Americans in a way that self-appointed radical spokesmen never could. Unfortunately, such voices have not been given a proper hearing, either by white or black Americans.

Other voices which seem not to have been heard are those of black law-enforcement officers who have been in the front line, not only of fighting crime, but also of concerning themselves with the means of preventing it.

Consider Grant Wright. How many Americans know that this thoughtful and hard-working black man recently retired as Chief of the National Park Police? Fewer, it seems clear, than know the Angela Davises and Stokely Carmichaels.

Grant Wright's career is itself testimony to the promise and opportunity of American society. A native of Fredericksburg, Virginia, Wright lost his mother at the age of three and ten years later lost his father. Despite these misfortunes, he managed to complete high school while helping to support himself and in 1936 enrolled in Virginia Union University, where he worked his way through without outside financial aid. At the University he was a member of the varsity football team and was elected President of the Student Government Association for the 1940 school year. He received his B.S. in Chemistry at the end of that year.

After a short period of employment with a Fredericksburg industrial concern, Grant Wright recognized the lack of opportunity for Negroes and resigned to accept a teaching position in the W. S. Creecy High School in Rich Square, North Carolina. After military service, further study at the City College of New York, and another teaching position in Washington, he was appointed to the position of a private in the United States Park Police.

As a Park Policeman, Wright performed duty in Washington and its surrounding area as a footman, cruiserman and motorcycle officer and in 1954 became the first Negro to be promoted to a supervisory position in the police force. Ultimately he was advanced upward through the ranks of Sergeant, Lieutenant, Captain, Inspector, Deputy Chief, and finally Chief of the 450-man police force.

Asked about the influence of militant and radical black spokesmen, Chief Wright noted that the press builds up the extremists, while tending to ignore the sentiments of the majority of black Americans. "Middle-class Negroes want to succeed, to escape from the ghetto," he states. "Unfortunately, they do not want to exert leadership. Often they are vocal only after the fact. Some moderates vent wrath against 'the Establishment' only to receive media support, and to become established as a black 'leader' or 'spokesman.'"

Wright asks the question of who really are black leaders. How are they chosen? "When I made Chief," he recalls, "Every newspaper ran a story. *Ebony* magazine ran four or five pages. Yet, later on, when that magazine selected black 'leaders' I was not among them. It is the professional and civic organizations, not the media, who should establish who leaders are."

Another prominent black law enforcement officer is Owen Davis, who retired in December 1972 as Deputy Chief of the District of Columbia Police Department.

A member of the Washington metropolitan police department since April 4, 1939, at his retirement Davis had served longer than any other member on the force. As a Negro, he endured the rigors and exclusions of a segregated force and a segregated city until things began to change in the 1950s. Asked if, in retrospect, he had any bitterness, he replied: "Hell no, none whatsoever. I know that sign down at the National Archives that says 'The Past Is Prologue' .... There is nothing to correct the past, nothing to change it."

Davis' career saw him rise from among the handful of black officers on the force in 1939 to become deputy chief 31 years later in charge of the city's patrol division, the highest position ever attained by a black policeman in Washington, D.C.

Born in Elkins, West Virginia, Davis came to Washington when he was about 13 and graduated from what was then called Armstrong Technical High School. He then worked for two years in Depression-era Civilian Conservation Corps camps in Virginia and Maryland and returned to Washington in 1936 where he attended Howard University. In 1939 he joined the police department.

Owen Davis challenges the thesis that the rapid increase in crime in the black community is due to poverty. He notes that two friends of his 16-year-old son have been involved in crime. "One's mother is a teacher, the parents of the other own a beach house, have three cars, are quite prosperous. How do you figure it out? I know a situation in which two boys in the same family turned out to be completely opposite. One dropped out of high school, and one is receiving his Ph.D."

Davis recalls that most prominent blacks of his own age—judges, lawyers, doctors— "were poor as church mice. Their parents couldn't send them to college. They waited on tables, did every conceivable kind of job to succeed. They must have thought their prospects were slim, but they did their best—and they made it."

Discussing the black militants and white radicals, whose demonstrations he had to keep orderly during the 1960s, Davis declares, "In my view the militant civil rights leaders and the leaders of the anti-war movement would not know a civil right if they stumbled across one. But what they do know is how to work the system . . . . Certain black 'leaders' do anything for publicity, such as the Black United Front which said that the murder of a policeman was 'justifiable homicide' . . . . Negroes often use the term 'brother' in a misleading way. Many are not interested in the color of your skin, but only in the color of your money. The false notion of 'black solidarity' has kept some Negroes from reporting such crimes to the police. They must understand that there is no such thing as 'brotherhood' where the criminal is concerned."

The rapid movement of blacks into urban areas, believes Davis, accounts for much of the problem. "Our ability to deal with new problems," he states, "is outstripped by urbanization. We must recreate the spirit of community . . . . When I was a kid, a student at my school broke into a store. The principal of that segregated school in West Virginia called an assembly about it, and it made an impression on all of us. Today, in an impersonal mass society, kids go around the corner and do something, and the parents never find out."

Owen Davis and Grant Wright are not alone. Of the nation's 400,000 policemen, an estimated 15,000 to 20,000 are black, and the number grows each year. Many have won citations for bravery, and in Miami a black sergeant named Robert Ingram was picked by fellow officers as "Policeman of the Year." More and more, black policemen have been performing roles both very sensitive and very dangerous.

Writing in the *Reader's Digest,* Trevor Armbrister reports, "In San Francisco . . . white policemen arrested a Black Panther in front of his party's headquarters. An angry crowd materialized. A white sergeant ordered the people to disperse and, when they refused, allegedly fired over their heads. Just as a serious clash seemed inevitable, a black sergeant named Henry Williams stepped forward. He admitted that his colleagues had acted hastily, promised that there would be an investigation. He asked everyone to go home to avoid further trouble. Because they knew and trusted him, they did."

Armbrister also reports that at a St. Louis housing project, a gang of teenagers stole several boxes of dynamite fuses. The detectives assigned to the case could develop no leads. Then the project's black citizens gave black Patrolman Everett Page vital information, and Page had the fuses within three hours. "The black policeman is sometimes more effective," Page says, "because he can relate to the community. He's a brother and most people feel that a brother will give them a fair shake. His mere presence helps keep down complaints."

Black police officers have become a particular target of militants in the inner city, where they are referred to as "Toms" and "tools" of the "white oppressors." In New Orleans, New York and other cities, black militants have targeted black cops for assassination. In Detroit, a black patrolman—Glenn E. Smith—was shot and killed outside a Black Panther headquarters.

Throughout the country, black officers have formed a series of new organizations: The Guardians in New York, Hartford, Pittsburgh, Philadelphia, Indianapolis and Detroit; the Bronze Shields in Newark; the Officers for Justice in San Francisco; the Afro-American Patrolman's League in Chicago. Unlike traditional police organizations, these groups don't push for higher-wages or better working conditions. Instead, they list as goals snuffing out discrimination in their own departments, upgrading professional standards, and above all establishing new links to the black community. In Newark, for example, the Bronze Shields have developed a program to locate troubled youths and assign them in groups of six to individual "counselors." "We're going to be the conscience of our departments," says Pittsburgh's Harvey Adams. "We're also going to be their salvation."

In St. Louis, blacks command two of nine districts. A black major supervises patrols covering one-third of the city, and blacks have accounted for more than 20 percent of recent promotions. In Detroit, black inspectors head three of 13 precincts. In Baltimore, black officers patrol every section of the city. In Washington, the department is hiring as many blacks as whites every month.

The increasing number of black policemen in the nation's major cities has produced a new willingness within the black community to work with and assist the police. In Newark, for example, Detective Carl Spruill, president of that city's Bronze Shields, was trying to make an arrest in a tough black neighborhood. The suspect, a large, powerful man, resisted him and began shouting, "Let's take him off; let's take him off."

"Suddenly," Spruill remembers, "three or four guys came out of the crowd and got between me and this fellow. They grabbed him and asked me what I wanted done. It was all over in two or three minutes, and I was able to call for a car. Then I went to thank those guys. One of them I knew; in fact, I'd arrested him before. I asked him why he'd helped. He knew about the Bronze Shields, he said. He knew what we were trying to do."

In New York City, the head of a black policeman's association says that crime prevention is often inadequate in many neighborhoods. Sergeant Howard Sheffey, speaking during a seminar on how to improve relations between the police and community, said: "It's quite evident to anyone who has been a victim of a crime that police coverage is not adequate in many areas."

Sheffey, head of the Guardians Association, urged that a forum be held where "community members can offer solutions to local problems." He spoke during the first day of the seminar held in March 1973, cosponsored by the National Conference of Christians and Jews and minority-group organizations in the Police, Housing Police, and Transit Police Departments.

Mrs. Gladys Burleigh, a member of the conference's planning committee, explained that questionnaires had been handed out to community residents by policemen a month before asking for suggestions on topics. "We were very pleased with the results," Mrs. Burleigh said. "Surprisingly, I thought the major issue would be brutality, but the black community has asked for more ranking officers. Apparently, many people feel that department testing eliminates blacks on upper and entrance levels."

Mrs. Burleigh said that drugs were also prominent as a topic. Mrs. Alicia Rivera, an East New York resident, said that police indifference was a major problem. "Patrolmen pass you by and act like they're afraid to talk to you. Young people rebel when they see this and that just adds to the problem."

At the end of the seminar, Sergeant Sheffey evaluated some of the things he had heard. "The most important issue to surface is the person-to-person contact situation," he said. "By eliminating the experts and community leaders, we're hearing from Joe Citizen. By identifying large areas of responsibilities that are most easily changed and thinking of interim solutions, we can accomplish things right now."

Increasingly, black leaders are turning to their own community, seeking to find within that community the causes of crime and violence, and the means to deal with them most effectively. Expressing this view, the *Philadelphia Tribune,* which serves that city's black community, declared: "There is a high degree of crime against the person and property within the black community. These are crimes committed by blacks with the victims also being black. Since it is not a problem caused by someone or something outside the black community, the cause must be within."

The *Tribune* noted, "The cause is fear, along with a lack of concern for fellow community members. A criminal cannot exist within a community whose members have decided to be without criminals. A criminal exists within a community if he is allowed. When the average community member is afraid to check, halt or question another community member, then criminal activity will have a high rate of occurrence. When the average community member is not concerned with the well-being of his neighbors, then his well-being is also in jeopardy."

In order to end such criminal activity within the black community, states the *Tribune,* "We must turn to working with one another. Each community member must be willing and committed to aiding fellow community members. Law and order forces, whether city police or National Guard, cannot be called upon to solve the problems occurring within our community. The community members must solve that problem themselves."

More and more black leaders have been making their voices heard in the fight against crime and narcotics addiction. In February 1973, New York Governor Nelson Rockefeller, recognizing that New York's narcotics laws had done virtually nothing to deter the sale and use of addictive drugs, asked state lawmakers for sweeping new measures that, among other things, would make illegal trafficking in hard drugs and crimes of violence committed by persons under the influence of such drugs punishable by life imprisonment.

Rockefeller proposed legislation which would block all avenues for escaping the full force of the sentence, including acceptance of a plea to a lesser charge, probation, parole and suspension of sentence. Nor would any distinction be made between adult and juvenile pushers, except that persons between 16 and 19 years of age would be eligible for parole after serving at least 15 years of a life sentence. The bill would authorize the state to pay a cash reward of $1,000 for information leading to the arrest and conviction of each pusher.

These proposals elicited loud protests from those who opposed such a "hard line" toward criminals and narcotics pushers. The *New York Times,* for example, ran a story by the father of a former addict, who bemoaned the fact that such measures could have landed his son in jail. While the white liberals opposed even the slightest step in the direction of firmer law enforcement and judicial policies, the same was not true among black leaders, whose communities bear the brunt of rampant drug addiction.

Four respected black civic and church leaders from Harlem, together with Dr. Robert W. Baird, a white physician who has been curing drug addicts in Harlem for over 20 years, held a news conference in Albany to describe for the press their view of the drug problem as seen in their daily lives. All of them agreed that the governor's program was desperately needed, long overdue and, if anything, should have been even more stringent.

Glester Hinds, the head of Harlem's People's Civic and Welfare Association, said that the legislature should pass a sterner law than Rockefeller's.

"As a matter of fact," said Hinds, "I don't think the governor went far enough. It should be included in his bill as capital punishment because these murderers need to be gotten rid of immediately. Yet because of these bleeding hearts that we have, the legislators try to be pacifistic in having laws that do not work. Now, we need a mandatory penalty for these people who are destroying the young generation."

Pleading for immediate affirmative action by the legislature, Hinds said that unless such measures are taken, "it means we have to have the National Guard do the job because it has gotten so bad that people cannot go out and shop after four or five o'clock in the afternoon. Why, Harlem used to be a showplace. Today it's a ghost town. You cannot go into some stores where the merchants are saying, "I've got to close; I've got to close; I don't know who's coming in.' This is what is . . . ."

Reverend Earl B. Moore, who is pastor of the St. Paul Baptist Church in Harlem and serves as deputy to the regional president of the Southern Christian Leadership Conference founded by Dr. Martin Luther King, Jr., agreed with Hinds' description of present-day Harlem, calling it "a land that is fast becoming a waste, howling wilderness."

Moore, a liberal who was the New York Coordinator of the Poor People's Campaign in 1968, said that under present legislation, "the addicts reign and the nonaddicts have become slaves and can barely exist."

He declared, "We come today believing that our governor, our chieftain, bears the mark of a hero. He bears the mark of a hero because he has stood on the walls of our state, he has stood on the walls of our homeland, and he has seen the preponderance of failure, of doom and devastation, and as he stands there, he has done something that is very hard to do, and that is to admit failure from all the other programs that we have tried."

"We have come," continued Reverend Moore, "to demand that our legislators . . . will back up this legislation so that the people of the land of desolation, the mothers of the land, the children of the land, the fathers of the land from whence I come may once again be able to walk towards the omega point of hope."

Dr. George W. McMurray, pastor of the oldest Negro Methodist Church in the United States, the Mother African Methodist Episcopal Zion Church, and head of the AME Zion Church nationwide—commended Governor Rockefeller for his "forthright stand" against narcotics addiction, which he called a "subtle form of genocidal execution."

"I have followed the Governor's regulation," McMurray said. "As a minister, someone says, 'McMurray, you are being a little too harsh.' " But, he said, if the pusher is left on the streets "out of sympathy, he's going to kill you, he's going to kill me. Then he's going to kill himself."

Continuing, McMurray said: "Where someone says, 'What you going to do with the poor little boy who is not 21 years of age? You mean you're going to send him up for life?' Yes. If this is his choice, then let him go for life." Only by doing this, said McMurray, will trafficking in drugs be deterred.

Describing the misery created by narcotics addiction, Reverend Oberia D. Dempsey, founder and pastor of the Upper Park Avenue Baptist Church in Harlem and a militant drug fighter, joined in the call for more effective sanctions.

"The nonaddict pusher," said Dempsey, "knows too well that his slave hard drug addict pushers are violating the rights of blacks and whites daily. Freedom of worship, a cherished right, and the right to work and earn a living have been, since the beginning of time, the most honored rights among human beings. Yet people in Harlem and throughout New York City and New York State have been completely barred from holding evening worship. Merchants have been forced to operate during daylight hours with their doors locked and employ armed guards to open and close the doors as a few frightened customers come and go. But the hard drug pushers don't care.

"All the nonaddict drug pushers know," he said, "that as long as we have weak and inadequate machinery in law enforcement and in our criminal justice systems, no antidrug program will succeed. We've tried many programs in the State of New York, many programs were tried because people were sincere, the state was sincere. But as long as these pushers realize that the machinery to deal with them is inadequate, the programs will not succeed."

The minister, who led a 1970 nationwide antidrug march on Washington, stated, "That is one reason why I know that Governor Rockefeller's proposed legislation . . . must be passed at once."

Commenting upon the articulate black support for a harsh policy against drug pushers, the conservative Washington newspaper *Human Events* noted editorially on February 17, 1973, that "at the very time when white liberal groups across the nation, including even such respectable organizations as the Consumers Union, are calling for increased availability of drugs for addicts through so-called heroin maintenance programs, black leaders from Harlem, the most drug-ravished ghetto area in the nation, are demanding a far different policy, one which results in the total and permanent removal of the drug pusher from civilized society."

Black Americans, by any objective standard, are the primary victims of the wave of crime, violence and narcotics addiction which has befallen the major urban areas of our country in recent years. And almost every poll which has been taken in the nation's black communities indicates that black Americans are even more concerned than their white fellow citizens about crime, and are more desirous than whites of added police protection in their neighborhoods. A number of these polls and surveys have been cited elsewhere in this text. One which is typical is the 1970 Roper survey of the black and white communities of Louisville, Kentucky.

The Louisville survey disclosed clear differences between black and white feelings about their living conditions—housing, crime and neighborhood improvement. While Louisville whites frequently answered "nothing" in response to the questions, "What are the real problems in your neighborhood?," Negroes reported many real difficulties.

Concerning "real problems" in the neighborhood, 41 percent of the black respondents listed juvenile delinquency, as opposed to only 14 percent of the whites. Thirty-nine percent of the blacks listed crime in general as their neighborhood's most serious problem. Only 12 percent of the whites responded in this manner. Similarly, in a survey on crime itself, 59 percent of the Negroes responded that breaking into houses was a "real problem" as opposed to 48 percent of the whites. Drug use among youths was listed by 38 percent of the blacks and 4 percent of the whites.

Roper concluded, "Almost without exception, every neighborhood problem on the list is less troubling to *lower* economic level whites than to *upper* level Negroes."

Polls dealing with Negro attitudes toward black organizations ranging from the NAACP and the Urban League to the Black Panthers also indicate clearly that the overwhelming majority of black Americans reject the idea that violence is the method through which political and economic advances are to be achieved.

In a poll on Negro feelings toward the Black Panthers taken among 494 Negroes in New York, San Francisco, Detroit, Baltimore and Birmingham in early March 1970 by the Opinion Research Corporation, the Black Panthers were shown to be a little more than half as well known to blacks as the NAACP. Asked whether they knew a list of organizations "very well or a fair amount," 73 percent responded that they were familiar with the NAACP, 53 percent were familiar with the Urban League, but only 39 percent were aware of the Black Panthers.

Asked about those organizations toward which their attitudes were "very favorable or somewhat favorable," 83 percent chose the NAACP, 66 percent the Urban League, but at the bottom of the list was the Black Panthers, with 37 percent.

In a poll taken by Louis Harris in the summer of 1971 blacks were asked, "Do you feel the Black Panthers represent your views or not?" Twenty-eight percent said that the Panthers did represent their views, 49 percent said that they did not, and 23 percent were uncertain.

In fact, the violent rhetoric and violent actions of the Black Panthers have met with so little support in the black community that the Panther organization has itself abandoned its militant and revolutionary approach. Writing in the *New York Times* of August 20, 1972, Paul Delaney notes, "Sixteen months ago, two Black Panthers, Ericka Huggins and Bobby G. Seale, were on trial for their lives in a Connecticut courthouse. Today, Mrs. Huggins is an elected member of the Berkeley Community Development Council, the California city's antipoverty agency, and Mr. Seale is a candidate for Mayor of Oakland."

Delaney points out, "Their political activity is indicative of a major change in policy and direction for the national Black Panther Party. Reports from two dozen cities show that its dominant faction has put down the gun and picked up the ballot as its new weapon."

"The gun itself is not necessarily revolutionary," Huey P. Newton, the party's supreme commander, has declared in leading the revision of policies. He added that the Panthers had "defected from black people" by becoming too militant and out of step with the masses of blacks.

While many white liberals continue to entertain the myth that the radical and violent rhetoric of the Panthers all through the 1960s was, somehow, representative of black thinking, the Panther leaders themselves are now quite clear in announcing that they were wrong—that their radicalism alienated them from the black community and made it difficult for them to have the influence they sought.

Seale declared, "It's about time we started getting things together." Conducting voter registration drives and running for local office are "part of our new program of going into politics at the grass-roots level," he added.

The fact is that the Panthers have changed course because of their almost total failure to attract support and followers within the black community for their violent rhetoric of revolution. Panther attorney Charles Garry states, "By participating in the system, the Panthers will be much more of a threat then they ever were when they were carrying guns. They will win many more friends, they will become more acceptable to all groups and they will attract many more members."

Implicit in such a statement is an admission that the path of violent revolution is the path of defeat and failure in appealing to black Americans for their support.

Admitting the overwhelming support for religion found in the black community, Bill Broadwater, Panther coordinator in Philadelphia, stated, "We go to church every Sunday because the church is a part of the community and we are trying to deal with the total community. We are working with the sisters in the church, the gangs on the corner, the addict in his misery and every other person in the black community,"

Sensing that the Panthers and others were right in their belief that the black community would not support those who worked outside of the system, and those who urged violence and upheaval, Washington black activist leader Julius Hobson also found himself expressing at least guarded optimism about America and the future.

In an interview with the *Washington Post* in July 1972, Hobson seemed to have mellowed a good deal. The man who ran for Vice President with Benjamin Spock on the Peace and Freedom Party ticket declared, "I consider myself an optimist . . . I can't buy the fact that America has gone crazy and that everybody has gone crazy. I came up in the thirties and forties when a nigger was like a rabbit in hunting season in Alabama, and there's a hell of a difference now. I'm not saying there isn't all kinds of crap going on to make you so mad that you ought to battle. But life is dearer now, black life is dearer now than it used to be. You can't shoot a man down. A white man can't just go out there and shoot a black man down on the street now without answering for it."

Turning away from his radical rhetoric and calls for revolution, Hobson pointed out, "If a black man goes to Harvard and doesn't get in the wrong civil rights organization, and keeps his skirts clean, he could end up an assistant secretary of something. I've seen it happen. When I went into government I would travel across town to see what a black GS-12 looked like; there weren't two in the government."

Summing up his position, Hobson stated that, "I'm still as militant as I used to be . . . I believe that the only way you can get the mule's attention is to knock the hell out of him with a two by four. But I also, after having lived so long and gone through that, realize that after you get the mule's attention you have to have something to tell him worthwhile—and in order to tell him that you've got to do a little homework and you've got to understand."

It is important to remember that the increase in black crime has occurred at the very moment when the rhetoric of violence and revolution was most widespread. Professor Walter B. Miller of the Joint Center for Urban Studies at Cambridge reported, "Young Negroes were provided incentives to violate the law by civil rights militancy and the riots. Suddenly, there was an ideological justification for crime—to compensate for injustice, to punish white society. Because you have been deprived for so many centuries, you have a right to take back what is yours. You help your race when you oppose the police 'pigs.' "

The violence of the 1960s was in large measure the result of a distorted media presentation of the black community. The overwhelming majority of black Americans not only opposed crime and violence, but were the primary victims of their increase. In many ways, in black communities across the nation, leaders sought to implement programs to fight narcotics addiction and violent crime. Such leaders went without publicity and recognition. Neither whites nor blacks, in many instances, were even aware of their existence.

Whether Americans have been aware of the fact or not, the reality of a black community fighting in a variety of ways, some effective, some not, against the nightmare of urban crime and violence has taken place against a backdrop of an ever deteriorating situation. In such a deteriorating situation it has been blacks who suffered most and whose suffering seems, in many cases, to be unappreciated. When we search for heroes, we would do well to consider those brave men and women in the nation's inner cities who stood against the tide of crime and violence and said "No!"

Chapter 7

Looking To The Future

In mid-September 1968, Attorney General Ramsay Clark testified before the National Commission on Causes and Prevention of Violence. After a few introductory remarks, Clark made this statement:

> Negroes, 12 percent of the total population, were involved in 59 percent of the arrests for murder; 54 percent of the victims were Negro. Nearly one half of all persons arrested for aggravated assault were Negro and the Negro was the primary victim of assault. Forty-seven percent of those arrested for rape were Negro and again studies show the Negro is the primary victim. Sixty-one percent of all arrested for robbery were Negro. Less than one third of the persons arrested for property crime are Negroes.

FBI tabulations upon which Ramsay Clark's statement was based disclosed that more Negroes than whites were arrested for murder, robbery, carrying concealed weapons, prostitution and gambling. Only the total number of arrests for each racial group is given for each offense, but since Negroes made up approximately 12 percent of the population, simple arithmetic would show that for the FBI's "index" crimes, the national arrest rate for Negroes was five times the arrest rate for whites, and for some violent crimes it was more than ten times as high.

In an extensive study of urban arrest data for 1964 through 1967, the FBI found that Negroes' arrest rates for violent crime were far higher than whites' rates—higher than most experts had guessed in their gloomiest moments. FBI figures showed that the Negro urban robbery rate was 16 times greater in 1967, and for the coming generation—those from ages ten to 17—the Negro rate was 20 times the white rate. In terms of arrest rates (the number per 100,000 persons per year), the national robbery rates in 1950 were 12.7 for whites and 68.8 for Negroes. By 1967 this had risen in the cities to 22.8 for whites and 368.9 for Negroes. Among the younger group, it was 27 for whites and 549.7 for young Negroes.

While many commentators express the view that the Negroes' low economic status is an important factor behind this rise in criminality, the fact is that the recent increase in crime came at a time of significant economic gain among blacks. A more psychological explanation for the recent upsurge is given by Professor Walter B. Miller of the Joint Center for Urban Studies at Cambridge.

Dr. Miller states, "Young Negroes were provided incentives to violate the law by civil-rights militancy and the riots. Suddenly there was an ideological justification for crime—to compensate for injustice, to punish white society. Because you have been deprived for so many centuries, you have a right to take back what is yours. You help your race when you oppose the police 'pigs.' "

Economics is not the explanation for the increase in crime. One of the first comparative studies of crime by blacks and whites of similar economic status was conducted by Professor Earl R. Moses of Johns Hopkins University in Baltimore as far back as 1940. It produced the conclusion that if Negroes and whites of the same socioeconomic levels are compared, the Negro crime rates are still higher.

More recently, a study detailing 10,000 Philadelphia juveniles by Marvin Wolfgang and Thorsten Sellin showed that when they sorted the white and Negro boys into groups according to their families' earnings and job levels, the Negro delinquency rates were found to be higher for every income bracket. The boys from high income Negro families, who had the lowest arrest rates, had higher rates than the white boys in the highest crime, lowest income bracket. The professors concluded that psychological and cultural influences outweighed economic ones in fostering criminality.

This theory gained further credence when Negro crime was found to have accelerated between 1964 and 1967, while the economic status of Negroes was improving dramatically. The number of nonwhites who lived below the government's statistical "poverty line" dropped from 10.9 million to 8.3 million during that time. In his volume, *The Self-Inflicted Wound, New York Times* correspondent Fred Graham declares, after reviewing this and other data, that "the inevitable con-

171

clusion is that 'wars on poverty' even if wildly successful will not greatly sap the growth of Negro crime."

Before considering some of the important affirmative steps that can and must be taken, it is important to remember what *not* to do, for the things which we must not do are, in fact, the very things we have been doing. Not only have such approaches failed to solve or ameliorate the problem, but, even worse, they have had a serious negative impact.

Since the problem we face is *not* economic, the solution cannot be economic. The programs of urban renewal, welfare, "the war on poverty" and similar expressions of the economic thesis have caused many of the problems with which we are now coping. Consider several examples.

The measures advocated for some time in the field of housing are an important example of the failure of the welfare state approach to solving our problems. Political conservatives have always opposed this approach, so that their opposition is expected. But today the former advocates of that approach recognize its own futility.

Jason R. Nathan, New York City Housing and Development Administrator, told former Senator Paul Douglas' National Commission on Urban Problems, "The entire concept of federal aid as we know it may be completely wrong." Nathan said, "Even if the federal government spent ten times the money they do now—which they won't—it would not be enough. After ten or 15 years of traditional programs, for example, we have not even begun to approach the problem in Bedford-Stuyvesant in Brooklyn." Urban renewal programs, as a case in point, were meant to ease the problem of low-cost housing scarcity. Exactly the opposite has resulted.

The United States Commission on Civil Rights found that federal projects in Cleveland had drastically reduced the amount of low-rent housing in the city and contributed to the creation of new slums. Out of the resentments that were produced a new bitterness grew, culminating ultimately in riots. Commenting on the Cleveland developments, Father Theodore Hesburgh, President of the University of Notre Dame and at that time a member of the Civil Rights Commission, said:

> These enormous federal programs . . . are coming in, supposedly to help the community. They want to rebuild our society. What has happened in many cases is that people who are presently in the worst situation have their houses swept out from under them by bulldozers, they are given very little help in finding houses and they generally do worse than where they came from. This is immoral.

Many former advocates of such liberal programs have come to the conclusion that they have not, in fact, solved any of the problems at which they were aimed.

In the mid-1950s, two agricultural sociologists, Charles P. Loomis and I. Allan Beegle, made a survey of depressed farming areas. They were, they found, exactly where they had been in the 1930s. The New

Deal and subsequent programs had passed over these areas without touching them.

Michael Harrington has noted that the liberal approach to government has produced "socialism for the rich" and "free enterprise for the poor." In *The Other America,* he writes, "The welfare state is upside down. The protection, the guarantees, the help all tend to go to the strong and to the organized. The weakest in society are those who are always disposed of in some congressional log-rolling session."

The welfare state philosophy has not given people a stake in their communities or the hope for a better future. Bayard Rustin, director of the A. Philip Randolph Institute in New York, said that the welfare state philosophy inherent in the war on poverty is an "immoral bag of tricks" amounting to a new form of slavery. He stated, "The problem for Negroes, Puerto Ricans and poor whites . . . is that America has no commitment to turn muscle power into skills."

In his *Autobiography,* Malcolm X said to white liberals, those he found most guilty of supporting the idea of a dole for poor blacks:

> If . . . [they] wanted more to do, they could work on the roots of such ghetto evils as the little children out in the streets at midnight with apartment keys on strings around their necks to let themselves in, and their mothers and fathers drunk, drug addicts, thieves, and prostitutes . . . . Or [they] could light some fires under Northern city halls, unions and major industries to give more jobs to Negroes to remove so many of them from the relief and welfare rolls, which created laziness, and which deteriorated the ghettoes into steadily worse places for humans to live . . . one thing the white man never can give the black man is self-respect. The black man never can become independent and recognized as a human being who is truly equal with other human beings until he has what they have, and until he is doing for himself what others are doing for themselves.

The fact that must be recognized is that the approach to urban problems inherent in the philosophy of the New and Fair Deals, the Great Society and even much of the thinking of the Nixon Administration, has not worked. We know this not only by the lack of results but also because the former advocates of these programs have told us so.

Expressing something of the growing disillusionment with big government on the part of its former supporters, Professor Hans Morganthau states, "The general crisis of democracy is the result of two factors: the shift of effective material power or decision from the people to the government, and the ability of the government to destroy its citizens in the process of defending them."

Daniel P. Moynihan, previously director of the Urban Studies Center at Harvard University, stated that advocates of big government must divest themselves of the notion that the nation, especially the cities, can be run from agencies in Washington. Because the federal government is "good at collecting revenues and rather bad at disbursing services," he said, federal money should be shared generously with state and local authorities on a "permanent, ongoing basis."

Moynihan also expressed support for the view that the voluntary sector of the economy should help to solve domestic problems. He said, "We must begin getting private business involved in domestic programs in a more systematic, purposeful manner. Making money is one thing Americans are good at, and the corporation is their favorite device for doing so. What aerospace corporations have done for getting us to the moon, urban housing corporations can do for the slums. All that is necessary is to enable enough men to make enough money out of doing so."

Urban renewal programs were meant to ease the problem of low-cost housing scarcity. Exactly the opposite has resulted. Richard Cloward of the Columbia University School of Social Work, in a publication issued by the Center for the Study of Democratic Institutions, offers this statistical summary:

> Since the public housing program was legislated in 1933, some 600,000 low-income housing units have been built, but in the last 15 years urban renewal and highway construction alone have demolished 700,000 low rental units . . . [owing to additional destruction through various privileges granted private realtors and contractors], it is estimated that probably one million low-income units have been destroyed . . . . In this same period, urban renewal has built at the most 100,000 new units . . . . So . . . the net loss in low-income housing is probably about 250,000 units.

The assessment by Professor Cloward was made in 1967. In 1973 a study was issued by the American Enterprise Institute, compiled by Professor John C. Weicher of Ohio State University. Weicher traces the development of urban renewal and shows how it has systematically failed to fulfill its promises.

As of 1965, according to Weicher's data, some 444,000 dwelling units had been scheduled for demolition, and only 166,000 had been scheduled to replace them—a net projected loss of close to 300,000 units. Since 1967 the basis of the figure has changed, but Weicher notes that on the new data the record is just as bad: from 1967 through 1971, urban renewal demolished 538,000 dwelling units and built 201,000—a net loss of more than 300,000.

The fact is, of course, that the dwelling units destroyed are usually occupied by people with relatively low incomes, primarily black, while those constructed are occupied by people with relatively high incomes, primarily white. It is for this reason that so many black leaders have declared that what Urban Renewal really means is "Negro removal."

Discussing urban housing, Michael Harrington, in his book *The Other America,* notes that in 1959 the Mill Creek area of St. Louis

174

was cleared as part of an urban renewal effort. In place of a Negro slum there arose a middle-income housing development. The majority of those evicted were forced to find housing within the existing, and contracted, urban ghetto. In St. Louis, 50 percent of the displaced families were lost to view altogether; of those whose movements are known, only 14 percent found their way into low-cost projects. In New York in 1954 there was one unit for every 7.1 eligible new families; in 1956, there was one unit for every 10.4 eligibles. The situation became worse, not better.

Most of the urban areas in which riots occurred were the very areas to which larger than average shares of federal aid had been given. Detroit had been allotted $100 million in federal funds for urban renewal since 1960, and was spending $30 million a year at the time disorders erupted. New Haven, Connecticut, had been granted federal funds amounting to about $800 for every man, woman and child. This is a figure almost 20 times greater than that for New York City.

The liberal disillusionment with the failure of their own programs was so great that commentator David Brinkley prepared this epitaph for the *Chicago Tribune* in 1967:

> In about three years we have seen the beginning and the end of another period of social experimentation in this the beginning and the end of another phase of the American flirtation with utopia. And when I say Great Society in this context I do not mean merely a series of bills proposed by the President and passed by Congress. Instead, I mean the whole breadth and depth of the American social attitude over the last few years . . . our flirtation with Utopia is over, at least for now . . . if all the bureaucrats had done everything right for 50 years and had spent ten times as much as they have, we would still have slums and crime . . . about all government can do is furnish a floor, a framework, a system of fairness, protection and order; and within that it is still up to every person to find the rest of it for himself. The government cannot produce a utopia.

While certain black leaders have supported programs such as those involved in the War on Poverty conducted by the Office of Economic Opportunity, others have recognized that such programs were not helping to make the urban situation better but, instead, often contributed to making it worse. One such black spokesman is Reverend Henry Mitchell of Chicago. Discussing those Negroes who launched a campaign early in 1973 to prevent the dismantlement of certain OEO programs, Reverend Mitchell declared, "These dudes have organized an antipoverty factory in the name of helping the poor by robbing the taxpayers. Quite naturally they will do everything in their power to keep their antipoverty factory in action."

He noted, "I live, eat and sleep in the ghetto. I'm raising my family in the ghetto, I pastor a church in the ghetto, the North Star Mission is in the ghetto, and I will call any man or woman a liar and prove they are lying if they say these programs have helped the poverty-stricken American."

In *The Star News,* the publication of the North Star Mission, Reverend Mitchell invited any person into his Lawndale area of Chicago to knock on any door and ask the question, "What has the so-called antipoverty program done to help you?"

"Ninety-five percent of the people," he stated, "wouldn't even know what you are talking about . . . . But if you knock on the door of any precinct captain, ward committeeman or alderman and ask them the question 'What has the antipoverty program done for you?' if they would be truthful they would say, 'It has created patronage jobs for certain people who are used by the crooked political machines to steal votes by misusing the rights of the voters and the programs and have lined their pockets . . . and stripped their hearts of honesty.' "

The fact is that far from seeking to help people to help themselves, the programs instituted by OEO sought to exacerbate already tense situations by urging violence and coercion and by legitimizing the activities of the least representative and most militant elements within the black community. A special two-volume manual, for example, was mailed to regional directors of the Community Action Programs in the fall of 1969. Sent out by D. C. Drohat, chief of the Program Management Division of the Community Action Program, this manual underscored the fact that some OEO officials sought to turn these community agencies into militant political action organizations.

The manual urged "boycotts and strikes" as levers for the community action organizations. Even more extreme was a recommendation for Community Action Programs to employ, as a perfectly ethical weapon, the threat of violence. It stated: "Threat power—the ultimate threat power is the riot. This is clearly against the public law . . . . But it is important that board members recognize the threat power of rioting is a very real power and possibility. The board's ability to act effectively and meaningfully in behalf of the poverty constituency will, to a very real extent, determine whether or not their constituency applies threat power . . . ."

The advice given in this manual was taken seriously by OEO operatives and organizations across the country. In Miami, the Black Afro Militant Movement (BAMM) in 1970 infiltrated the Economic Opportunity Program, Inc. Thirteen EOPI employees gave instructions on the manufacture of fire bombs to neighborhood youths in the South Miami area while they were employed by EOPI. A board member admitted in the press to starting the June 1970 Brownsville riot.

In May 1970, between 75 and 100 young militants invaded a meeting of the executive committee of the Perrino Neighborhood Center Board. During the disruption many of the regular board members left. No resignations were submitted and no elections were held. Shortly thereafter, the EOPI executive director received a letter allegedly signed by the president of the Perrino Neighborhood Center Board stating that new officers had been elected, and listing the officers. The "former" board president denied to investigators signing the letter or knowing its contents.

On March 17, 1971, Director J. Edgar Hoover of the FBI, in testimony before the House Subcommittee on Appropriations, said, "Many black extremist groups, local in character, have been encouraged by the success of the Black Panther Party in propagating revolution and racial violence. These combines of self-proclaimed revolutionaries emulate the Panthers by stockpiling arms and ammunition, engaging in violent confrontations with law enforcement officers and spouting rhetoric. One such organization is the Black Afro Militant Movement (BAMM) which was formed in 1970 in Miami, Florida."

In St. Louis, the Economic Development Agency designated the city as an economic development district after the Bureau of Labor Statistics found it to be the area of highest unemployment of blacks in the nation's 14 largest central city areas. A $900,000 OEO special impact grant was made for the period June 1, 1969, to May 31, 1971. At the time of the inspection, a year after the grant was approved and halfway through the two-year period, it was found that none of the three major projects for which this money was earmarked had been put into operation.

One additional example relates to the Mission Rebels Action program in San Francisco, which received a $496,760 grant in 1968 for "Operation Motivation," a program designed to use "hard-core" counselors to help disadvantaged drop-out-prone youth to cope with school problems.

A counselor was promoted by Operation Motivation ten weeks after he was cited by school authorities for breaking windshields of two police cars with an axe. The promotion document praised "his outstanding ability to communicate . . . with adults regardless of background."

This same counselor was arrested with other Operation Motivation employees for transporting handguns into California from Nevada. That same counselor later attempted to kill the Operation Motivation project director because the director balked at dummying payroll records to provide funds for the purchase of weapons for a militant organization.

GAO auditors found six names on the Operation Motivation payroll who were no longer associated with Operation Motivation. One such name was the former director, whose name still appeared six months after he began serving a jail term for rape.

At one time Operation Motivation was headed by a convicted armed robber and former narcotics addict who gambled during working hours at a Reno, Nevada, gaming house, and was arrested in 1968 in San Francisco for carrying a concealed weapon. OEO funding of Operation Motivation ended in January 1970. Mission Rebels remained a delegate agency of the San Francisco Economic Opportunity Council until January 1971.

Examples of this kind abound—in all parts of the country. The fact is that programs such as OEO have been dismal failures. White liberals and other well-meaning supporters of such approaches to the problem of black crime and poverty are doing the black community no favor in encouraging the most irresponsible elements of the inner city. Rather than assisting people to gain the kinds of skills that will lead them to independent and meaningful lives, they are indoctrinated in the philosophy of welfarism, that somehow they have a "right" to the incomes of others and that their most important life-goal is to receive from the government the maximum amount of funds they can.

More than this, however, is the encouragement of violence as a legitimate means for achieving power and influence. When the government itself is funding what is, in effect, an indoctrination campaign in such terrorism it is difficult to accept the seriousness of government spokesmen who, at a later time, express "shock" at the crime and violence which exists in the nation's cities.

The problem is that expensive government programs in most areas of concern are inevitably failures, precisely because government itself is not equipped to solve problems which people must, in the long run, solve for themselves. This point was made in an interview Walter Lippmann had upon his 83rd birthday in March 1973. Asked about the idea of government involvement in all aspects of society to create, in effect, a "utopian" situation—one without crime, poverty and other forms of unhappiness—he replied that the concepts upon which this philosophy rested represented "something that is incapable of being achieved in human society. They are philosophically and morally untrue. Man is not naturally good, nor is his nature perfectable by economic means. The Jacobin philosophy is being repudiated in every advanced society because it involves attempting to do by taxation things not possible to do. It's not possible by government action, or any other action I know, to create a perfect environment that will make a perfect man . . . . It's not the effort to achieve reforms that's wrong, but the inner ideological content of these particular efforts. This is where the fallacy lies—the belief in human perfectability through government."

A program that relates to the effort by government to eliminate the alleged "causes" of crime in the inner cities is that dealing with the growth of narcotics addiction. Discussing this program, the National Commission on Marijuana and Drug Abuse warned the nation that government is compulsively spending more than $1 billion a year to fight the drug problem without knowing whether the money is directed "toward the achievement of success" or the mere "perpetuation of government activity."

In the second of two reports to the President and the Congress in March 1973, the commission charged that the creation of "a drug abuse industrial complex" has led to "a rapid growth in bureaucracy" which needs evaluation because it focuses on the evils of drugs rather than the conditions in society that promote their use. The report observed that what is now offered as "treatment" for drug abuse would be more accurately described as substitutes for punishment, since the medical therapies suggested by the word "treatment" do not yet exist. Indeed, it says, even the assertion that methadone maintenance programs reduce crime is highly questionable because analysis of the evidence cited to support this claim is questionable.

A recurrent theme of the report is that the private sector make greater efforts to control drug-induced behavior and turn to government only as a last resort.

Initially, in looking to the future, we must understand that what we do *not* need is more government programs seeking to redistribute wealth and attempting to deal with the economic question which, as we have seen, is not at the root of the problem of black crime. Such programs have not only failed to achieve any of their stated goals because the economic question is not the problem but, more than this, they have even failed to deal with the economic question for their major thrust has been in favor of welfarism, not self-help. In too many instances, government programs—such as urban renewal, welfare and the Community Action Program of OEO—have made matters far worse.

Those who are concerned with the economic question, which is different and distinct from the question of crime, should turn their attention to the valid criticisms of governmental paternalism from such black leaders as Dr. Thomas W. Matthew, founder of the National Economic Growth and Reconstruction Organization (NEGRO). Dr. Matthew has criticized the present welfare system as a "glorified WPA for Negroes." The welfare state, according to Dr. Matthew, has produced a black population of "kept citizens" and is contributing toward the increasing frequency of riots and violence in the black community.

Roy Innis, National Director of the Congress of Racial Equality, has repeatedly called for programs of self-determination and an end to government "Mickey Mouse programs" that only perpetuate Negro dependence upon a paternalistic white government.

The current welfare system involves an act of condescension by the white society toward its black citizens. Only through programs designed to help people to help themselves and become independent is there any hope of solving the problem of urban poverty.

In concerning ourselves with the problem of black crime, however, it is important to remember that such crime does not exist in a vacuum. All of the forces which stimulate lawlessness, lack of respect for authority and a philosophical approach of moral relativism operate in both black and white communities. Until the society as a whole once again comes to believe that men are responsible for their actions and must pay a price for wrongdoing, it is unlikely that crime will decline.

In recent years the burden of sympathy and concern in American society has been for the perpetrators of crime, and not their victims. Professor Sidney Hook points out that "accompanying this increase in violence and crimes of violence has been an impressive, sympathetic concern—some have unfairly called it a 'preoccupation'—with the human and civil rights of criminals . . . . The potential victim has to have a fair trial and a skillful defense. As a citizen, most of the interfered with and outraged as the person accused of such crimes has to have a fair trial and a skillful defense. As a citizen, most of the rights guaranteed me under the Bill of Rights become nugatory if I am hopelessly crippled by violence, and all of them become extinguished if I am killed."

Professor Hook expresses the view that no matter how we seek to escape from acknowledging it, there is a direct conflict between the rights of the criminal and of persons accused of crime and the rights of their past and potential victims. "For example," he writes, "the right of a person out on bail when he is charged with committing the same type of violent offense, and to be granted bail even when he is charged with committing the offense a third time—a right which he legitimately claims since he has not yet been found guilty of the first offense—conflicts head-on with the rights of his victims who can legitimately claim that they suffered this violence because the person at bar enjoyed his constitutional right to be free on bail."

The problem of crime and lawlessness in American society, believes Dr. Hook, can be solved only if we "begin the quest for intelligent solutions . . . to reorient our thinking in the current period to the rights of the potential victims of crime, and to the task of reducing their number and suffering."

As long as individuals feel that they can commit crimes and escape any serious punishment for them, one of the major causes of crime remains. This, in reality, is an important part of the issue involved in the question of capital punishment.

Beyond the legal questions involved is the question of whether punishment is really bad and whether "rehabilitation" is the only valid and legitimate purpose for our penal institutions. It is popular at the present time to say "yes," but what is popular is not necessarily correct.

In her important volume, *The Need for Roots*, the French philosopher Simone Weil, dipping deeply into her own roots, which were both Jewish and Christian, expressed the view that "punishment is a vital need of the human soul . . . . But the most indispensable punishment for the soul is that inflicted for crime. By committing crime, a man places himself, of his own accord, outside the chain of eternal obligations that bind every human being to every other one."

Miss Weil, as if responding to those who urge "rehabilitation," states that "punishment alone can weld him back again; fully so, if accompanied by consent on his part; otherwise only partially so. Just as the only way of showing respect for somebody suffering from hunger is to give him something to eat, so the only way of showing respect for somebody who has placed himself outside the law is to reinstate him inside the law by subjecting him to the punishment ordained by the law."

There is an unfortunate tendency in American intellectual circles to judge questions such as that of capital punishment not on the basis of whether it is right or wrong, but on the basis of whether it is something which an "enlightened" and "progressive" man in this time and place can "afford" to believe. A great deal of compassion is expended, as a result, on the murderer and the rapist, with little left for the innocent victims who, because of our legal system, must often face the same murderer and rapist time and time again. Thus, the compassion of such individuals is very selective—and very limited.

The herd instinct of American intellectuals is nothing new. Soren Kierkegaard discovered the same approach to important questions in Europe at a different time. He wrote: "The truth. No; by nature man is more afraid of the truth than of death—and this is perfectly natural: for the truth is even more repugnant than death to man's natural being. What wonder, then, that he is so afraid of it? . . . For man is a social animal—only in the herd is he happy. It is all one to him whether it is the profoundest nonsense or the great villainy—he feels completely at ease with it, so long as it is the view of the herd, or the action of the herd, and he is able to join the herd."

Crime, in the black community and in the society as a whole, will never be eliminated or lessened until American society makes it clear that men and women will not be permitted to commit crimes and escape punishment for them. Until the permissive atmosphere of the present period is reversed, the problem will continue.

While citizen action is essential to create the proper atmosphere within inner city neighborhoods, the police and other law enforcement agencies also have an important part to play and, in many instances, they have been operating in a manner much less effective than is necessary.

There is a feeling on the part of many citizens that their protection is low on the list of police priorities. While police may be observed during the daylight hours placing parking tickets on automobiles on city streets, the same streets which are heavily ticketed during daylight hours are with a minimum of police protection at night when danger and criminals appear. Similarly, honest citizens read with interest and dismay of the gangland slayings in New York and other cities and wonder why it is that men can be identified as "well-known criminals," and yet not be in prison. A sophisticated society such as ours, which can produce nuclear weapons and can reach the moon, can surely prosecute Mafia chieftains. Or so many honest citizens suppose.

In April 1972 a two-day conference was sponsored in Washington, D.C., by women from George Washington University to discuss rape defenses and aftereffects in response to two recent assaults on that university's campus. One woman, who said she had reported being raped to District police, termed the subsequent investigation "as bad as the rape itself. Their questions and attitudes are humiliating and it makes aftereffects worse." Sergeant James Wainwright, a sex-squad member of the District Police Department for six years, said that although "one rape is one too many," women "should not be as alarmed as you are this morning." He said that 410 reported rapes in 1971 were "not many" when compared to the half-million female population of the city. He advised women that most rapes could be prevented if women "have companions with them when they go out at night" and "take cabs instead of walking."

Here we have an unusual situation. Official spokesmen declare that 410 reported rapes represent nothing about which to be alarmed, discounting, of course, the number of unreported rapes, which may have been quadruple that number. Honest citizens are told that they cannot walk the streets alone, should take taxi cabs or find companions. These same police, however, spend a good deal of time on tasks which have no relationship to protecting citizens, which is the primary function of police.

A special committee of the American Bar Association issued a report in March 1972 suggesting practical changes in the law that would free men and money to fight the crimes really worth fighting. Members of this committee included such well-known defense lawyers as Edward Bennett Williams and Samuel Dash, prosecutors such as New York's Frank Hogan, former Assistant Attorney General Fred Vinson, and federal appeals judge Edward Tamm. The result of their year's study was a long report on urban crime that recommended abandonment of the prosecutive approach to heroin addiction and the repeal of criminal laws covering "victimless crimes." In nearly all states, laws prohibit gambling, prostitution, consensual "deviant" sex acts, possession of narcotics, public drunkenness and other forms of "nuisance" activity.

Yet in all these "crimes" no participant considers himself hurt. Those who commit the acts may be arrested, prosecuted, fined and jailed. But no one is directly or immediately harmed by what they do, and it is clear that the laws that make such acts criminal have been passed not to protect victims, as is true of laws against rape, assault, murder or robbery, but, instead, "to codify morality in the criminal law."

The time and money which police, prosecutors and courts spend in chasing numbers runners, entrapping prostitutes or their customers and disposing of drunks becomes unavailable for tracking down robbers, rapists and murderers. The American Bar Association report cites the FBI's 1969 statistics showing that almost one-quarter of U.S. arrests were for drunks in 1969. New York City spent $229,000 to arrest and prosecute 172 gamblers in an average month in 1968. (No one went to jail, and the total fines imposed came to $5,000.) It is impossible to tell how many physical assaults and burglaries might have been solved or prevented if law enforcement were not preoccupied with conduct which, as the ABA noted, "presents little, if any, threat to society in general."

Government is involved in many areas of society for which its Constitutional justification is slim indeed. Where in the Constitution, for example, is government really given authority to subsidize farmers and businessmen, to impose wage and price controls, to nationalize education? It is, on the other hand, clear that one of the basic roles of any government is to provide for the public safety and to make the lives and property of its citizens secure. In this task government and law enforcement agencies have failed. Unless crimes of violence are given their proper place of priority, and until courts and the judicial system are as concerned with the rights of victims as with the rights of the perpetrators of crime, such failure will continue.

We face an equally serious problem, of course, in the attitude of so many well-meaning and socially conscious individuals who have tended in recent years to accept the proposition that society itself is responsible for crimes, and not the individuals who have committed them. According to this thesis, the *victims* of rape, murder and theft are as responsible as the perpetrators of such acts for they have helped to create a social atmosphere in which certain individuals are victimized by racism, poverty and an unhappy family life. This attitude, however well meaning, completely ignores any concept of good and evil, and the idea that men are responsible for their actions. In effect, it denies the humanity of the individual who has committed an illegal act.

Discussing the effect of environment upon individual action, Freud once said: "Try and subject a number of strongly differentiated human beings to the same amount of starvation. With the increase of the imperative need for food, all individual differences will be blotted out, and in their place, we shall see the uniform expression of the one unsatisfied instinct."

Challenging the idea from his own personal experience in Nazi concentration camps, Austrian psychiatrist Victor Frankl responded in his volume, *The Doctor and the Soul:* " . . . in the concentration camps we witnessed the contrary: we saw how, faced with the identical situation, one man degenerated while another attained virtual saintliness." Similarly, Robert J. Lifton, writing in the *American Journal of Psychiatry* about American soldiers in North Korean prisoner-of-war camps, comments: "There were examples among them both of altruistic behavior as well as the most primitive forms of struggle for survival."

Frankl declares, "Man is by no means merely a product of heredity and environment. There is a third element: decision. Man ultimately decides for himself." Those who today set forth the view that society—and not the criminal—is responsible for the criminal act are simply stating that man is not a unique, thinking and feeling individual, but is simply an automaton who can be programmed in any manner society chooses to use. Such a view, of course, is simply a "sophisticated" presentation of the material view of man believed in so fervently by Hitler, Lenin and other advocates of totalitarian government.

A view similar to that held by Victor Frankl has been expressed by Harold H. Titus, the U.S. Attorney for the District of Columbia. He stated, "I believe in free will. I believe there is such a thing as an evil, bad man." Until our society returns to this view, and commits itself to the protection of its citizens, our streets will remain unsafe and our lives will continue to be in danger. This is certainly the case today, and it will continue to be the case until the swift prosecution of violent crimes is made our first police and judicial priority.

The seriousness of the crime problem has, unfortunately, been minimized by many political spokesmen, often to indicate the manner in which they have succeeded in fulfilling their own campaign promises concerning such crime. In March 1973, for example, President Nixon announced that "the hour of crisis is past" in the nation's cities. Senator Abraham Ribicoff of Connecticut was selected by the Democrats to respond to the President's optimistic assessment of life in our urban areas. He declared, "Anyone who lives or works in or visits the cities knows that the crisis is still with us. If the crisis is over, as the President claimed, why has serious crime gone up 30 percent in the past four years?"

There is, of course, a good deal of narrow, partisan politics in all of this. Since the President was in charge, he wanted to paint an optimistic picture. Since the Democrats were out of power, they wanted to be as grim as they could. Nevertheless, the facts tell a story of their own—despite the efforts of politicians to tailor them to their own use.

At the very moment when President Nixon was claiming that the crisis had ended, New York Police Commissioner Patrick V. Murphy was releasing the crime figures for 1972 in the nation's largest city. The figures showed that murder cases were up 15.3 percent, to 1,691; rape was up 35.4 percent, to 3,271; and aggravated assault was up 9.6 percent, to 37,130. The only decrease to be found was in the category of "robbery," which includes muggings, holdups and purse-snatchings. Even here, the gains were challenged. Representative Mario Biaggi, a former New York policeman, said that he was "apprehensive about the accuracy of the figures. As a former police officer and a member of that department for 20 years, I am familiar with the administrative gimmickry that can be used to come up with more favorable numbers."

How do police departments manupulate figures to make it appear that crime is really being lessened while, in fact, it is growing at a rapid pace? Crime statistics can be and have been manipulated by police departments for political reasons. One method is to list crimes of special concern in categories where they will be less conspicuous. A purse-snatching, depending on the circumstance, can be classified as a burglary or as "criminal mischief." Another way statistics can be manipulated by police is to increase the number of "unfounded" crimes—those that were reported by citizens but that police investigation indicates did not occur.

The *New York Times* reported that the proportion of "unfounded" robberies, burglaries and grand larcenies sharply increased in April 1972. Despite their best efforts at manipulation, however, the rapid increase in crimes of violence could not be covered up.

Also at the same time that President Nixon was hailing an end to the "urban crisis," the FBI released its national figures for 1972. The bureau's statistics showed that crimes of violence—murder, rape, robbery and assault—increased by one percent during the previous year. While this increase represented a lower percentage rise than previous years, it was nevertheless an increase, not a decrease.

While Americans were wondering what political leaders meant when they discussed an end to the "urban crisis," 1.5 million subscribers to the *London Sunday Times* magazine were reading a 14,000 word article entitled, "New York: A Lesson for the World." The article discussed "New York's degeneration" and the "hopeless," "intolerable," "inhuman conditions" in "virtually every aspect of municipal life." The article is sprinkled with grim statistics on crime, narcotics addiction, welfare recipients, corruption, pollution, education, housing and population shifts. "Much of the 1.1 million-pupil system," it observes, "can be compared to a collection of Borstals [reform schools] teetering on breakdown."

Mayor John Lindsay, whose own failure to govern the city was made evident when he was forced to announce that he would not be a candidate for reelection, called the article "outrageous." The author of the article, George Feifer, a New Jersey native who has lived in London for six years, responded, "I'm willing to bet that anyone who calls it exaggerated lives in a safe area of Manhattan and earns over $20,000 a year."

For most Americans, the problem of crime and violence in our urban areas not only continues, but continues to get worse. Most urban residents keep their doors locked and stay home at night, and largely discount those who make political capital out of the plight of the cities.

Yet, the fact that the problem of violent crime will not be corrected until the atmosphere of our society changes, until men are held responsible for what they do, until standards of right and wrong are restored, until the legal system is as concerned for the rights of victims as for the rights of the perpetrators of crime, does not mean that concerned citizens either can or should sit back and wait for such a change. Whatever change does come will only be the change which we ourselves produce. There are things to be done, and no place are these actions more needed than within the black community, which is most victimized by crime and most involved in its perpetration.

Discussing the need for members of the black community actively to fight crime within their own neighborhoods, black author Orde Coombs declares, "Just as we took to the Southern streets to protest in the sixties against segregation, so should we now stand in our Northern streets to insist that our tax dollars flood our neighborhoods with lights and policemen. The latter will perhaps never learn the difference between brutality and firmness, but we need their presence to give us a breathing spell while we devise plans to rid our communities of the ambushers who are emboldened by our silence."

Calling for a tough stance on the question of crime, Coombs writes, "If the liberals cry about constitutional rights, chase them back to Scarsdale, for they do not quake every time they saunter out of doors. Of course, I know that if this is done to addicts, it can be done to alcoholics, to homosexuals and all the blacks. But we can only fight one battle at a time, and we are fighting now for our lives. The addicts of Harlem now control more turf than they did ten years ago in spite of the millions of dollars spent for rehabilitative programs .... We can no longer excuse crime because of society's inequities, for we will not live to see the end of those injustices. We stand menaced by our kith and kin. All our nobility and all our endurance, which have brought us to this place, will be corroded by the unremitting fear of the muggers who hide behind every lamppost."

In Washington, D.C., Tilmon B. O'Bryant, assistant chief of operations and the highest-ranking black in the metropolitan police department, said that "the black community must work hand in hand with the police. If you see a person rob a store and don't report it, you're giving the robber immunity."

Speaking to an audience of students, faculty, citizens and metropolitan and special police officers at a colloquium on the administration of criminal justice and the black community at Howard University, he declared, "The community must make a civic contribution to the police. If not, the community is subject to the wrath of crime.... Ninety percent of robberies, rapes and housebreakings are committed by blacks on other blacks."

In addition to having blacks work with the police and work within the community to fight crime and narcotics addiction, it is essential that whites who are involved in the black community—as policemen, as teachers, as social workers and in other capacities—not patronize those with whom they are in contact.

It is, in part, because of the failure of the schools in the black inner city that so many people in the black community are ill-prepared for constructive lives in the larger society. The problem with the education of blacks in many of our large cities is not that they are singled out for poor treatment, but that the predominant philosophy of progressive education, when applied to them, leads to a negative conclusion.

This point is effectively made in the book *White Teacher in a Black School*. In it Robert Kendall, a young man who taught for two years in a predominantly black school in Los Angeles, describes the problems he encountered in his attempts to provide his children with hope for the future and the tools for their own development. "In education," he writes, "I felt the standard of excellence was just as vital as the free education factor which extended literacy among our people as no other nation had." His problems often came from the children themselves, and their families, but this Mr. Kendall was able to understand.

It was the attitude of the school administration which proved most troublesome, and which should appear most dangerous to us. Progressive educational ideas, as applied by many school administrators, mean simply an acclimation of the child to his environment. What this means for the black child in a slum environment is, of course, clear. It means a future of despair, frustration, and futility.

Early in his career Mr. Kendall found that one of his students, called Captain Smith, was retarded to the extent that he entered the room crawling on both hands and feet. He had, however, advanced to English B-9. Bringing the matter before the school principal the teacher pointed out that Smith did not belong in a regular classroom and was obviously in need of special attention. To this he received the following reply: "You know the philosophy of progressive education and our social adjustment policies, don't you? . . . Captain Smith has made some measure of improvement every year so he has been advanced every year . . . ."

Replying, the teacher said that if he gave passing grades to children who could neither read nor write with any degree of skill he would be helping them to get a diploma which meant nothing, meaning that education in such schools, in effect, meant nothing. The simple reply: "You're taking this thing much too seriously . . . . Just see to it that your kids all pass their grades."

Where is the equal opportunity for a child whose teachers do not care whether he learns or does not learn, and who are compelled to give him passing grades regardless? Kendall summed up part of his philosophy this way: "Whether children are born in Boyle Heights or Beverly Hills . . . every child on God's earth should be given equal opportunity to make something of his life . . . . And yet, where was the inspiration that would lead a child into doing this? Society preaches conformity. Educational policies dictate 'life adjustment' . . . . But wasn't this policy only encouraging an attitude of defeatism? . . . Wasn't this a true crushing of any dormant spirit which might lie within in a person to forge upward and onward to a better life, a better world?"

While many white liberals believe that it is proper to assist black children in the inner city to speak "their own" dialect and to "adjust to" ghetto conditions rather than seek to rise out of them, black spokesmen have a far different view. While a minority of black militants—the ones who dominate the media—advocate educating black children toward separatism, the majority of concerned black citizens express the opposite view.

Former Brooklyn Dodger baseball star Joe Black expresses the view that it is bigotry to exalt the so-called special language of blacks. "What is our language," he asks, "Foteen' for 'fourteen,' 'Pholeeze' for 'police,' 'Raht back' for 'right back,' 'We is going.' To me any man, white or black, who says whites must learn our language is insulting. What he's saying is that every other ethnic group can migrate to America and master English, but we, who were born here and whose families have all lived here for more than a century, don't have the ability to speak proper English."

Speaking to a black college audience, Joe Black admonished them to "wear a dashinki or an African hairdo, but in the name of common sense learn the English language. It is your own."

Dr. George Roche III, President of Hillsdale College in Michigan, described the manner in which both white and black Americans have been provided with a distorted picture of the Negro past and current condition in America. He noted, "An imaginary version of Negro history and life has gained such currency in many quarters that people assume all blacks to be dope fiends and criminals with no moral sense, no family ties and no self-respect. This tendency is especially prevalent in today's fictional work, fiction often written by black authors."

He points out, "Perhaps a taste of ugliness is so common in today's fiction, television and movies that we have come to accept the stereotype which it offered us. However this came about, it is the black community itself which is the loser. There are sound and solid Negro citizens all over this country who share a strong sense of tradition, a love of family and friends, and a respect for self. These people have every right to resent bitterly the abuse which we hand them with such a patronizing attitude."

A black member of the English Department of South Carolina State College has provided a somewhat different version of the Negro past:

Daddy wasn't a numbers runner, Mama wasn't a loose woman, my two brothers were neither pickpockets nor pimps, and I have never seen heroin in my life.

When I read reviews of current fiction by and about black Americans, I wonder if I should turn in my membership card, or better still I wonder how I'll ever be able to become a member of the black community. I mean where are my family, friends, schoolmates, teachers, the deacons, missionary sisters, usher board members and choir that made up the world that I inhabited in rural Durham County, North Carolina, in the mid-20th century? Were they phantoms, fantasies, dreams that somebody dreamed?

My classmates and I went to school, learned to read, ate our biscuit sandwiches, the envied ones brought "light" bread and cold sweet potato lunches, popped the whip, and sang in "chapel" every day. We went to Sunday School on Sunday, staying once a month for preaching.

I could never bear to read Faulkner and other writers like him because I hated the image that he portrayed of blacks. But I could intellectualize him by saying that he didn't know any better. But how to explain . . . how to explain the images currently jumping out of the pages of fiction by blacks? Is this all there is? Where are we residents of Durham County? Rural black farmers and factory workers, domestic workers, common laborers all. Don't our lives have meaning? Are we not worthy of being celebrated in song and story? Or should we turn to drugs and crime before we can exist in the pages of literature?

The false image presented of the black community has had a dramatic impact both upon white society and upon youngsters growing up within the black inner city, as has a false and patronizing liberalism which tends to characterize the educational and welfare establishments with which so many blacks are in touch—often their single official relationship with the larger society.

The *Chicago Tribune*'s black columnist, Vernon Jarrett, asked a question which more and more blacks are asking: "Why is it that in the big cities of the North it is exceedingly difficult to teach poor blacks to read, when blacks who grew up under the most exacting of economic and civil deprivation did learn to read and write and speak clearly?"

Jarrett was thinking of this seeming anachronism when he entered the Hill Supermarket on Jefferson Street in Nashville, which runs past two black colleges, Fisk University and Tennessee State University. As he wandered up and down the aisles, an aging woman passed by, wearing dark glasses.

He writes, "There was something faintly familiar about the way

189

she held her head. I was compelled to take a second look, and when she turned toward the cashier, another look at her profile struck a chord. She could have been my eighth-grade teacher back in Paris, Tennessee. Even though I hadn't seen her in over 30 years, something forced me to circle the aisle and see her face once more. I took a deep breath and clumsily asked the question: 'Don't I know you? Aren't you Miss Porter?' "

The old woman smiled. "My name is Mrs. Blanton," she said. "Don't you remember I got married?" Then she ran her fingers over Jarrett's face, and the smile got bigger. She grabbed his shoulders with both hands and began shaking him with joy. "I can't think of your name, there were so many," she said.

Noting that she was now nearly blind, Jarrett wrote that "she was seeing with that special kind of sight available to people who have given their lives to the young. Before I could pass the first syllable of my name she finished it for me, and began shaking me by the shoulders again. This was an indescribable experience."

Later on, he reflected on the day, just about the same time of year, "when Miss Porter slammed down a textbook and rushed to the back of the classroom, grabbed me by the shoulders, and gave me another shaking. My friend Paul Buchanan and I were talking while she was trying to teach. She announced what our punishment would be but looked us straight in the eye and seared into our minds—as so many other teachers had done—the meaning of education to people who were not only black but poor. And then she sent us to the principal to get a whipping. In those days, if you got a whipping at school you got another one at home."

Lamenting that times have changed in the schools, Vernon Jarrett concluded that "teachers like Miss Euria Porter Blanton did make a difference."

Before young people in the black inner city will turn away from the wasted lives of crime and narcotics addiction they must have their sights raised for them. They must understand the vast opportunities which are available to them, and must know that American society has made a commitment to provide all of its citizens, regardless of race, with the chance to go as far as their abilities will take them.

For every Archie Moore or Charles Lloyd or General Chappie James who tells black youngsters the truth about today's American society, there are innumerable black militants and white liberals to tell them a far different story. In fact, New Left white liberals and civil rights leaders have deliberately thrown "a blanket of silence" over data indicating the advancement of most black Americans into the middle class, according to an article in the April 1973 issue of *Commentary* magazine.

The authors, Ben J. Wattenberg and Richard M. Scammon, who

also wrote the volume *The New Majority,* contend that black leaders are aware of gains made by blacks in employment and education, "But they have elected as a matter of policy to mute any public acknowledgment or celebration of black accomplishments in order to maintain moral and political pressure on the administration and on public opinion."

As examples, they cite a statement by Julian Bond, a Georgia state senator and civil rights leader, who said that blacks were worse off in 1973 as compared with whites than they were previously. They also cite a 1971 speech by Senator Edmund Muskie of Maine, who described what he called the "failure of American liberalism." "How can they go around saying, 'We've failed but give us some more money anyway?' " asks Wattenberg.

The authors claim that a majority of blacks are now in the middle class, according to statistics from the U.S. Census Bureau's 1970 census and subsequent surveys. They picked a median family income of $8,000 a year as the line between lower and middle class in the North and $6,000 a year in the South. By that definition, 52 percent of the blacks are now in the middle class. Nationally, blacks in 1971 had a median family income of $6,440 as compared with $10,672 for whites.

Scammon and Wattenberg acknowledge that by various tests blacks still lag behind whites on the economic scale. For example, black median family income was only 63 percent of white family income in 1971, but that remains a gain of 10 percentage points in a single decade.

Among other statistics cited were the following:

- Between 1960 and 1970, the number of blacks with four years of high school increased from 36 to 54 percent.
- During the same decade, black family income increased by 99.6 percent (as opposed to a 69 percent increase for whites) and brought black family income from 53 to 63 percent of that of whites.
- Among younger blacks outside the South, families in which both husband and wife work now earn 4 percent more than a comparable white couple.

Wattenberg and Scammon charged that the New Left stress on helping ghetto blacks could have a backfire effect: "By refusing to acknowledge the facts of success, liberals give further currency to the old stereotypes of blacks—slums, rat-infested dwellings, a self-perpetuating welfare culture—and thereby help to confer legitimacy on the policies of those who would shirk the hard task of social . . . integration."

Until the black self-image is made to have some relationship to the reality of the black condition, the motivation for achievement within the black community will remain lacking. It is far more important to improve the psychological makeup of black youth than to look only at their physical surroundings. Crime and narcotics addiction are the products of what many falsely believe to be the hopelessness of their condition, and are not the result of poverty as those who seek easy answers so often tell us.

Just as many in the black community misunderstand their opportunities because those who are in a position to inform them of such opportunities—teachers and welfare workers, both white and black— seem more interested in preaching despair and seem to have their own masochistic self-hatred of American society to overcome, so many in the black community also misunderstand the history of their country.

One of the charges made most frequently against American society and one which tends to meet the approval of large numbers of men and women is that "America is a racist society." The very acceptance of this idea is an indication that the message of American history has been lost.

Andrew Greeley, for example, has speculated that the historians of the 23rd or 24th century, looking back to this time, will find that apart from the great population increase in the world, and its Westernization and industrialization, the most extraordinary event was the fusing of cultures in America.

He writes, "The historian of the future will find it hard to believe that it could have happened that English, Scotch and Welsh, Irish, Germans, Italians and Poles, Africans, Indians, both Eastern and Western, Danes, Armenians, Croatians, Slovenians, Greeks and Luxembourgers, Chinese, Japanese, Filipinos and Puerto Ricans could come together to form a nation that not only would survive but, all things considered, survive reasonably well. I further suggest that the historians of the future will be astonished that American sociologists, the product of the gathering of the nations, could stand in the midst of such an astonishing social phenomenon and take it so for granted that they would not bother to study it."

Our country has made mistakes, and it has many shortcomings that we must continue to strive to correct. Ours was the last Western nation to abolish human slavery. This is a deplorable fact of our history. But our country is one which, from its beginnings, welcomed the diversity of people. Discussing the mission of America, Ralph Waldo Emerson said that "the office of America is to liberate, to abolish kingcraft, priestcraft, caste, monopoly, to pull down the gallows . . . to take in the immigrant, to open the doors of the sea and the fields of the earth."

To a remarkable degree, America has performed that task. We have fashioned a nation from what poet Emma Lazarus referred to as the "wretched refuse" of Europe's "teeming shores." Writing to the Hebrew Congregation at Newport, Rhode Island, George Washington told them that in America each man might "sit under his own fig tree," and "there would be none to make him afraid." There has been none to make him afraid. Freedom of speech, religious freedom, freedom of the press—these are realities and have been since American independence.

"America," Eric Hoffer has said, "is the only new thing in history." American nationality has been unique, based not upon common race, common religion, or common ancestry, but on a common belief in and commitment to freedom. Yet, despite all this, Americans themselves seem willing to think the worst of their country and their tradition, to accept the false charge of "racism" as the final commentary on the American tradition.

One of the bases upon which radicals, both black and white, argue that America is a "racist" society is because they hold it to be a tenet of faith that capitalism causes racism. If they were not illogical, they would seriously seek out empirical justification for their thesis by investigating racism in "socialist" or "communist" societies. The most cursory investigation of the U.S.S.R., for example, reveals that the Chechen, Ingush, Karachai, Balkar, Crimean Tartars and Jews are the victims of far greater racism than any known in the United States. Indeed, it is government-sponsored racism, the most pernicious because it leads to pogroms and concentration camps.

The mystical and unmaterialistic Orient would provide equally fertile ground for comparison studies. Here we find feared and despised Chinese minorities in countries such as Thailand and Indonesia. The persecution of Hindus in Pakistan and of Moslems in India is well known. In Africa, Nigerians despise Biafrans because they are short and ambitious. In South Africa, it is not only whites and blacks who fail to live in harmony. Indians and blacks live in mutual suspicion which occasionally explodes into violence. In Latin America, Indians and mestizos regard each other as less than human.

It may be said that we should not compare ourselves to these underdeveloped peoples but to the "advanced" populations of Europe. Such an objection is in fact racist itself, but, more than this, it is badly taken. Slovaks hate Hungarians, Poles hate Germans and Russians. Finns are at odds with Swedes and Russians. The Serbs, Croats and Slovenes have long been in conflict. The Irish hate the English, and the English have reciprocated. In fact, the Irish of County Cork dislike the Irish of County Connaught. Darker Italians from the South are treated as inferiors by northern Italians. These webs of hatred, of man's inhumanity to man, have led to genocide, committed not only by the Germans in World War II, but by the British in Tasmania, the Dutch in South Africa, the Portuguese in Brazil and the Russians in Hungary.

Despite the fact that radicals claim that racism is an American institution or is unique to our society, or even dominant here, the fact is that racism is so much and so unfortunate a part of man's history that Brewton Barry, in his work *Race and Ethnic Relations,* states that racial harmony is itself a special exception. In the three cases he cites, unusual factors apparently play a large part in causing it. In the case of the Tungus and the Cossacks of Manchuria, for example, the cause of harmony seems to be their shared hatred for a third race, their Chinese neighbors.

Shakespeare has one of his characters declare: "There is a stranger, throw a rock at him.' " Kipling wrote, "Everyone like us is we, and everyone else is they." The differentiation between man and all those who differ from him is as old as man himself.

What is new is not "racism" or prejudice or discrimination. A fair look at the world would show that the United States, although far from perfect, is one of the least racist countries in the world. Our civil rights laws go further and have more teeth than those of any other country. Those against discrimination in jobs and housing are practically unique.

Great Britain is usually considered by Americans to be largely free of racism. Yet, Brian McArthur of the *London Times* has said that "one often wishes that the same sincere commitment to equal job opportunities for minority groups that exists in America could be detected in Britain."

An indication of how much change has occurred in our country in recent years may be seen in the August 1971 issue of *Ebony* magazine, which is devoted to "The New South." One of its significant discoveries is that American blacks are returning to the South in large numbers, and they are pleased with what they find there.

Ebony cites "a change in the attitudes of whites which was not dreamed of ten years ago" and adds, "Whites who once said they would not let their children attend school with Negroes are doing so today. Whites who said they would never sit beside a black man on a bus are doing so today. Whites who once thought that blacks could do little else than clean, cook, plow, chop cotton and strip tobacco are now begrudgingly admitting that blacks can sell shoes, operate cash registers, take shorthand, operate punch presses, and successfully fill other jobs that had previously been closed to them."

Is America, in the light of our historical condition and present reality, really a "racist" society? In the play "Fiddler on the Roof," the story is told of a group of Russian Jews being forced to flee their country during a pogrom. As they packed their belongings and prepared to make new lives for themselves, there was only one word on their lips: "America."

America was promises to all of the dispossessed all over the world. Whether today's young radicals and their older supporters know it or not, America has kept most of the promises. If it is permitted to do so, it will keep those same promises for this generation of young people growing up in the nation's black inner city areas. It will not be permitted to do so, however, if the philosophy of welfarism persists and if black young people are told by white liberals and black militants that dependence upon governmental paternalism is, in some sense, a substitute for hard work—and for taking advantage of opportunities.

The rate of public assistance has been rising rapidly in every large city without making a dent in any of the problems that need to be solved. Instead, many of these expenditures have been a positive disservice. Professor S. M. Miller of Syracuse University states, "Welfare assistance in its present form tends to encourage dependence, withdrawal, diffused hostility, indifference, ennui."

The present system of welfare is self-perpetuating. Far from relieving dependency, it encourages dependency. A study of public assistance in New York State, made by the management consulting firm of Greenleigh Associates for the Moreland Commission, reported that existing policies and procedure lead to *increased* dependency. A national study of the Federal Aid to Dependent Children Program, made by M. Elaine Burgess and Daniel O. Price of the University of North Carolina for the American Public Welfare Association, called for major changes to long-term dependency to prevent the continued development of second generation dependents. In his volume *Crisis in Black and White,* Charles Silberman laments that "one sometimes has the feeling that welfare agencies almost welcome failure, for failure, if repeated frequently enough, only demonstrates the need to expand their services still more."

Silberman writes, "Negroes, like every other group, can really be helped in only one way: by giving them the means with which to help themselves . . . in the last analysis their rejection of the conventional offers to help—the resentment they show—springs less from the injustice per se than from their sense of inadequacy and impotence."

Mary Burch, a distinguished educator and civic leader in Newark, New Jersey, states of these black young people: "They've always been on the receiving end. They have to learn how to give if they're going to develop into responsible adults." For the same reason Mrs. Burch refuses to dole out money to any of her youngsters. If a child needs eyeglasses, for example, the Leaguers will finance the purchase—but the youngster is required to take on some job that will enable him to earn enough to repay the advance.

The problem of crime in the black community is intrinsically linked to all the problems of American society—rootlessness, permissiveness, moral relativism, a court system more solicitous of the desires of criminals than the rights of honest citizens. It has, in addition, its special elements—a media which portray only a minority of militants, a welfare system which encourages dependence, a pervasive narcotics problem which gets worse each year.

A first step toward solving some of these problems, at least to the degree that they can be solved, is for those blacks who oppose the militants, the advocates of crime, the encouragers of second-rate education, the advocates of welfare dependency, to make themselves heard. As we have seen, these are the overwhelming majority of black Americans. For too long, the black middle class—the black silent majority—has been content to let events take their own course. If they continue, if the natural leaders of the black community do not assume that leadership role, the problem will only continue to deteriorate.

In the long run, the problem of black crime will correct itself only as the total American society returns to a system of values and ceases to follow the advice and the policies of its least realistic and least responsible elements. We are, for better or worse, in it together— black and white. We are, together, responsible for the problem and only together can we work to reverse the present trend. We will succeed only if we learn the lessons the history of our recent past so clearly teaches us. Americans have ignored the lessons of history before, at a very great cost. We cannot afford to do so again.

Index